SNI~~TCH~~

SNITCH!

A History of the Modern Intelligence Informer

STEVE HEWITT

continuum

2010

The Continuum International Publishing Group Inc
80 Maiden Lane, New York, NY 10038

The Continuum International Publishing Group Ltd
The Tower Building, 11 York Road, London SE1 7NX

www.continuumbooks.com

Library of Congress Cataloging-in-Publication Data
Hewitt, Steve.
Snitch! : a history of the modern intelligence informer / Steve Hewitt.
    p. cm.
  Includes bibliographical references and index.
  ISBN-13: 978-1-4411-0082-5 (hardcover : alk. paper)
  ISBN-10: 1-4411-0082-2 (hardcover : alk. paper)
  ISBN-13: 978-1-4411-9007-9 (pbk. : alk. paper)
  ISBN-10: 1-4411-9007-4 (pbk. : alk. paper)
  1. Intelligence service—Case studies. 2. Informers—Case studies. 3. War on Terrorism, 2001—Case studies.`I. Title.

  JF1525.I6H49 2010
  327.1209—dc22   2009024738

ISBN: HB: 978-1-4411-0082-5
    PB: 978-1-4411-9007-9

Typeset by Pindar NZ, Auckland, New Zealand
Printed in the United States of America

Contents

Acknowledgements

First and foremost, I would like to thank Marie-Claire Antoine of Continuum. She has displayed extraordinary confidence in this project and in me, and for that I am extremely grateful. Thanks as well to others involved in the production of the book. Two other women inspired this book, in fundamentally different ways. One, active in a career within the Canadian government, informed on me to the Royal Canadian Mounted Police over a matter of Canadian national security. This led to my being visited by the police in June 2000 and, although nothing came of the investigation, because I had done nothing wrong, it did instil in me a sense of a betrayal and a curiosity as to what motivates people to snitch. The other woman is Katharine Gun, the antithesis of an informer in that as a whistleblower she willingly put not only her career but also her freedom at risk in an effort to stop the illegal invasion of Iraq in 2003. Her courage is an inspiration.

Several others helped me directly with this project. Michael Burns provided invaluable research assistance in 2005 and without his labours this book would not have been possible. I am also appreciative of the University of Birmingham for granting me study leave in 2005–2006, during which time parts of this manuscript were written. Friends took the time to read and supply feedback on various stages of the manuscript. In this respect, my gratitude goes to Warren Johnston, Ceri Morgan, Reg Whitaker and Maria Ryan for their time and help. Any remaining errors emanate entirely from my own numerous shortcomings and despite the best efforts of Isaac and Flora to assist me with the bibliography.

I also wish to acknowledge the help of other friends and colleagues. Topping this list is Mary Hawes of Chesterfield, Ontario, Canada who, through her perpetual good humour and fundamental generosity, has long been an influential figure in my life. This book is dedicated to her.

I am truly blessed to work with several wonderful individuals, in particular Danielle Fuller, Scott Lucas, Michele Schweisfurth and Corey Ross, who have become even greater friends. I wish to single out Michele Aaron and Christabelle Sethna, whose friendships over the last few years have meant a great deal to me. Special thanks as well to the wonderful Julie-Anne Wright, Gaye Bye and Margaret Conway for their help and encouragement.

Finally, there are those closest to me. My siblings, parents and children, including the newly arrived Gwily Gob, have helped, supported and inspired me more often than I could possibly recognize across a hundred books. This is doubly true of Ceri Morgan who, through the force of her love and her wild Welsh ways, turns ordinary days into extraordinary ones.

CHAPTER 1

Introduction

Stories about them and their activities abound. Since 2005, when this book began, informers present and past have received widespread attention. There was Denis Donaldson, a long-time and senior member of Sinn Féin who, in December 2005, outed himself as having been an informer; although the British media repeatedly referred to him by the inaccurate but perhaps less pejorative label of 'spy'. Four months later, while he was living without formal police protection, assailants killed him with three shotgun blasts as he begged for his life. Then it was the turn of the original or archetypal informer, Judas Iscariot, for a round of publicity. Through a recently discovered ancient scroll, there emerged once again the suggestion that Judas was, in effect, a double agent, or a turned informer, who supplied information to the Romans not for 30 pieces of silver (the ultimate motivation of any betrayer being money) but because Jesus Christ encouraged him to do so. This was the version of Judas depicted in Nikos Kazantzakis *The Last Temptation of Christ*, where Judas is told by Jesus that his is the most difficult task of all because of the fate that will befall the one who is the betrayer.[1] Then there were the informers in the 'war on terror'. Between May and August 2006, alleged major terrorist plots would be foiled in Canada, the United Kingdom, and the United States. Although the media coverage emphasized the use of electronic surveillance against those arrested, such as by monitoring their postings in Internet chat rooms, it soon emerged that informers played significant roles either in first bringing the alleged plots to the attention of authorities, or in maintaining coverage of their operations, or both. An informer in the Canadian plot would even become a public figure after he revealed his secret work for the Canadian state in front of a television camera.[2]

Despite the significance of informers for efforts by state agencies, such as police forces and intelligence services, analyses of their activities remain scattered. Major studies, although extremely useful, are limited in number. Much of what has been written is of the popular and sensational variety, often penned by journalists or police officers.[3] In the confessional society that is the US, some informers have written of their work and experiences.[4]

The scholarship that does exist follows national narratives, concentrating on developments within specific countries. Some of it is superb, in particular the work of Gary T. Marx, one of the first to recognize the significance of informers to the work of American domestic intelligence. In the UK, Steven Greer has built upon Marx's insight in an effort to develop a systematic model for understanding informers. Then there is the late Frank Donner, who thoughtfully reflected on the use of informers by the 'red squads' of American police forces, and Finnish sociologist Malin Åkerström's exploration of the importance of betrayal in the world of informers, an approach developed in his studies of Finnish prisons. Much earlier than these publications came the writings of Georg Simmel, a German scholar, on secrecy.[5]

More recent efforts, after the end of the Cold War, have moved away from informers, putting their focus on technology and, in the process, in some ways writing humans out of the story of surveillance. A spate of books, with titles like *The End of Privacy*, *Database Nation* and *The Unwanted Gaze*, have appeared since the 1990s, all with the common theme of the danger that technological surveillance poses to the general population in liberal-democratic societies.[6] The omnipotence of technological surveillance, coupled with the inherent sexiness of some of the equipment being wielded, makes for a compelling attention-grabber. In the UK, for example, plans are on the table that will allow the government to monitor the daily movement of millions of vehicles in the country and maintain those records for up to five years. Already, such technology has been deployed in British counter-terrorism efforts.[7] To put it bluntly, in certain parts of the world, we are close to a society where there is, in the title of one publication from the genre, 'no place to hide'.[8]

There is no denying the significance of technological surveillance, both as a tool for the state and as a threat to civil liberties. This emphasis is driven in part because conceivably everyone could be subject to this form of surveillance. It ignores, however, the reality that humans continue to play a crucial role in watching over us for the state — and not just by sitting behind CCTV monitors. One reason for the neglect is the perpetual veil of secrecy that surrounds informers and informing. The secrecy has implications for the researcher. Simply put, it is difficult to get access to specific and detailed information in a comprehensive way. It is the equivalent of having a large jigsaw puzzle where several crucial pieces are not missing but locked away forever. As a result, this study attempts not a micro examination of the subject — excellent examples of these, primarily focused on policing and criminality, already exist — but to attempt something different: a broad, international and accessible survey of informers that historicizes and contextualizes them and their work. The survey mainly concentrates on informers operated by intelligence agencies, who supply information on intelligence matters instead of crime. In doing so, it makes no claim to be comprehensive. For instance, informing is not just a practice encouraged and carried out by police and intelligence services. Governments, in a variety of ways, such as through snitch lines to report welfare fraud, encourage citizens to inform on each other. The uniqueness of this study arises instead from its recognition that, variations aside, there are common aspects to informing that cross boundaries. This is true, both of the present and of the recent past. These universal factors include the nature of informing, how informers are recruited, why they are recruited, their impact, their importance and the wider popular perceptions of them.

What follows then is a series of detailed snapshots using available source material. Chapter 2 offers a general description of informing, including elements related to motivation and the relationship between handlers and informers. The third chapter offers an historical discussion of the rise of the modern informer, particularly in the twentieth century. Chapter 4 provides a series of detailed case studies of famous informers. Chapter 5 considers informer states, like the late German Democratic Republic, where large numbers of citizens served as informers. The subsequent chapter looks at the use of informers in the 'war on terror' while the Conclusion reflects on past, present and future trends in informing.

Finally, one additional point about state informing requires elucidation. Regardless of where one positions oneself on the issue, it is not a neutral activity. It is a useful function carried out on behalf of the state, be it in the service of intelligence agencies, police forces or other government bodies. Informing aids the state in the pursuit of a goal, whether that is through the tracking of alleged terrorists or infiltrating groups considered by the state to represent a threat in some form. Equally, however, the type of surveillance being used is not without consequences. Informing by humans comes at a cost. That price is borne not just by the individuals being spied upon and those close to them, but by the informers and even the families of informers. Having a friend, colleague or even family member secretly spying on oneself engenders a crushing sense of betrayal and, unsurprisingly, strong reactions. Informers and informing are powerful tools that profoundly affect those doing the spying and those being spied on.

CHAPTER 2

'Inherent in the Conditions of Human Society'[1]: The Nature of Informing

Informers toil around the world in different forms and places. Wherever they are active, however, there are common characteristics, both in the present and in the past. These include why they are used, the impact that they have on those targeted for surveillance, how they are recruited, why they inform, how that informing occurs and how the informing is received. This brings us to the book's first major point: informers are extremely valuable to the state in a variety of ways. That value is frequently two-fold: first, informing allows the state, through its security institutions, to watch the activities of its citizens, whether concerning subversive, criminal or terrorist activity.[2] Sometimes the monitoring is done on a widespread scale, in what amounts to an 'informer state' in which large numbers of citizens actively spy not just on dissidents but also on the wider populace. For democratic political systems, informers serve a different role, one that clearly varies from the most common uses of electronic types of surveillance. They usually do not target the population as a whole but are deployed by the state in a more specialized sense to work against narrowly defined targets, either by police forces or intelligence services.

Second, informers play multiple parts. When their presence is known or suspected, they can affect the behaviour of others. Although it is more commonly applied to the impact of electronic forms of surveillance, such as CCTV cameras, the knowledge of the existence of secret spies can correspond to Jeremy Bentham's famous Panopticon. Bentham, an English social theorist active in the latter half of the eighteenth century and the first part of the nineteenth century, sought to design a model prison. In a 1791 book, *Panopticon or the Inspection House*, he struck upon the idea of a structure using bars to enclose cells surrounding a large tower in the middle that would allow all of the prisoners to be potentially observed, without their knowing whether in fact they were or not.[3] The system allowed the many to be watched by the few. In turn, French academic Michel Foucault developed Bentham's notion into a theoretical model in which the Panopticon in hierarchical societies represents a disciplinary force on wider populations. Although the Foucauldian model is most often applied to technological surveillance with the potential to affect everyone, the notion of its disciplinary power also relates to the use of informers in authoritarian states in general and in democratic states among certain marginalized groups or communities subjected to extensive and intensive human surveillance.[4] The awareness of the mere possibility that informers may be present in the midst of groups or individuals serves as a controlling force, out of recognition that agents of the state are observing actions. This is a key aspect of why the state, even while being completely resistant to revealing the identities of individual informers, is not at all reluctant to make it clear that informers operate in the wider society, since such knowledge affects behaviour.[5]

Accordingly, informers in societies purporting to be democratic do not represent a threat to the liberties of the entire population; they are not a form of surveillance like a computer database sweeping up all in their path, the technological equivalent of a drift net dragging the bottom of the sea, unable to distinguish between fish of value and those that are superfluous. Instead, they are something much more exact. They serve as a discriminatory tool for the state to target communities and individuals who are, or have historically been, in some way marginalized (such as for their political views or because of the advocating of violence) or 'othered' as existing outside of dominant discourses: Catholics, Muslims, Communists, Socialists, workers, union leaders, feminists, various ethnic minorities, Aboriginals, Black nationalists, Gays and Lesbians and countless others, including those on the far right. In some aspect or other the state has deemed or continues to deem these categories, several of them having been at one time or another on the margins of orthodoxy, as a threat, either real or imagined, to state power or some type of societal status quo and, therefore, subject to extensive monitoring. In truth then, all do not experience surveillance equally, in whatever form it comes. David Lyon captures this well when he notes that much of the popular literature speaks of the impact of surveillance in 'individualistic terms as a potential threat to privacy' and, as a result, misses 'one of the key aspects of contemporary surveillance: "social sorting."' '[C]ategorical suspicion of everyone (or at least everyone within a particular category)' is how Gary T. Marx describes the same phenomenon. Regardless of the terminology, the reality is that certain groupings experience surveillance disproportionately.[6]

The impact of informing can grow ever larger if the actions of informers expand beyond largely passive monitoring into playing the role of an *agent provocateur* by actively working to undermine said plans. In that sense, as former Central Intelligence Agency (CIA) Director Admiral Stansfield Turner has recognized, informers are 'employed to do what technical systems cannot do'.[7] One way they can do that is by actively seeking information. Whereas a microphone can sit buried in a wall waiting, perhaps in vain for the announcement of when and where a secret meeting might occur, an informer in the room can simply ask for the details and then relay them to his or her covert employers.

Several other points pertain to the use and impact of informers. Some are more particular and applicable to the present and the specific, while others are universal and eternal. Informers are valuable for more than just monitoring a targeted community, group or individual. They serve as an efficient weapon for damaging the interests of said targets by creating suspicion or paranoia or, in some cases, by actively undermining a cause targeted by the state.[8] Their use even creates the potential for dividing communities or groups, with intelligence agencies poised either to pounce on divisions in order to recruit more informers or to use existing informers to further exacerbate schisms. During 'the Troubles', British intelligence came to believe that once they recruited informers from the Catholic community it was a sign of the increasing isolation of the Irish Republican Army (IRA).[9] Similar trends have occurred in Israel, with the playing off of Palestinian factions against each other, and in Iraq when, after the 2003 American invasion, some communities, either because of violence against Muslims, national pride, or the largesse of American taxpayers (or a combination in some form of the three), turned against the Iraqi version of al-Qaeda, resulting in an increased flow of intelligence.[10] For democratic societies, writes Victor Navasky, the use of informers is destructive. In his study of the impact of McCarthyism in the early Cold War on Hollywood, *Naming Names*, Navasky argues that informers 'pollute the public well, . . . poison social life in general, [and] destroy the very possibility of a community' since the informer reflects 'principles of betrayal' whereas the community 'survives on the principle of trust'.[11] Those who employ informers, who in the past and present have included private companies in addition to state agencies, needless to say, see the phenomenon differently.[12]

Simply having informers within an organization, even if their presence is unknown, or whether they have served as *agents provocateurs*, still has the potential for affecting the targeted organization. Gary T. Marx illustrates the nature of the impact in gendered language (which is likely accurate in that, with certain exceptions to be discussed later, informers tend to be men):

> The most passive informant, of course, has some influence on the setting by his mere presence. His presence can make a movement seem stronger than it actually is. If nothing else, he may provoke the kind of information he is looking for. He may pass on to authorities false, exaggerated, or misinterpreted information. This may move through several police agencies and bureaucratic levels, and can lead to police actions with self-fulfilling effects.[13]

Damage through suspicion or through the information supplied to authorities is not the only variety of harm that can be done by informers. Accusations of informing against individuals can be even more destructive for those on the receiving end. Sometimes these emanate from failed efforts at recruiting, whereby intelligence agencies, in attempting to coerce individuals into informing, use the implicit or explicit threat that if they do not cooperate, rumours will be spread that they are providing assistance anyway, thus inviting retaliation. This was done by the British in Northern Ireland as a contrivance for signing up informers in the IRA among those who were in police custody. Because of a growing awareness of this tactic, released prisoners resorted to admitting that British intelligence had approached them, thus putting the matter out in the open, lest they face retribution.[14] Then there are false accusations designed to encourage dissension or worse within an organization. In the 1960s, the Federal Bureau of Investigation (FBI), as part of the tactics of its Counter Intelligence Program (COINTELPRO), employed a tactic known as 'snitch-jacketed' or 'bad-jacketed'. This involved agents leaking false information that certain targets, often serving in leadership roles and sometimes those who had spurned efforts to recruit them as snitches, were police informers. The police sought not only to discredit the individuals in question but also to invite retaliatory attacks against them, which demonstrates clearly the powerful response sparked by informing.[15] As an illustration, in 1968 an FBI agent in New York proposed to J. Edgar Hoover the following course of action against Stokely Carmichael, Black Panther member and former leader of the Student Nonviolent Coordinating Committee (SNCC):

> . . . consideration [should] be given to convey the impression that CARMICHAEL is a CIA informer. One method of accomplishing [this] would be to have a carbon copy of informant report reportedly written by CARMICHAEL to the CIA carefully deposited in the automobile of a close Black Nationalist friend . . . It is hoped that when the informant report is read it will help promote distrust between CARMICHAEL and the Black Community. . . . It is also suggested that we inform a certain percentage of reliable criminal and racial informants that 'we have

heard from reliable sources that CARMICHAEL is a CIA agent'. It is hoped that these informants would spread the rumor in various large Negro communities across the land.

In September 1970, Huey Newton accused Carmichael of being a CIA informer.[16] A year earlier, a Black Panther in California named Fred Bennett was 'bad-jacketed' and murdered as a result.[17]

A related tactic involves police forces arresting selected individuals and releasing them without charge, thus creating the suspicion that they had been recruited as an informer. A recent study offers a succinct commentary on the impact of the knowledge of the existence of informers in Northern Ireland: 'The effects of the informer war are profound: the level of violence is reduced; the republican community is rendered increasingly paranoid and must eliminate a proportion of its own membership in an attempt to regain its integrity.'[18]

The impact of informers stretches even beyond this, however. Informers can shift into becoming *agents provocateurs* on behalf of the state, actively thwarting or discrediting a movement or individuals. Such disruptive measures clearly have appeal to intelligence and police agencies since these, along with similar tactics, represent moving from being reactive to proactive, particularly on the intelligence side where there is not always the ready resort to arrests, as there is in fighting crime.[19] One version of *agent provocateur* disruption efforts consists of encouraging more radical actions on the part of groups to justify a crackdown by authorities, while delegitimizing the group's cause. The simple awareness of such a possibility had an impact, as E.P. Thompson wryly noted in *The Making of the English Working Class*:

[O]ne Jones, of Tottenham, . . . accused (mistakenly) of being a spy, because of his violent resolutions which were alleged to be for the 'purpose of entrapping the [London Corresponding] Society'. Jones (the genuine informer, Groves, reported with wry relish) complained:

If a Citizen made a Motion which seemed anyways spirited he was set down as a Spy sent among them by the Government. If a Citizen sat in a Corner & said nothing he was watching their proceedings that he might the better report it . . . Citizens hardly knew how to act.[20]

Comparable reactions occurred elsewhere. In the mid-nineteenth century a Belgian socialist lamented the effect of informers: 'The associations had disappeared; public gatherings and even private ones were from that moment on difficult to hold. You were frightened of your neighbour and had lost all hope . . . Everyone was suspected of being a spy.'[21] Observing a similar impact that the knowledge of the existence of *agents provocateurs* could have on a targeted group was a Canadian labour politician in the 1930s: 'Again and again visiting in the mining camps in the west [of Canada] I have had labour people come to me and say: "If there is any suggestion made in the way of provoking trouble be careful, because that suggestion comes from an agent of the government"'.[22] In a more recent case, involving the second wave of American feminism, historian Ruth Rosen describes the impact of FBI informers thus:

> Fear of provocateurs paralyzed some protestors. Fear of agents and informers eroded trust. Given the widespread assumption of infiltration, feminists sometimes found it easier to accuse one another of being informers than to accept the inevitable differences among them that, even without the FBI, would naturally result in different feminist perspectives and different ideas of sisterhood.[23]

The influence of informers is then two-fold: knowledge of them can act as a check on behaviour and their actual activities can be used by state agencies to undermine all varieties of causes. This can take the form of encouraging more radical or violent behaviour, even going so far as to entrap the unsuspecting, thus discrediting the movement while providing the state with an excuse for cracking down on those targeted. Ironically, in the short term, argues Gary T. Marx, an informer could assist the organization that he or she had infiltrated:

> The movement may sometimes benefit from the presence of an agent. Specious activists may help perpetuate a protest group by offering the

kinds of resources and more support that are often in short supply among those who take highly unpopular positions and engage in illegal actions. Because of their need to be accepted, agents often work very hard, are often very successful at gaining new recruits for the movement, and even at starting new branches of a movement.[24]

The intelligence informer brought a particular 'zeal' to the job because he or she alone knew that they did not face the risk of arrest for their radical activities and, therefore, could operate with immunity.[25]

Then there are other reasons why informers are deployed. Precision, particularly in comparison to technological surveillance, is one clear advantage. Equally significant is that in democratic societies, it is often easier to employ informers than forms of shadowing involving technology. A scandal erupted in December 2005, when the *New York Times* revealed that the administration of President George W. Bush had been conducting warrantless communications interception.[26] The 1978 Foreign Intelligence Security Act (FISA), passed by the US Congress, created a special body, nicknamed the FISA Court, which requires the US government to acquire a warrant either before initiating electronic surveillance against a set target or within 48 hours of having done so.[27]

No similar requirements exist for the deployment of informers.[28] The committee of Senator Frank Church, which in the 1970s investigated wrongdoings by American intelligence agencies, noted this anomaly:

> There is no specific determination made as to whether the substantial intrusion represented by informant coverage is justified by the government's interest in obtaining information. There is nothing that requires that a determination be made of whether less intrusive means will adequately serve the government's interest. There is also no requirement that the decisions of FBI officials to use informants be reviewed by anyone outside the Bureau. In short, intelligence informant coverage has not been subject to the standards which govern the use of other intrusive techniques such as wiretapping or other forms of electronic surveillance.[29]

The Church Committee added that at the time the only (loosely enforced) restrictions on intelligence informers were internal ones included in the FBI's 'Manual of Instructions', which it did not publicize. The specific proscriptions on the collection of information by informers related to communications between a lawyer and his or her client, 'defense plans or strategy' on the part of a legal team, 'employer-employee relationships' of the type associated with a labour union, and 'legitimate institution or campus activities'.[30] Currently, the Canadian government requires its main intelligence agency, the Canadian Security Intelligence Service (CSIS), to get special political permission, including retroactively, if necessary, when informers are utilized against sensitive targets, such as university campuses and churches and mosques, but these uses still do not involve the obtaining of a warrant. CSIS's predecessor in security matters, the Royal Canadian Mounted Police (RCMP) from the early 1960s on was not allowed to recruit informers on campuses but it could accept 'volunteered' information.[31] Since 2000, the Regulation of Investigatory Powers Act (RIPA) in the UK has governed the deployment of informers in investigations, including who has authority to authorize their use, but there still is no requirement to obtain a warrant.[32] Informing then is a type of state surveillance that does not necessitate such legal approval. Indeed, the US Supreme Court has legitimized the use of informers in more than one legal decision.[33] Three Supreme Court decisions in the 1960s, the most famous of these, *Hoffa v the United States* involving the then head of the International Brotherhood of Teamsters labour union, the still missing James 'Jimmy' Hoffa, imposed no legal limits on the exercise of informers by the US government.[34] In the union leader's case, the decision went against him, stating clearly that this form of human surveillance differed from its technological cousin since the subject of the intelligence gathering opted to supply the information directly to the government spy.[35] This 'assumption of risk' principle had previously been articulated by Justice William Brennan in a dissent in another case when he made a strong distinction between technological and human surveillance:

For there is a qualitative difference between electronic surveillance, whether the agents conceal the devices on their persons or in the walls or under beds, and conventional police stratagems such as eavesdropping and disguise. The latter do not so seriously intrude upon the right of privacy. The risk of being overheard by an eavesdropper or betrayed by an informer or deceived as to the identity of one with whom one deals is probably inherent in the conditions of human society. It is the risk we necessarily assume whenever we speak. But as soon as electronic surveillance comes into play, the risk changes crucially. There is no security from that kind of eavesdropping, no way of mitigating the risk, and so not even a residuum of true privacy.[36]

The FBI weighed in on the issue of requiring warrants for the use of informers in the mid-1970s during the Church Committee hearings. Not surprisingly, the Bureau opposed any policy change for several reasons, including, probably somewhat disingenuously, concern for freedom of speech rights of informers:

Concerning warrants, a warrant requirement for the use of informants appears impractical and may be unconstitutional. It is impractical because probable cause usually is not available when the informant technique is initiated and the submission of an affidavit in application for a warrant would increase the hazard of exposure of the informant's identity. Such a limitation might be unconstitutional because it would limit the First Amendment rights of the informant to communicate with the government. Existing legal restrictions required guided informants to recognize the same legal limitations as would be applicable, in the same circumstances, to those directing the informants. An informant can legally do no more than an Agent is permitted to do.[37]

Ironically, the Church Committee openly warned in 1976 of the risks that the use of informers represented to American civil liberties, particularly freedom of speech, because of the lack of the review and checks on this type of intelligence gathering that applied to other methods:

The intelligence informant technique is not a precise instrument. By its very nature, it risks governmental monitoring of Constitutionally-protected activity and the private lives of Americans. Unlike electronic surveillance and wiretaps, there are few standards and no outside review system for the use of intelligence informants. Consequently, the risk of chilling the exercise of First Amendment rights and infringing citizen privacy is increased. In addition, existing guidelines for informant conduct, particularly with respect to their role in violent organizations and FBI use of intelligence informants to obtain the private documents of groups and individuals, need to be clarified and strengthened.[38]

The Church Committee aside, the continuing concern by civil libertarians and others about technological surveillance rather than informing is striking, and is a tendency that extends to the present. A trawl of the bookshelves reinforces this emphasis, with numerous tomes having appeared in the UK and US since the end of the Cold War documenting the threat of technological-based intelligence collection. Popular culture has weighed in with movies like *Enemy of the State* and *Minority Report* that present, through expensive and sexy special effects, technological surveillance exercised by the state, including in the former case, by the American government's National Security Agency (NSA), as a tremendous threat to personal liberty. Technology has not simply vanquished personal privacy in these cinematic outings, it has extinguished it. These more recent cinematic depictions echo a theme raised by director Francis Ford Coppola in his superb 1974 movie, *The Conversation*, in which microphones and other audio equipment are used to conduct surveillance and invade privacy. At the end of the movie, the lead character, a surveillance expert, is left helpless to evade being spied on in his apartment through a hidden bug.[39] This skewed emphasis even extends to academia. In the UK, an academic association related to surveillance and society focuses almost exclusively on the use of technological surveillance, thus ignoring older types of information collection.[40]

Then there is a matter of resources. Professional technological surveillance in whatever form it takes is expensive. The NSA and the National Reconnaissance Office (NRO), the agency that handles satellite surveillance for the American government, combine together to represent approximately a third of the US intelligence budget compared to roughly 10 per cent for the CIA. In a direct comparison, the NSA's budget is double that of the CIA's and it has three times as many employees.[41] Technology is costly and its use is complicated — even in 2006, basic technological surveillance of a subject, which still on occasion involves physical access to the targeted group or individual's property or body, can involve up to a dozen people performing a variety of tasks.[42] All of these factors make this type of spying by the state, in most democratic nations, complicated and unwieldy. In the US of the 1960s, for example, bugging someone required either a warrant to enter the premises, thus paperwork and legal expenses, or an illegal entry, as the FBI did on more than one occasion. Also involved were technicians to ensure the equipment worked properly and then, in an often ignored but crucial aspect of the activity, individuals to spend hours listening to often mundane conversations as they carefully typed up transcripts for investigators to read, an aspect effectively depicted in the movie *Das Leben der Anderen* (*The Lives of Others*).[43] This is why a study by the US government's General Accounting Office (GAO) in the mid-1970s found that, whereas the FBI used informers in 85 per cent of its domestic intelligence investigations, it deployed electronic surveillance in only 5 per cent.[44] In that sense, Hollywood's emphasis is frequently inverted in proportion to the type of intelligence gathering actually used by intelligence agencies and police forces.

An additional practical aspect pertains to why intelligence agencies, or police forces for that matter, find it useful to employ informers. This rationale has long been around but it is even more relevant in the increasingly multicultural world of today: it allows the state to increase its reach. Government agencies simply cannot always be diverse enough to have expertise in every language and/or culture present in many countries today — think of cities like London, New York and Toronto that literally have representatives of every corner of the globe. As of 2004, Toronto had the second highest percentage of foreign-born citizens of any city in the world, after Miami.[45] New York is almost as multicultural — witness the scene from Spike Lee's

2002 heist movie *Inside Job* in which bank robbers are recorded speaking a language the police do not recognize, so they broadcast it to a crowd of bystanders in the successful hope that someone will recognize it.[46] It is for this reason that the FBI is becoming increasingly reliant on informers for intelligence-related investigations, more so than for normal criminal work, particularly as a starting point into terrorism investigations.[47] In the UK, there has been a drive to recruit more informers from among Muslim communities because of the difficulties the police and the Security Service (MI5) have had in penetrating them from within their own ranks.[48] Historically, the lack of diversity within security agencies has also applied to gender. Into the early 1970s, the two main domestic intelligence agencies in Canada and the US, in part reflecting that policing and intelligence work historically has been gendered male, still did not have female agents or officers. Despite this limitation, they still managed to conduct detailed espionage against women's groups, including all-female gatherings. This could not have occurred without the utilization of informers.[49]

The usefulness of informers extends to overcoming efforts to avoid surveillance. Those involved in radical or criminal activities have long been aware of the possibility of electronic surveillance and have sought to thwart it by not using the telephone or through employing encrypted email or other electronic means of communication that the state can not monitor or not crack. Informers represent a different type of surveillance that in some ways is more difficult, although not, of course, impossible, to counteract as it comes in the form of a friend, colleague or even family member. Some targets did and do attempt to employ methods to counter informers. Moving to smaller cells, with each having little knowledge of the activities of the others, is one such method. Questioning members about their backgrounds and political convictions is another. In the 1960s, it might involve having to partake of drugs as proof of one's counterculture credentials.[50] An additional technique is to require serious criminal activity as a test of commitment to the group and out of the belief that an informer would not engage in such actions.

Finally, informers serve as an instrument of precision in comparison to technological surveillance. The latter, involving considerable resources, widely deployed could potentially vacuum in everything, producing too much information.[51] An informer, on the other hand, is a more accurate weapon — a sniper rifle instead of a shotgun. He or she, through the coaching of a handler, can ascertain specific plans and, if necessary, shift into the role of a direct *agent provocateur* and actively work to undermine said plans.

This brings us to this book's definition of an informer. Essentially, an informer represents anyone who furtively supplies information to a state security agency, as opposed to a spy who provides information to a foreign intelligence service. An American who clandestinely helps the FBI is an informer; one who covertly aids Russia's *Federalnaya Sluzhba Bezopasnosti* (FSB) is a spy. This point applies to their use in foreign countries by occupying forces, such as the recruitment of informers by the US military in Iraq. Before the fall of Saddam Hussein, an Iraqi working for the US was a spy. During the American occupation, anyone supplying intelligence to the occupiers is an informer.

One key aspect of this definition is secrecy. Informers normally do not have their assistance publicized or, if that relationship does emerge from the shadows, pains are made to protect the identity of the person involved. This aspect differs from those well-publicized cases of individuals, such as former members of the mafia or so-called 'supergrasses' in Northern Ireland. These latter were members of the Irish Republican Army who later testified in high-profile trials.[52] They may well have been informers at one time, but their act of open testimony does not represent informing, because it is being done in a full glare of publicity even if ultimately their identity remains hidden.

Offering a general definition of an informer is not to suggest that all informers are the same. They clearly are not. A Canadian government enquiry in the 1970s into criminal activities by the world-famous Royal Canadian Mounted Police offered a helpful categorization of the various types of informers, including the use of the term 'source' as a label for those who inform:

TABLE 2.1 Types of sources[53]

Type	Description	Payment	Nature of handling
Volunteer	Person who volunteers — could be anyone supplying information, often on a one-time basis	Usually none	Infrequent meetings
Undeveloped casual source	Source who occasionally supplies information — examples on campus include security officers, secretaries, personnel in registrar's office	Usually none	Recruited — periodic contact
Developed casual source	More permanent source	Occasional, especially expenses	Recruited after considerable planning — source has specific handler who makes frequent contact
Long-term penetration source; sometimes known within the RCMP as a 'secret agent'	Most important source — described in Canadian government report as the 'bread and butter' of security work;[54] source either already in a targeted organization, or injected into one by police force or intelligence agency	Paid	Recruited after development of relationship between Mounted Police member and target for recruitment; extensive handling ensues — strong relationship often formed between source and handler; recruited after lengthy profiling and concerted effort to form relationship

Dutch police have their own categories of informers: 'one-time informants, opportunity informants, professional informants, provocateurs, and civilian informants.'[55] One major US city police force officially lists four different types of informers: a 'source of information' who provides casual information; 'paid confidential informant' who assists the police in return for compensation; 'defendant informant' whose assistance is motivated by a desire for assistance with an impending trial; 'other informant' such as those involved in criminal activity who are looking to assist the police.[56] In 1994, in the UK, the Association of Chief Police Officers (ACPO) offered a broad definition of an informer as anyone who provided 'information about crime or persons associated with criminal activity, such information being given freely, whether or not for financial reward or other advantage'.[57] Four general categories of informers are proposed by sociologist Steven Greer: 'inside single-event informants', who consist of the 'confessor' and the 'accomplice witness'; 'outside single-event informants' like a 'casual observer'; 'multi-event informants' such as the 'agent provocateur' and the 'supergrass'; and the 'outside multiple-event informant', that being the 'snoop'.[58] Victor Navasky also reduces intelligence informers to four broad categories with names that reflect motivations for informing: 'the informer as patriot', 'the espionage informer', 'the conspiracy informer', and the 'liberal informer'.[59] What several of these definitions have in common is recognition of the diversity of informer types and the importance of motivation in explaining why they do it. The focus of this study is on the more serious long-term informer, but it does not ignore the casual.

In doing this study, another reality must be acknowledged — the subject matter does not generate a plentiful supply of information. Rather, it is a secretive field because of the controversial nature of the work — and it is work — that informers do, and what they represent. Informing is associated with betrayal. This leads to negative public perceptions. Think of the general terms applied to informers: grouse, snitch, fink, dobber, stool pigeon, stoolie, rat, canary, finger, narc, grass, supergrass, squealer, tout — and those are just English-language terms.[60] In a study published in the 1960s, two American police officers described the perception of informers in criminal cases among the public:

> 'Informer' is a dirty word. In the underworld, he is scum or something that crawls out from under stones. He is the most hated creature because he is the underworld's most dangerous threat . . . One might suppose that this fact would make the public pause in accepting the underworld's derogatory appraisal of the informer. But it does not. This is part of a curious phenomenon which arises in part, we suppose, from the fact that few of us possess an entirely clear conscience. Too often we identify ourselves with the underworld rather than the law. Special antagonism to informers may be attributed also to our American

revolutionary heritage and to the fact that the forebears of many of our citizens came to this country one jump ahead of the process of the law. Many Americans of today have a sort of atavistic hatred of the informer derived from a grandfather who evaded the 'Black and Tans' in Ireland or the Kaiser's conscriptors in Germany.[61]

The same points apply generally to the portrayals of informers in popular culture. An exception is *On the Waterfront*, in which inform- ing is portrayed as heroic. Elia Kazan, vilified by many in Hollywood after he 'named names' of former Communist associates in 1952 in front of the House Committee on Un-American Activities, directed the film. The film's screenwriter, Budd Schulberg, also provided names to Congress.[62] In contrast, cinematic depictions of informers and informing have frequently been negative. The movie *Spartacus*, penned by Dalton Trumbo, himself a victim of the blacklist but who, unlike Kazan, refused to offer up names and went to prison as a result, offered a rejoinder to *On the Waterfront*. In a now iconic scene, a Roman leader offers a group of prisoners their lives in return for betraying their leader, Spartacus. Instead of informing, they stand up one by one and declare, 'I am Spartacus.'[63]

Betrayal figures prominently in other motion picture portrayals. Some of the films introduce a degree of nuance, as in the example of *The Molly Maguires*, a 1970 film directed by Martin Ritt, also a victim of the anti-Communist Hollywood blacklist. In that movie, Richard Harris portrays an Irish-American Pinkerton's Detective who infil- trates a radical group of Irish-American miners, serving as an *agent provocateur*, albeit one with conflicted loyalties between the men he spies on and his employers. Similarly, another mining movie, this one set in West Virginia, John Sayles' *Matewan*, has a central character who is an *agent provocateur* on behalf of the coal company, actively working to sow divisions among the miners. More recently, in 2007, two films focusing on informing won Academy Awards. The best picture Oscar went to Martin Scorsese's *The Departed*, loosely drawn from the real-life case of mobster and FBI informer, James 'Whitey' Bulger. It interweaves the stories of two informers: the 'good one', a role taken by Leonardo DiCaprio, who infiltrates the mob on behalf of the Boston Police while the other, the 'bad one', portrayed by Matt Damon, infiltrates the Boston Police on behalf of a James 'Whitey' Bulger-like mobster, himself simultaneously working as an informer for the FBI. The other film, *Das Leben der Anderen*, a German film about the surveillance of dissidents in the former German Democratic Republic (GDR) in the 1980s, captured the Academy Award for best foreign language film. In that film, the partner of a playwright under surveillance is pressured by the GDR's infamous intelligence service, the Stasi, to become an informer against him.[64] Interestingly, and as a means of distinguishing them from movies about technological surveillance, the theme at the heart of each Oscar-winning film is less about omnipotent surveillance and a loss of privacy than it is about human betrayal. This speaks to the power of the reaction that informing generates. In both, the lead characters who engage in treachery end up dead.

On television, the long-running animated series, *The Simpsons*, has had more than one episode focusing on informing, including one in which family patriarch Homer Simpson becomes a prison snitch in return for favours; his first bit of information that he relays to prison officials is that Homer Simpson has become a snitch. In another, Simpson attempts to entrap his friends at their local bar on behalf of the American state. In a third episode, and an obvious spoof of *The Departed* right down to the appearance of a symbolic rat at the end, Bart Simpson finds his plans to cause chaos at his school repeatedly disrupted because of the presence of an informer among his friends. In the post-9/11 world an entire series called *Sleeper Cell*, concentrating on an FBI informer operating within a group of terrorists in Los Angeles, would appear. An Australian series called *The Informant* focuses on the life of an undercover operative working for an elite Australian police force.[65]

The negative representations clearly outnumber the positive, which reflects wider societal perceptions. Indeed, controversy erupted in the early twenty-first century, when t-shirts with the caption 'Stop Snitching' began to appear on the streets in parts of inner-city America. In the UK, even police forces have played on the negative associations connected to snitching with a campaign entitled 'Rat on a Rat', designed to encourage the supplying of information about drug dealers.[66] The message conveyed is in keeping with the wider negative opinions of informers that stretch back centuries. Pro-informer campaigns in Stalin's Russia, or the lionizing of informers and informing in McCarthyite America, which Navasky labels as having raised the informer from a 'rat to a lion', demonstrate this wider truth since, if informing was properly embraced, states would not have to encourage the activity. These portrayals of state inform-ers indicate that the legitimacy of the state is still under challenge by older traditions that prize and emphasize ties to communities, tribes and families. In that sense, campaigns against informing, regardless of motivation, represent a form of resistance to state power.

Those employing informers are well aware of these associations, since they often share these impressions,[67] yet they also actively seek to combat them since improving the standing of informing and informers is clearly in the interest of the state in two respects: a positive image will aid in the future recruitment of informers, while affording more legitimacy to those in the present. One method is to stress the positive benefits of informing to society, as J. Edgar Hoover did by invoking patriotism to attack those who criticized such assistance to the state: 'They stigmatize patriotic Americans with the obnoxious term "informer," when such citizens fulfil their obligations of citizenship by reporting known facts of the evil con-spiracy to properly constituted authorities.'[68] Navasky points to an appeal to a 'higher loyalty' as a means of countering the calumnies associated with informing.[69] Language plays a role in this strategy. Hence, a concerted effort by those who use them to 'redefine [the] informant from a shadowy image to that of a good, dutiful citizen'.[70] Writing in the 1960s, two American police officers called for a change in terminology to encourage a reconceptualizing of informers: 'We should eliminate the word informer where we can, because it has such poor connotations. We can substitute words like "source" or "com-plainant" or "special employee" or some more euphemistic term.'[71] Increasingly, in a trend identified by Frank Donner, intelligence agen-cies and police forces have sought, in their discourses on the topic, to apply neutral or positive labels to informers, such as 'source', 'human source', 'covert human intelligence source', 'asset', 'confidential source', or, in the words of MI5 about informers in Northern Ireland, 'national assets'.[72] Hostility is, of course, relative. While the practice of informing is generally perceived in negative terms, the actual role of informers within certain groups may not be viewed by those untargeted, in equally negative terms, depending on the nature of the group and the context of the time. Wider acceptance for infiltrating the Communist Party of the United States of America by FBI informers would likely have existed in the 1950s than in the 1970s, for instance, although not among American Communists. Similarly, few would now protest the use of informers by the FBI against the Ku Klux Klan, although in the 1960s, opinion in the American south would have been more divided, particularly in communities where racial prejudice was endemic.

Still, in the hostile environment that can surround their actions, informers choose to remain anonymous and their handlers work to protect their identities. There is, of course, the aspect of safety — and this cuts both ways. Employers seek to ensure the obscurity of an informer in part to protect the safety of that individual, partially out of a sense of loyalty. A secret collaborator engages in betrayal and this engenders powerful human emotions including revenge. Denis Donaldson, who assisted British intelligence in Northern Ireland is one such example of being targeted, in his case by the Real IRA, but there have been other revenge attacks on both real and imagined informers.[73] Donaldson's former organization, the IRA, killed seven or eight alleged informers ('nutting' them in IRA slang) between 1979 and 1981 (and additional ones before and after this period), a number higher than IRA members killed by British authorities during the same period.[74] In India, Maoists guerillas regularly execute suspected informers, including at least 20 in 2005, prompting the police to raise compensation offered to potential snitches to counterbalance the risk.[75] An estimated 1,000 Palestinians were executed by their fellow citizens between 1987 and 1993 because of alleged assistance to Israel.[76] Attacks occur not just on informers. Families can be at risk as well. A brother of the individual rumoured to have informed the American military of the location of Saddam Hussein's sons, Uday and Qusay, in return for a $30 million reward, was later murdered, apparently in retaliation.[77]

There is, however, a much more practical and self-interested reason why handlers seek to protect the identity of the informers and it has nothing to do with safety. It is done out of necessity to ensure the continued recruitment of informers in the future. If a particular agency is shown to be unable to protect the identity of an informer, let alone their personal safety, no individual will willingly submit to being one, out of fear of exposure. This is a long held principle of intelligence agencies and police forces, hence the desire for perpetual secrecy. In the US, courts have recognized this factor and have provided authorities with the power to avoid revealing the names of informers, even during trials. In *Irons v Bell*, a court ruled that publicizing an informer's name served as an 'unwarranted invasion of personal privacy'. More significantly, it added that such a course 'would cost . . . society the cooperation of those [informers] who give the FBI information under an express [or implied] assurance of confidentiality'.[78]

With all of the potential negatives associated with informing, there remains the matter of how such a useful asset is recruited in the first place. Informers play a helpful role for state agencies but their deployment first requires recruitment, and that frequently entails finding individuals either willing to cooperate or who can be convinced by handlers to collaborate. Why such people assist is frequently complex, and often, contradictory, and is affected by location and era. It also may differ depending on the agency that is signing up informers — for example, the main motivational tools may fluctuate depending on whether it is a police force or an intelligence service doing the recruiting. In that respect, as two British criminologists argue, motivation is 'not a property of the informer but a socially constructed property of the detective-informer relationship. Officers have power over informers because they can translate that power into dependency'.[79]

Clearly, this is not a relationship founded on equality. The imbalance is most obvious when looking at police forces and their informers. Career criminals who inform for the police are at a perpetual disadvantage in that they face a return to jail and are in a continually inferior position to those employing them. The example of intelligence informers in a liberal-democratic society is more complex. Arguably, in some cases the imbalance of power flows, at least initially, in the direction of the informer or potential informer. Intelligence services perpetually detest publicity with rare exceptions, such as the head of Sweden's internal security branch announcing publicly in 2001 that his agency was seeking informers from within the ranks of anti-globalization protesters.[80] An individual doing the recruiting has to be sure, therefore, that his or her potential target will not rebuff the offer or, even worse, reject it and go to the media with the information, as one did in April 2009, along with a recording of the potential handler's approach.[81] The power imbalance particularly applies in cases where the social status of the potential recruit exceeds that of the recruiter, as with university faculty being recruited by police officers to spy on students or other academics.[82]

Considering the dangers and negative associations attached to informing, why are some willing to do it? Numerous motivations for informing have emerged over the years. The classic categorization of the reasons for informing was developed not about informers but about spies who betray their countries. Soviet KGB defector Stanislaw Levchenko set out four classic motivations for betrayal in what he called MICE (money, ideology, compromise and ego).[83]

Money, or some other type of reward, is obviously a leading motivation. This is especially true on the criminal side, but it is not insignificant for those dealing with intelligence investigations, when it comes to encouraging betrayal. 'Mrs. Fischer asked me to submit to my superiors her offer to apply them with intelligence in return for funds' was how an agent of the FBI described the approach of a German émigré in the US with an offer of information on members of her community.[84] In 1975, half of 1 per cent of the FBI's overall budget was set aside to pay 'all types of security informants including those in the foreign counterintelligence field'.[85] In New Zealand, police paid more than $1 million (NZ) to informers between 2000 and 2003.[86] It is common for informers involved in high profile drug cases in the US to receive annual payments in the hundreds of thousands of dollars.[87] One such FBI informer on the criminal side not only received $135,000 in a two-year period but he additionally received a cell phone, and money for car repairs. The FBI even rescued his dog from the local pound. Working against terrorism also does not go without its rewards. For one informer in a terrorism case, the FBI spent over $1 million on him and his family. In Canada, the Royal Canadian Mounted Police informer, in a 2006 terrorism case that led to the arrest of a group of Toronto men, received several hundred thousand Canadian dollars.[88]

Despite these high profile payments, when it comes to financial reward, not all informers are equal. Arguably, a class system along capitalist principles exists, even in informing with a small number of people, depending on the significance of their position and the concomitant quality of the information supplied, being well compensated while those at the bottom with little valuable to offer, receive little in return. In the early 1970s, FBI informers earned roughly $100 per month.[89] A 1996 study in the UK found payments to informers normally were about £100 in exchange for information received.[90] Around the same period, Dutch police made on average 200 payments a year, ranging from 500 guilders all the way up to 100,000 guilders.[91] Payments to informers by Israel's General Security Service, known as Shin Bet or Shabak, are deliberately small since, in the words of its former head, 'sudden riches arouse suspicion'.[92] An offer to pay off student loans was the appeal made by a Scottish police officer to a member of an environmental protest group in 2009 because, according to the recruiter, 'UK plc can afford more than 20 quid'.[93]

In spite of the financial incentive, informing is also not solely about money. Malachi L. Harney and John C. Cross, based on their American policing experience, suggest a number of motivations: financial reward, 'the Fear Motive', 'Revenge Motives', 'Perverse Motives', 'Egotistical Motives', 'Mercenary Motives', 'The Detective Complex', 'Selective Law Enforcement', 'Repentance or Desire to Reform', 'Appreciation or Gratitude Toward Police or Prosecutor', and 'Demented, Eccentric or Nuisance Type Individuals'.[94] Academics who have studied the matter emphasize additional motivations such as ingratiation, envy, love and hate, self-interest, dealing with criminal competitors, disgruntlement and even the simple thrill derived from trafficking in secrets.[95] Sociologist Steven Greer offers his own broad-ranging list of what he sees as the key incentives: 'patriotism/ideological opposition to the group in question'; 'coercion'; and 'inducement; activist disaffection'.[96] Some of the inspirations are context specific — ideology, for example, clearly played a greater role during parts of the Cold War than it does now.[97] Malin Åkerström and others mention the excitement of betrayal or the fantasy associated with a life of secrecy and illicit behaviour as factors. This impetus was acknowledged by an informer he interviewed, who explained his choice of career: 'I love to do this. I'm, like, addicted now.'[98] Other stimuli include nationalism, revenge and prejudice.[99] The type of informer also affects the motivation. Some casual informers may act simply out of a sense of public duty. Those who volunteered on the intelligence side during the early Cold War often did so because of ideology or their personal circumstances or a combination of the two. The same point applies at times to the current 'war on terror'.[100] Criminal informers are distinct from intelligence informers, with money being even more important for the former, along with other, unique factors such as reduced sentences and revenge against rivals.[101]

Then there is duress.[102] In 1955, J. Edgar Hoover claimed that '[u]nlike the totalitarian practice, the informant in America serves of his own free will, fulfilling one of the citizenship obligations of our democratic form of government'.[103] Clearly, however, coercion in a variety of forms, including blackmail, is deployed on occasion, and not only in non-democratic states. It is particularly used in contexts where power imbalances are in place (arguably the majority of recruitments) or where vulnerabilities exist — Denis Donaldson said he was recruited by British intelligence 'after compromising myself during a vulnerable time in my life'.[104] Prisoners, including those under arrest, whether due to criminal or political activity, for example, are in a particularly vulnerable position. Some handlers prefer coercion and regularly employ it, because the tactic provides continual leverage over the snitch. For that reason, paying money to informers who do not seek financial reimbursement allows for greater control, such as the possibility of blackmail, particularly if the money is not declared for tax purposes.[105] A British study found that, in its sample, 84 per cent of police informers had either been in custody or facing charges when they were recruited and in 85 per cent of the examples it was the handler who launched the recruitment.[106] In 15 cases from the early 1970s involving the recruitment of intelligence informers, Gary T. Marx discovered that six had been recruited under duress, including through the threat of arrest.[107] In recent times there have been several cases where the threat of being sent to Guantanamo Bay was used as a recruiting sergeant.[108] New immigrants to a country who require state approval to gain citizenship or to be allowed to stay are equally vulnerable, doubly so since intelligence agencies may require those from such backgrounds to penetrate existing communities.[109] Another context pertains to dictatorships where state agencies had and have almost complete power over the lives of citizens. At times, this can lead to brutal behaviour, such as the alleged case of Egyptian security personnel raping two children whose fathers were in an Islamacist group and then blackmailing them into becoming informers.[110]

Although coercion is obviously being utilized, its extent may be overestimated, for one main reason: coerced informers are not as effective as those who do it freely. This has been a consistent experience of intelligence services, even those operating in non-democratic states. If compulsion is deployed initially as a tool of recruitment, the handler may seek to change the nature of the relationship in order to encourage more effective assistance — the idea being that those who willingly participate will supply better information than those who do so under duress. This is not to suggest that the relationship would become an equal one — clearly a power imbalance would remain.[111] Some of the emphasis on coercion as the method of choice for recruitment involves retrospective efforts, particularly in Eastern Europe, by those who once informed to absolve themselves of responsibility for their actions by portraying themselves as victims in a similar fashion to those on whom they spied.[112]

Motivation is only one part of the process. More significant are the actual enrolment of informers and the maintenance of them as sources. The competent recruiting of such workers requires skilled efforts by trained handlers. In turn, effective handlers need characteristics such as patience, commitment, flexibility, intelligence and knowledge of human psychology. Modern intelligence services have developed detailed handbooks to aid their employees in the recruitment and maintenance of informers.[113] Some employ psychologists to assist in the recruiting and retention of informers. Once a potential source is selected, a relationship will slowly be developed with him or her, while the person's suitability is simultaneously evaluated. The FBI, for instance, does a background check on potential informers, examining all available records. A former member of Shabak compares this process to a game of chess in which the handler has all of the valuable pieces and the potential collaborator only pawns.[114] 'The Shabak guy talks in Arabic to [the suspect] without an accent, or appears as an Arab guy himself', explains a witness to Israeli recruiting. 'Shabak already knows everything about them, and that is such a shock to them. So they are afraid, and they will tell Shabak everything.'[115]

Ironically, that suitability has to include a number of characteristics that in some ways represent the fundamental opposite of the values inherent in the work of informing: honesty and loyalty. Potential informers also reflect the characteristics of the targets they are being directed at in order for them to do their job without attracting undue attention. As a result, and because it is cheaper, it usually makes sense to avoid using regular police officers or intelligence agents as informers. Instead, it is more effective to find someone either already in the targeted organization or someone who could credibly be a member of the said organization.[116]

Effective informers need certain skills. The potential source has to be able to weather an underground life since this profound confidentiality and dishonesty generates considerable pressure on the individual, along with the risk of exposure, weakening the impact of their work or causing them to crack and potentially embarrass the agency employing them.[117] The skills extend to the target of their activity. Providing information on criminals, for example, requires a familiarity with criminal activity. Alternatively, those toiling on the intelligence side often need to have a different form of awareness, frequently in the form of specialized political knowledge, since the groups they infiltrate are frequently dominated by ideology.[118]

What accompanies informing, plants additional ethical landmines for those doing the handling. For instance, what type of criminal activity would be tolerated on the part of an informer or, for that matter, an intelligence informer? This question is particularly germane for the simple fact that being credible among criminals, or even amid radicals seeking to test loyalties, might involve participation in criminal activity. This reality puts police forces in an especially difficult position as they can be forced to countenance seemingly illegal activities in order to potentially prevent crime. In the province of Alberta in 1998, the RCMP blew up a building in order to develop the credibility of an informer, as part of a determined police effort to arrest an activist suspected in a series of attacks against the oil industry.[119] The same point relates to some intelligence investigations, particularly those involving violence. The FBI, in the 1960s and 1970s, instructed its informers that while they should be fully involved in the New Left they 'should not become the person who carries the gun, throws the bomb, does the robbery or by some specific violative, overt act become a deeply involved participant'.[120] Nevertheless, evidence exists of Bureau informers having participated in and, arguably, even having encouraged the use of violence during this time period. A different issue arose with the action of a CIA informer in Guatemala during what amounted to a civil war between the country's indigenous population and US-backed government forces. A member of the Guatemalan military, the CIA informer was connected to the murder of two people, one an American citizen and the other the spouse of an American citizen.[121] When this involvement became public, a so-called 'scrub order' was issued by the CIA requiring the recruitment of anyone with a dubious human rights or criminal record to be approved by a committee.[122] The restriction was dropped after the attacks of 9/11 after criticism that a credible informer inside a terrorist group might need to have blood on their hands.[123] The reality is a little more complex, as Harney and Cross point out: 'There is an old police saying that "One does not get criminal information from preachers." This, we think, is a slander on the acumen and sophistication of the clergy. We have found them to be among the most reliable and realistic of sources.'[124]

The actual recruitment, principally on the intelligence side, often occurs after the cultivating of a relationship in some form between the objective and the handler. This may involve meetings, long conversations, meals or other encounters. For the handler, these discussions serve as an opportunity to assess the suitability of the individual being targeted in terms of the information they could access. It also extends to the level of their trustworthiness and reliability with respect to the information they would be supplying and whether they would remain quiet about their work or the initial effort to recruit them. Additionally, an opportunity to meet the individual in person would allow a pitch to be developed. Did the person have enemies? Racial prejudice? Super patriotism? Financial need? Hidden secrets? A mixture of several motivations? The pitch needs to be tailored to each individual case. During periods in the Cold War, an obvious appeal to patriotism could be made, but this became less useful as the struggle between communism and capitalism dragged on and then finally ended. A coerced recruitment, by its very nature, would entail applying pressure in a variety of ways on the individual being targeted. Again, once recruited, the handler will frequently downplay the coercion while emphasizing other motivations, such as financial reward, as a means to ensure the coerced informer becomes a willing or at least partially willing informer.

Once signed up, the employer becomes very familiar with his or her new employee. Many agencies, both in democratic and non-democratic states, require newly recruited informers to sign contracts. This document is useful in several respects. It indicates a willingness to cooperate, plus the recruiter could brandish it in the future, depending on the circumstances, as a tool to ensure cooperation or silence on the part of former informers. In the case of the latter, an FBI informer from the early 1970s reporting signing 'a security clearance and an oath swearing not to divulge anything I might observe or report to anyone but the FBI . . . If I violated my oath, I'd be liable for prosecution and a maximum fine of $2,500'. In doing so he became a 'subcontractor' and not a full FBI employee, thus preventing him from being listed on the Bureau's payroll.[125] After the fall of communism in Eastern Europe, contracts of this type would come back to bedevil many of those who signed them.[126]

To ensure an efficiently run operation, thus reducing the potential for informers to be exposed, agencies like the FBI and RCMP centralized the running of informers. At one point, FBI agents had to complete a form known as an FD-209 on a monthly basis to keep informer files up-to-date.[127] The Security Service in the UK has similarly developed an elaborate system for handling those who supply information, according to a former member:

> For each source report, there are three copies. One remains with the originating section, G6. Two further copies–one white, one blue–go to the desk officer, who checks the names of those who appear against service records. The officer then assesses, grades and comments on the new intelligence. The desk officer's white copy is filed on an investigative and/or personal file. The blue form is then returned to the agent-running section to provide feedback to the agent's handler. Once there, it is filed with other reports produced by the same agent.[128]

Wherever they are employed, regular direct and indirect meetings occur at which information is supplied verbally or in writing by the informer and collected by the handler. Part of the handler's job is to motivate the informer to continue his or her covert work while also pressing for additional or more specific information depending on the needs of the handler's employer. In the background, an evaluation would be occurring to ascertain the value and accuracy of the information, at times through the use of additional informers. One potential danger is a form of 'Stockholm Syndrome' whereby the informer comes to identify too closely with the group he or she has infiltrated or is already a member of. Frank Donner detailed the example of an infiltrator of the Black Panthers who gradually became sympathetic to the cause and then racked by guilt at his deception. In turn, this led him to become more militant in recompense for his betrayal.[129] Still, being well integrated into a targeted group is sometimes useful. American examples exist of informers who had sexual relationships with those they were spying on in an effort to create a full cover for themselves or possibly as an *agent provocateur* to sow divisions within.[130]

For handlers there is the additional risk of being intentionally or unintentionally misled by those supplying the information. Potentially, this could come from a 'double agent' with the aim of damaging intelligence efforts. To control for manipulation, or simply to ensure that the work of the informer has some degree of truthfulness and usefulness to it and the individual is not a 'bullshitter', requires the use of multiple informers, regular review of the information coming in, clear rules and instructions, centralized control of informants, tight supervision by individual handlers and possibly surveillance against informers. Some intelligence agencies also oblige their covert employees to undergo polygraph tests to ascertain the veracity of their claims.[131] In his autobiography, William C. Sullivan, a senior FBI agent and Hoover deputy, warned of the reliability of informer reports and how to address the issue:

> After they've been working for us for a while, informants get to know the kind of information we want and many of them tailor their stories to suit the occasion. . . . That's why we always try to have more than one informant in the same group. Three in a group of thirty would be ideal. Each would be unknown to the others, of course, so that we can compare three separate reports of the group's activities.[132]

Policemen Harney and Cross similarly advise that '[i]nvestigators should never lose sight of the fact that the informer, as a witness, is at best an irregular. He should never be taken at the face value accorded to an officer, even though he has a record for reliable performance.'[133] The same point applies elsewhere, reflecting the widespread nature of the informing experience. When it came to the secret police of the German Democratic Republic, historian Barbara Miller points out, the 'Stasi could never have functioned as it did if it had been constantly fed erroneous and fabricated information. In order to ensure that the information was "true, complete, current, original and testable" it was to be checked and double-checked'.[134]

Because of the regular meetings and the all-prevailing secrecy surrounding their assignation, close relationships, not dissimilar to an illicit affair, frequently develop between handlers and informers. Ironically, trust is all-important in a relationship built on betrayal. After retirement one Canadian intelligence officer continued to see his past informers socially, despite no longer being in contact with his regular work colleagues.[135] Another Canadian informer never told her husband of her lengthy and intimate involvement with the police because 'he never succeeded in gaining my confidence'.[136] In some cases, often on the criminal side where a fundamental power imbalance prevails, the relationship between the handler and informer can become sexual, potentially unwillingly on the part of an informer already coerced by the police to assist in the first place.[137] Less frequently, the manipulation can run in the opposite direction. In a celebrated case, an FBI agent became the lover of his Chinese-American informer, unaware that she was in fact a Chinese intelligence agent.[138] The relationship can also spin out in other directions. James 'Whitey' Bulger used his relationship with his childhood friend, who was also his FBI handler, to discover the identity of police informers within his criminal organization and have them murdered.[139] On occasion the connection could be over more diverse things, like the MI5 handler who regularly purchased heart worm pills for her informer's dog, or the Shabak agent who arranged gynaecological treatment for the wife of his informer.[140]

Law enforcement agencies and intelligence services recognize that the close relationships between informers and handlers invariably lead to risks, hence the repeated efforts at introducing rules and enforcing them to provide outside scrutiny of these relationships. As part of their training, Dutch police are instructed never to meet individually with an informer but to do so in pairs. In the early 1990s, the FBI was advised to tighten further central control over informers and handlers by employing managers who would directly oversee the use of informers and, in the process, help ensure that agents keep a balance in using informers.[141] The Bureau did bring in reforms in 2001 after the Bulger case,[142] as did the Boston Police, which enacted the following regulations governing handling:

All planned meetings or significant contacts with the informant shall be documented by recording all records of payment — if any, and the filing of debriefing reports. Debriefing reports shall not identify an informant by true name, but shall include the date of the meeting, the code number of the informant, the names of the officers who met with the informant, a summary of the information the informant supplied and what payment, if any, was made to the informant.

Officers shall only hold planned meetings with an informant, or potential informant, with another officer present both for corroboration and for backup.[143]

In the UK, police forces are required to register informers in criminal matters. The records are kept centrally as a means of maintaining security and ensuring proper procedures are followed.[144]

Rules are one thing, but compliance is a distinctly different affair. Because of the covert nature of informers, their handlers and their activities, ensuring rules are being followed is that much more complicated. This is especially true since the traditional priority appears to be on the quality of the information obtained, not on how its collection occurred. Since the terrorist attacks of *9/11*, this emphasis has only grown. Studies in both the UK and the US found non-compliance when it came to following through on new rules governing the use of informers. A 2005 US Department of Justice study of FBI compliance in 120 informer cases, performed in the aftermath of the celebrated mistakes on both the west and east coasts, found that the Bureau broke the rules in 87 per cent of the cases, including cases where informers engaged in illegal activity.[145] A study in the UK similarly discovered that some police officers in the field were not following proper procedure when it came to registering informers.[146]

Despite the human element (or perhaps because of it), informing in the present has evolved into a science — a highly organized, thought out and consistently practised activity around the globe. Although differences exist, particularly in the scale of informing, there remains identicalness to the activity in how it is perceived, how it is organized by those in charge of it and the nature of informers themselves, including why they do it. These practices and activities have evolved over time, particularly with the development of modern states. The historical context to the world of informers is the subject of the next chapter.

CHAPTER 3

Informing History

He has the plague all over him, and like other infected persons, desires to spread his venom and infection, and kill as many as he can; and therefore all that know him, avoid him, as the pestilence.
— Edmund Hickeringill, *The Character of a Sham-Plotter or Man-Catcher*, 1681.

No man admires an informer. There is in the human breast implanted a sentiment of fairness and justice which reprobates the action of the man who tells against those who have been partners in his guilt.
— *New York Times* editorial, 25 February 1883

If informers are active in the present, they have been equally evident for centuries, for the simple reason that they are essential tools for collecting information. In an age before the electronic compiling of the present, human intelligence (HUMINT) through informers represented not only the best type of intelligence collection, but almost

the only version. What has changed over time is the institutionaliza-
tion and routinization of informing as a practice. This began in the
nineteenth century with the rise of the modern state, through the
development of increasingly professionalized police forces and intelligence agencies; a trend that continues to this day.[1] Informing went
from being haphazard in the way it was conducted to representing
a structured activity similar to other forms of information gathering
carried out by the state. Explored herein are some of the developments
within the context of Europe and North America.

The archetypal, but undoubtedly not the original informer
appears in the Bible: 'And Judas Iscariot, one of the twelve, went unto
the chief priests, to betray him unto them.'[2] And, typically of many
informers, he did it for the money. It is not just in the Bible, however,
that informers appear in ancient times. Reflecting the life-and-death
world of the oppressed, the Talmud offers stark penalties for Jews
who informed on other Jews to Gentiles: torture, including mutila-
tion, perhaps as a warning to others considering a similar course, and
even death. To this day, loss of life is the ultimate retribution meted
out to those viewed as having betrayed, in part because sometimes
the informing itself, can lead to death.[3] Even in the afterlife, there
was eternal punishment for those who betrayed. In Dante's *Inferno*,
Judas is relegated to the worst level of hell.[4]

Those who relied on informers also meted out harsh punishments.
A 415 BC law in Ancient Greece regulated and encouraged informers
through a carrot and stick approach: a reward for accurate information and brutal justice, specifically death, for that which was not.
Typically, individuals who were best in position to supply information
enjoyed connections to those they informed against.[5]

In an age before formal police forces and intelligence agencies, the
reach of the state was inherently limited, especially in what passed as
the private sphere. As a result, informers represented the eyes and the
ears of those with power. In Ancient Rome, they were known as *delatores*, prominent freedmen or other officials hired to collect material,
especially of the private variety. Their testimony, including in treason
trials during the reign of Rome's first emperor, Caesar Augustus,
proved crucial in convictions. As a reward, they often received

the property of those who suffered as a result of their testimony. Additional factors, however, also explain the motivation of those who informed. Some did it out of animosity. Others did so because of a sense of loyalty to their friends or family. Some *delatores* may have participated because of their place within a hierarchical system that demanded such activity. Then there were those who informed in pursuit of greater power.[6] Regardless of why they did it, common to perceptions of informing elsewhere, those writing about *delatores* viewed their activities in highly negative terms. Chroniclers of the era, such as the historian Tacitus, 'othered' informers so that they became associated with being outside of the Roman norm, linked to deviance and criminality and even to disease and pollution.[7] Then there were those who knew and did not particularly care for individual informers in Ancient Rome: 'You are a *delator* and false accuser,/ And you're a swindler and a dealer,/ And you're a cock-sucker and gladiator trainer. I wonder why/ Why you don't have cash Vacerra.'[8]

In later centuries, during times of crimes and plotting surrounding religious and political conflict, the significance of informers only grew. In England, for instance, the judicial system relied heavily on informers, or 'approvers' as they were called for a period. There were important inducements to encourage informing. The individual coming forward received an exemption from the consequences if he or she participated in the same nefarious activities that they reported on, while possibly sharing in any reward on offer. On the other hand, false information provided could lead to execution.[9]

Their importance to the crushing of plots, the breaking up of criminal gangs and successful prosecutions involving harsh penalties for the guilty, plus the possibility of false or exaggerated accusations, made informers a prime recipient of vitriol. Sir Edward Coke, an English jurist and parliamentarian in the early seventeenth century, referred to the 'vexatious informer' who as 'viperous vermin' did 'vex and depauperize the subject and commonly the poorer sort, for malice or private ends, and never for love of justice'.[10] This negative association had an echo in (or, conversely, echoed) popular culture.[11] Playwright Ben Jonson, active as Queen Elizabeth I's reign came to an end, wrote this blurb about those who indulged in spying:

Spies, you are lights in state, but of base stuffe,
Who, when you have burnt your selves down to the snuffe,
Stinke, and are thrown away. End faire enough.[12]

In his poem 'Venus and Adonis', William Shakespeare depicts jealousy as 'This sour informer, this bate-bearing spy'.[13]

Because of growing problems associated with informing, the government of Elizabeth I sought to standardize the practice in 1576 through a parliamentary statute. Included in the legislation were licensing requirements for those informing and the punishment of a £10 fine and pillory, an often brutal form of physical punishment. These were to be applied each time individuals made false accusations. Another measure regulating informing passed in 1589.[14]

Despite the controversy associated with them, informers proved especially useful in dealing with real and imagined threats to the state. The England of Elizabeth I experienced growing divisions along religious lines that, in turn, intersected with national divides. That environment led to the deployment of informers against a particular marginalized entity: the remnants of the persecuted and frequently underground Catholic community. Frequently, Catholics spied on other Catholics. Anthony Tyrrell, a Catholic priest, was just such an example. His informing would eventually bring him to the attention of the Queen. Born in 1552, he entered the priesthood in the late 1570s and found himself in and out of English prisons. During his third stint in jail and facing the possibility of serious punishment for involvement in a plot, he contacted officials offering 'to become a Judas in kind'.[15] They readily accepted and Tyrrell offered information on associates, some of whom would later be executed. With the encouragement of his handlers, he continued as a priest while still in prison, passing on information he received from Catholic prisoners through conversations and, apparently, confessions. Later, suffering from guilt, he would become unreliable and confess to his treachery.[16]

Elsewhere, among those recruited to inform were unemployed graduates from the Universities of Cambridge and Oxford who needed the income. Philosopher Francis Bacon, who had a debt to address, became an informer for financial rewards. Sir Francis Walsingham, Queen's Elizabeth I's spymaster, led the organizing of informers, even paying their salaries out of his own pocket.[17]

The use of informers for political policing only grew in the seventeenth century. This was an age of plots, particularly centred on restoring Catholicism to its dominant religious position or during an era of English republicanism with the rise of Oliver Cromwell. Finding it difficult to keep track of radicals, Cromwell's government expanded resources devoted to intelligence collection and relied heavily on informers, both their own infiltration agents and those who were either recruited or volunteered to report. What initially was £1,400 a year to cover intelligence operations grew to £4,000 annually in the period from 1668 to 1675.[18]

As ever, there was a pattern to informers. Those doing it, often drawn from the lower echelons of English society, usually initiated the contact, even if later the government asserted control over them. Financial remuneration, including future patronage, served as the leading motivation for supplying information. In 1692, for instance, the Sheriff of Yorkshire employed six informers at £15 each to monitor former Cromwellian soldiers. Informing provided others with the opportunity to seek revenge against enemies. Some actively toiled as *agents provocateurs*. One such individual interpreted his role as to 'help . . . [the radicals] forward in any plot against [the] Government, and then reveal it'.[19]

Whatever the reason for informing, the potential existed for the supplying of false or exaggerated information in pursuit of financial or other rewards.[20] '[N]o sooner [was] one sham discover'd, but a new one [was] contrived to sham that', warned a pamphleteer writing in 1681 about those he condemned as the 'brutish and degenerate part of mankind.'[21] Still, in order for informers to receive their benefits from betraying, some accuracy usually pertained to the details being supplied. The real danger, according to historian Richard Greaves, lay 'in their ability to distort and misinterpret conversations, sermons, and private meetings. Innuendo and guilt by association were commonplace in their reports'.[22]

In England at that time, informers were widely used in criminal

and political matters for the simple reason that there was not a clear
system of law and order in place through formalized police forces
and/or intelligence services. Until the nineteenth century, a system of
local constables, whose duties were first codified in 1285 under the
Statute of Winchester, dominated instead.[23] The 1817 revelation of
informers acting as *agents provocateurs* against the Chartist movement and others sparked an outcry in Great Britain and contributed
to a continuing negative perception of police forces and secret police
forces. These agencies and their tactics were more often associated
with the continent, specifically the France of Napoleon Bonaparte.[24]
Two other English-speaking nations, Canada and the United States of
America, would inherit the English style of policing and the concerns
about a strong and centralized police force.[25]

Negativity aside, the British government through the Home
Office repeatedly employed informers in the late eighteenth and early
nineteenth centuries against selected political targets. They worked
against some of those involved with the 1780 anti-Catholic Gordon
Riots, the Luddites, who attacked factories and machinery between
1811 and 1817, and the reform-seeking London Corresponding
Society (LCS).[26] Some were volunteers, occasionally military men who
sought promotion as payment for their assistance, who contacted
the Home Office with information. Others clearly desired financial
remuneration.[27] Patriotism motivated still others, albeit with a note
of caution:

> You know my Zeal in the Cause, and my Readiness to support
> Government; and therefore I need not say anything on that subject,
> neither do I hesitate to say that I shall at all times be ready to inform
> Government of any Proceeding or Opinions of a dangerous Tendency,
> conceiving it my Duty as a Member of that State in which I enjoy
> Protection, to contribute to its Support; and this I shall do without any
> Recompense — but I must decline entering into any Engagements to
> give more minute or personal Information, particularly under the Idea
> of being paid for it; as I should not like to risque [sic] the odium which
> would necessarily attend a Discovery; to say of the unpleasantness of
> such a Task.[28]

Those of a similar inclination signed their reports to the British government with pseudonyms such as 'Patriot' or 'Lover of Liberty and
Order'. Remaining anonymous allowed snitches supplying information to avoid recriminations, in response either to real or false material
that they contributed. One discovered first hand the opprobrium that
went with being an informer. George Lyman, a member of the LCS,
served as government informer — reports he prepared for the LCS
were written in duplicate with the extra copy going to the government. Eventually, his treachery emerged and he bore, as his brother
described it, the consequences of his action: '. . . [his] reputation and
character were destroyed . . . [He] was deserted by his friends and
relations and frequently insulted in the streets which so preyed upon
his mind and both he and his wife's days were thereby shortened.'[29]
Not just informers received widespread scorn. The Home Office came
in for public criticism with the disclosure of its use of informers, especially when some were revealed to be *agents provocateurs*. As Clive
Emsley illustrates, however, the Home Office with its limited ability
to gather intelligence was dependent on informers.[30]

Whereas informing in Great Britain frequently had an amateurish quality to it, across the English Channel in France was where
the beginning of the modern use of informers emerged. Already in
the eighteenth century, police in Paris, in addition to covertly spying themselves, began to recruit informers as a tool for ensuring the
maintenance of the social order through creation of the fear that the
eyes and ears of the police could be anywhere.[31] Famously, the Paris
chief of police boasted to King Louis XV that if 'three people speak
to one another in the street, one of them will be mine'.[32] Eventually,
the chief's men in the streets would number as many as 3,000 and
be divided into three categories: '*observateurs* (observers), *espions*
(spies), and *basse-mouches* (informers).'[33] The King received a regular
intelligence briefing that then found wider circulation as a *bulletin
politique ou d'espionnage*.[34]

The system continued into the time of Napoleon Bonaparte and
his Minister of Police, Joseph Fouché. Fouché, who had served in a
similar position before Napoleon seized power for himself, added
300 informers to the payroll in Paris alone when he took charge. He

strongly believed in the efficacy of informers, often recruited from the bottom of French society. From the information generated by *mouchards*, the popular name for the snitches, he prepared a regular digest to pass on to Napoleon.[35]

In that context, the father of the modern informer in France was a convicted criminal named Eugène Francois Vidocq. As a young man, Vidocq worked first as a police informer while serving a prison sentence. He then went on to join the Paris police as part of the system of informers established by Fouché. From here, in 1812, he took charge of the *brigade de sûreté*, a special division for criminal investigations. The chief tactic he exploited was the professionalized and systematic use of *mouchards*, paid out of hidden funds. He believed, a reflection of his personal experience, that best placed to discover inside information on criminal activity were those who toiled in secret. His approach achieved a number of arrests and successes against crime and brought him fame partially generated through his own self-promotion.[36]

The approach to security of Napoleonic France influenced developments elsewhere. In 1809, Justus von Gruner employed the French model while restructuring first the Berlin police and then the police force of Prussia. Among the changes was the recruitment of informers, known as *Vigilanten*. Several German states later created police institutions to keep watch on radicalism and radicals as the anarchist movement was thoroughly penetrated. By the end of the nineteenth century, the police in Berlin actively employed informers as part of their operations. Police forces elsewhere around Germany issued instruction books on the proper management of informers, including both how to ensure their loyalty and that they not cross the line into becoming provocateurs. A handbook about the police force in Hamburg even included photos of its members undercover.[37] Not everyone was enamoured with the covert police operators, however. Otto von Bismarck complained of their tendency to 'lie and exaggerate in a most inexcusable fashion'.[38]

Brussels represented a comparable evolution to Germany. In 1835, there were but a few informers at work. Fifty years later, the state had informers including *agents provocateurs* operating, taking up 85 per cent of the police budget in 1889. In the process, they affected the free exercise of speech, as radicals had already discovered in England.[39]

Great Britain eventually followed the French trend, initially with the creation of a professional police force followed by the formalized use of informers. Under the leadership of Prime Minister Robert Peel, the British government established police forces. Part of the ongoing reforms involved the embracing of uniforms in a measure aimed at preventing policemen from working as spies.[40] In fact, the police eventually implemented methods tried elsewhere, including the use of undercover detectives from 1842. Later, the Criminal Investigation Department (CID) was formed in 1878 in Scotland Yard. Representing a familiar trend that would develop widely and which continues into the twenty-first century, the use of informers against certain marginalized groups, who represented real and imagined threats to the state beyond ordinary criminal activity, began. Specifically, in 1883, an organization focused on the growing threat from Fenianism was set up in London. Known originally as the Special Irish Branch, it would later become just Special Branch as its mandate expanded to encompass other threats to the state.[41]

Britain had previously used informers in its American colonies during the Revolution, triggering a backlash against the practice in the fledgling republic.[42] This experience, coupled with the English tradition of local constables, worked against the development in the US of a French model and, in particular, extensive undercover operations. Nevertheless, with growing urbanization, American cities began to develop their own police forces to ensure order. Especially significant as an inspiration for the use of informers, suggests Gary T. Marx, was the increasing ethnic diversity in big American urban centres. Whereas police forces could handle cities that were ethnically homogeneous since its members did not radically differ from those they policed, growing ethnic diversity suddenly divided police officers from those they targeted for policing. In an example that would be replicated elsewhere over the subsequent decades, including in Canada and the UK, American police recruited informers as a primary tool for policing immigrant and ethnic communities. Restrictive hiring practices at the time meant that members of these communities could not hope to be regular members of police forces or intelligence agencies. Instead, their expertise, through their skill with languages and their ability to blend in, put their services in demand. In the US, this provided opportunities to Chinese-Americans, African-Americans, and Jewish-Americans, all victims of discrimination. Of course, they were in demand out of necessity and not because of any growing enlightened tolerance on the part of the police.[43]

Equally, argues an historian, for ideological purposes in the US there was a privileging of the private over the public sector. In practice, this translated into the resorting by state and private interests to the use of both private security forces and informers.[44] Allan Pinkerton worked as a private detective for the Union during the American Civil War, and, in its aftermath, he established his own private detective agency. The name Pinkerton would soon become synonymous with undercover work, and, in relation to the labour movement, with strike breaking and repression. Most famously, a Pinkerton detective named James McParland spent two years working as a coal miner named James McKenna in order to infiltrate and spy on the 'Molly Maguires', a group of militant mineworkers purportedly responsible for a series of attacks in Pennsylvania against exploitative mining companies. Through his testimony, McParland helped convict several men, including 10 who were hanged in 1877. McParland's controversial role as an informer and, allegedly, as an *agent provocateur* would later became the subject of a Hollywood film in which Richard Harris played the Pinkerton detective.[45]

With the rise of the modern state and its institutions, state informers may not have grown in number but their use became more professionalized. A key influence was World War I and the arrival of a previously unheard of emphasis on domestic security. Practices were slowly developed and applied in what amounted to turning snitching into a science. The head of the Canadian national police force, the Royal Canadian Mounted Police (RCMP), distributed detailed instructions to his men at the end of the war, warning that handlers should 'be constantly on their guard against being purposely misled by the informants'. He recommended that two informers be employed to cover events in order to compare the veracity of the one against the other.[46]

In general, the war saw a dramatic expansion of state power in a number of countries and new efforts at monitoring and controlling the movement of individuals. 'Enemies within' became a particular concern to political and social elites. These consisted of ethnic groups drawn from nations now at war with countries like Canada and the US, but also featured workers and radicals, often with the three categories overlapping. With the 1917 Russian Revolution and the desire on the part of Bolsheviks to spread their revolution through support for domestic Communist parties in various nations, radical-ism and radicals became the main concern of those responsible for domestic security. Again, however, this overlapped with ethnicity and social class. Many of those who belonged to radical groups, espe-cially the rank-and-file members, came from non-English-speaking minorities. This posed a major problem for Anglocentric security agencies in increasingly ethnically diverse countries, such as Canada and the US.

In the case of Canada, the RCMP actively recruited inform-ers drawn from ethnic minority communities. The most celebrated Mountie of the interwar period was an informer named John Leopold. Born in Bohemia, he emigrated to Canada as a farmer but failed in that profession. The Mounted Police then recruited him because of his ability to speak several Central European languages and because his appearance did not match the dominant stereotype of what a proper Mountie looked like (even after decades of work for the police, he would still be regularly challenged to show his identification when entering headquarters). Despite being too short and not a naturalized Canadian citizen, he, unlike other informers, managed to become a regular member of the RCMP for the simple reason that the police desperately needed his linguistic skills. The informer soon put his abilities to work infiltrating the predecessors to the Communist Party of Canada (CPC) and then the newly formed party itself begin-ning in 1921. John Leopold became Jack Esselwein, a Communist activist renowned for his devotion to the cause. Throughout the 1920s, he actively reported on Communist Party activities while simultaneously engaging in disruption tactics, such as destroying party flyers. Continually living a secret life, however, inevitably took a toll on him and he increasingly turned to alcohol for comfort. Consequently, this led to disciplinary problems. He proved difficult for his handlers to control and mistakes occurred, leading to his eventual exposure. The next time many of his former party comrades saw him was inside a courtroom when he appeared in police uniform to testify against them in a case that saw several leading Canadian Communists sent to prison in the 1930s.[47]

Equally keen to use informers was the American Bureau of Investigation (in 1935 to become the Federal Bureau of Investigation [FBI]) under its new, young and dynamic leader, J. Edgar Hoover. A lawyer for the Department of Justice during World War I, Hoover became the Department's expert on communism and read voraciously the major Communist tracts, becoming thoroughly convinced for the rest of his life of the threat that an international Communist conspiracy posed against the US.[48] Hoover's new outfit already used informers against non-criminal targets and this had begun even before his arrival in the director's chair. By 1919, the Bureau, with no African-American agents of its own, had signed up African-American informers to spy on leading Black Nationalists such as Booker T. Washington and Marcus Garvey. Hoover had monitored their activities while he was still at the Justice Department.[49] A number of informers, with codenames such as '800' and 'WW', worked for the Bureau against Garvey. The former was James Wormley Jones, a past member of the US military, who became a leading figure in Garvey's Universal Negro Improvement Association (UNIA). Among the ranks of snitches were a friend of Garvey's, who was a Harlem businessman, and a 'confidential informant' connected to the Los Angeles Branch of the UNIA. The latter supplied detailed information on the organization's activities and membership levels. Others offered assistance to the Bureau when approached, while insisting on anonymity.[50]

Still, the Communist Party represented the chief target for the FBI as it did for the Security Service (MI5) in the UK and the RCMP in Canada.[51] In 1922, an FBI informer codenamed K-97 cast the deciding vote in the decision of the Communist Party of the United States of America (CPUSA) to become public after having been underground.[52] The concern about communism only grew in the 1930s. The key expansion of the FBI's use of informers for political policing occurred in that decade, specifically in 1936 when President Franklin Delano Roosevelt provided Hoover with the presidential authority to go after the CPUSA.[53] Hoover had initially shown reluctance, in 1932, to concentrate on the CPUSA out of a concern that his organization would be accused of employing *agents provocateurs*.[54]

One area of FBI focus in its hunt for Reds during the Depression was higher education, often at the forefront of progressive causes, and a location where informers would prove especially valuable. Their use and significance were evident at the University of Michigan. In its pursuit of intelligence about the left-wing American Student Union (ASU) the FBI obtained information from 'two confidential sources', a member of the Ann Arbor police department, the chief of police, the secretary to the dean of students, a professor, the university president, and from another 'confidential source' in the university's administration. In the final example, the informant supplied the investigators with intelligence on one ASU student leader's academic difficulties, including the reaction of the student's father during a discussion of his son's troubles. The labelling of some informers as 'confidential sources' indicated a longer-term relationship with the FBI, in contrast to others who might have provided information on a one-time basis. The Bureau received information on students or student activities from sources at as many as 43 universities during the 1930s. Informers operated where the police could not easily tread.[55]

World War II proved an even greater informing windfall than the Depression, to both the Bureau and the US Army. In January 1943, Roosevelt appealed to organizations and individuals to provide the FBI information about 'espionage and related matters'.[56] As part of this drive, the FBI and the US Army developed extensive informant networks in selected areas. The latter, for example, through its Counter Intelligence Corps, had at its height, approximately 250,000 informers.[57] The FBI using its contacts in the American Legion set up an informer recruitment program that contacted tens of thousands of people and in the end counted upwards of 43,000 in its ranks during the war.[58] The program continued into the Cold War. By the end of the Korean War in 1953, the number of FBI part-time informers through its American Legion Contact Program peaked at 108,000.[59] Overall, one scholar has the FBI employing at least 37,000 informers between 1940 and 1978.[60] Additionally, by the 1950s, the FBI had a special category of informers known as 'Special Service contacts' who provided 'valuable services to the Bureau including the furnishing of information on Security Index subjects, the saving of money and time in connection with transportation costs and installation of equipment, and the furthering of the good will toward the Bureau throughout the country'. There were almost 200 of these across the US in 1953, including Joseph P. Kennedy, the father of the soon-to-be president, John F. Kennedy, whose story is profiled in the next chapter.[61]

The FBI strengthened its focus on the CPUSA in the aftermath of the war, with as many as 1,000 informers infiltrating the organization in the late 1940s and early 1950s.[62] One estimate puts the number of FBI informers in the Communist Party at 20 per cent at one point in the 1950s.[63] Nearly 17 per cent of the CPUSA's paid membership by the early 1960s (1,500 out of 8,500) remained secret employees of Hoover's men.[64] Nor was it just the CPUSA on the left that occupied the FBI's attention. Trotskyists, through the Socialist Workers Party (SWP) and the Young Socialists (YS), had been infiltrated since 1940. Between 1960 and 1976, as many as 55 FBI informers occupied positions on YS or SWP committees, providing the Bureau with considerable sway over the radical groups.[65]

Searching for spies was one reason why the FBI targeted the far left. However, it had little success in this area for a number of reasons, but principally because of the Bureau's illegalities in the form of 'black bag jobs' that prevented it from submitting relevant evidence to a court.[66] The real focus was on the more nebulous field of subversion, a pattern the FBI shared with the RCMP in Canada and MI5 in the UK.[67] Informers would prove crucial in these campaigns against communism. For the purposes of testifying, the American Department of Justice kept a number of individuals on the payroll, prompting the *New York Times* to observe in 1954 that the 'cult of the paid informer is growing in the Federal Government'.[68] At the time, the American Department of Justice had 83 former Communists in full-time pay at a rate normally used to compensate scientists and academics; another 53 were employed part-time so as to keep them available for use in trials.[69] Some laboured for money; others did it out of a sense of patriotism; still others were pressured into assisting the FBI. Motivations, of course, could and did overlap.[70] Nor did they toil as ordinary informers. Intelligence-motivated investigations were far more intrusive than criminal ones. Material supplied often proved innocuous and pertained to legal and constitutionally protected activities, particularly the exercise of free speech. The informers also obtained and turned over to the FBI internal information from groups being targeted, including membership lists and financial records.[71]

The widespread use of informers by the Bureau was not without its controversy. This was hardly surprising, because of the negative associations such work has garnered historically, and because of publicity associated with the use of snitches in trials as witnesses. Hoover, however, would not hear of such criticism, and in June 1955, a defence of the tactic appeared under his byline in the *Federal Bureau of Investigation Law Enforcement Bulletin*:

> Experience demonstrates that the cooperation of individuals who can readily furnish accurate information is essential if law enforcement is to discharge its obligations. The objective of the investigator must be to ferret out the truth. It is fundamental that the search include the most logical source of information — those persons with immediate access to necessary facts who are willing to cooperate in the interest of the common good. Their services contribute greatly to the ultimate goal of justice — convicting the guilty and clearing the innocent. Necessarily unheralded in their daily efforts, they not only uncover crimes but also furnish the intelligence data so vital in preventive serious violations of law and national security. There can be no doubt that the use of informants in law enforcement is justified. The public interest and the personal safety of these helpful citizens demand that zealous protection of their confidence. Unlike the totalitarian practice, the informant in America serves of his own free will, fulfilling one of the citizenship obligations of

our democratic form of government. The criminal and subversive under-
world has long sought to destroy our effective informant system . . .[72]

Hoover's take on the motivation of informers was particularly
interesting. Informers often had a connection with secret police
forces which, in turn, were associated with dictatorships, including
America's Communist enemies. To differentiate, the FBI Director
made it clear that American informers performed out of a sense of
patriotism, raising the controversial practice to the level of a proper
citizen's required duty. In that sense, it was not hard to motivate the
interested to serve as informers during this period of the Cold War.
Fear of communism plus patriotism produced famous informers,
whose ranks included Herbert Philbrick, Harvey Matusow, Elizabeth
Bentley, Louis Budenz and many others, some of whose activities are
profiled in the next chapter.

Their uniqueness as informers related only to the extent of the
fame that they achieved. Many others remained anonymous, as the
FBI blanketed the CPUSA with informers in the 1950s. Collectively,
they provided the Bureau with comprehensive information on the
workings of American communism, a movement in rapid decline for
a variety of reasons, but also because of labours against it by what
amounted to an American secret police. In 1956, the same year that
Nikita Khrushchev denounced Stalin, a pivotal event in the history
of international communism and one exploited by western intelligence agencies, the FBI launched its Counter Intelligence Program
(COINTELPRO) against the CPUSA. This moved the FBI from a
relatively passive position of monitoring Communist activities to
an aggressive program designed to destroy the Communist Party.
Informers played a pivotal role in the campaign, working as *agents
provocateurs* with the deliberate mission of sabotaging the CPUSA.
It targeted the CPUSA not as a criminal entity but as a political one,
hence the resort to illegal tactics such as break-and-entries. This
represented a shift in the FBI's approach and was in part a reaction
to the public face of informers from the late 1940s and early 1950s.
The Bureau now avoided following proper legal practice because
prosecutions meant the exposure of informants within the targeted

organization. It had lost over 100 such individuals in a variety of trials during the late 1940s and early 1950s.[73] The RCMP had similar qualms. It considered but ultimately rejected an anti-Communist crackdown in 1951 because such a campaign would have exposed its numerous 'human sources' within the Communist Party of Canada. Instead, it engaged in disruptive tactics. One such operation consisted of the police creating and distributing a fraudulent letter designed to sow dissent within the CPC in the aftermath of Khrushchev's denunciation of Stalin.[74] In the UK the Communist Party of Great Britain (CPGB) was thoroughly infiltrated by MI5, which was especially effective at recruiting membership secretaries within the CPGB and its covertly affiliated organizations.[75]

The social turmoil of the 1960s and 1970s sparked an increased importance for informers, particularly in the sectors experiencing the highest levels of unrest. In North America these included universities, which saw the rise of student power movements beginning in the early 1960s. Student protest intersected with the civil rights movement and eventually the anti-war movement, Black Power, Red Power, and Gay and women's liberation. In the US, infiltration of said movements mainly but not exclusively involved the Bureau since both the American military and the Central Intelligence Agency (CIA) employed informers of their own to monitor domestic dissent. In the case of the former, by 1968 an estimated 1,500 informers laboured on behalf of their military handlers. Beyond the efforts by the federal government came state and city police forces, as documented in the work of the late Frank Donner.[76] These bodies utilized yet more informers to target the far left, the far right, and politically marginalized groups.

Leading the informer charge was, however, the institution dominated by J. Edgar Hoover since the 1920s. By the end of his tenure in the 1970s, the Bureau had two general categories of informers. There were 'paid and directed informants' and also 'confidential sources', a label applied by the Bureau to unpaid individuals who provided information based on their occupation, such as landlords or employers. So-called 'panel sources' were deployed to attend 'public gatherings on behalf of FBI for intelligence purposes or as potential witnesses' in the event of prosecutions. In 1975, the FBI operated around 200 panel sources, 605 'confidential extremist sources' and 649 'confidential subversive sources'.[77]

Because of its centrality in protest movements of the 1960s and 1970s, the New Left became a priority target for penetration by the Bureau. Midway through 1968, all FBI branches in the US had informers among the ranks of the Students for a Democratic Society (SDS) and other New Left organizations. Some of these attended the Democratic National Convention in Chicago in order to report on the activities of Democrats and demonstrators and there were even rumours that an informer or informers lowered the US flag in Grant Park, touching off the now infamous Chicago police riot. Whatever the case, intelligence supplied by snitches would be used in prosecutions against the protest leaders and these same individuals in the ranks of SDS were later put to good use in encouraging divisions within the organization's ranks.[78] The FBI recruited hundreds of secret spies to target the New Left; handlers instructed their snitches to take principal roles within the organizations in order to control their activities. 'In many ways I was a product of the Federal Bureau of Investigation', was how one informer, William Tulio Divale, recounted his spying days.

> The Bureau had 'recruited' (solicited) me when I was a political virgin. At the time I had no politics of my own and little of anyone else's. It was the FBI that pointed me toward membership in the Communist party, urged me to penetrate the W.E.B. DuBois clubs and to infiltrate SDS . . . It had moulded me to political consciousness.[79]

The presence of some Bureau informers like Divale actually fuelled radicalism because, to be credible, the informers had to be enthusiastic and committed to the cause. Since they were financially self-sufficient, thanks to their police income, they also had more time on their hands to organize than did real members. Groups with covert police operators could thus be pushed into escalating confrontation with those holding power. A student at an Illinois college who threw the school president off the stage was an FBI spy. He was also the only Weather Underground recruiter on campus and the finder of students to participate in 1969 protests in Chicago. Another, working in upstate New York, actually kept an SDS organization functioning when otherwise it would have faltered and disappeared.[80]

Repeating experiences elsewhere, informers frequently shifted from passive reporting to actively disrupting New Left groups. David Cunningham in *There's Something Happening Here* documents several instances of such activities as part of the FBI's COINTELPRO-NEW LEFT that launched in 1968. In 1969 and 1970, these included having an informer in Cleveland cause a New Left group 'to appear excessively militant' during a television appearance and sending informers to New Left meetings in Detroit and San Jose 'to promote factionalism'. The Chicago office used an informer to encourage conflict between SDS and the Black Panther Party (BPP). Another informer in New York City was ordered to destroy the literature of a New Left group, while a secret employee in Washington, D.C. was instructed to launch a petition with the specific goal of obtaining SDS members' addresses and handwriting styles.[81]

Overall, student protest bedevilled the FBI throughout the 1960s and 1970s, particularly because, as Cunningham points out, the FBI could not relate to those in the movement. As the sixties went on, the FBI faced increasing hostility on campuses and growing restrictions on their open activities at universities. Instead, they turned to campus informers for information they could no longer obtain directly themselves, particularly about the anti-war movement.[82]

In Canada, campuses similarly represented a contested terrain and the RCMP too faced hostility. In the latter half of the 1960s, the Mounted Police actually started an informer recruitment program because they had lost a number of their sources through retirement and graduation. The preference for informers was not students, who came and went and were less reliable and trustworthy, but permanent staff, especially academics, who had a long-term presence on campus and an interest in controlling unrest.[83] A senior Mounted Policeman at the time described a program to enlist faculty members as informers. It involved developing relationships with those who had served as references for background checks and appeared reasonably sympathetic toward the police:

When the foregoing plan had been pursued over an extended period of time, some rather pleasant developments took place. The most significant of these was in the number of professors, etc., who eventually offered their full cooperation on all matters of interest to us. Many, without prompting on our part, volunteered, or at least chose to discuss, the activities and political views of a number of their colleagues.[84]

More threatening than student protest from the racialized perspective of those in authority was the emergence of a Black Power movement in the 1960s that eschewed the non-violent rhetoric of Martin Luther King, Jr and his followers (who the FBI targeted, nonetheless, for extensive surveillance).[85] The FBI and urban police forces, with their lack of African-American members, would turn to informers not just to cover such a movement but also to participate in efforts to destroy it. Malcolm X was an early target in this respect. When assailants shot and fatally wounded him in 1965, the bodyguard who administered mouth-to-mouth resuscitation was a police informer.[86]

The FBI turned its attention more fully to the Black Power movement as the 1960s went on. In 1967, COINTELPRO-Black Nationalists was launched and Hoover's Bureau actively used informers to encourage divisions and open conflict between various African-American factions. Rumours of leading members being snitches were planted to try to discredit or, apparently, to cause harm to come to the individual. One Black Panther Party leader who suffered from the impact of informers was Fred Hampton, whom the Chicago Police shot to death under suspicious circumstances. The police knew where to find Hampton when they raided his apartment because an FBI informer in the BPP had supplied a hand-drawn layout of the flat.[87]

The growing unrest in American cities in the 1960s, particularly the Watts Riot in Los Angeles in 1965, led the FBI to instigate its crudely titled 'Ghetto Informant Program' in 1967. Ultimately, the Bureau employed more than 7,000 informers in African-American urban communities across the US, although one account by an insider suggests that FBI agents vastly inflated this figure because of pressure to meet snitch quotas.[88] Hoover's agents began the venture at the behest of the White House, with the almost colonial idea that the individuals, who included taxi drivers and barbers among their ranks, would serve as 'listening posts'.[89] Eventually, however, the informers, acting on orders from the FBI, would become more proactive, attending meetings and rallies and reporting on the distribution of perceived radical literature.[90] The FBI also sought to use its informers elsewhere. It instructed its handlers to 'immediately ascertain among all Negro informants, including ghetto informants, which informants are planning to enter college this fall and would be in a position to infiltrate black power groups on campuses. Bureau desires that we furnish them with the identities of these informants and the colleges they plan to attend.'[91] At universities in 1970, the FBI expanded its coverage of African Americans through informers to include African-American student unions.[92]

The same lack of expertise applied to surveillance of the women's movement in Canada and the US. All-male patriarchal security agencies had no choice but to rely on women to spy on other women. In her history of the post-1945 American women's movement, Ruth Rosen notes succinctly the extensive activity on the part of female informers: '[F]rom San Diego to Vermont, from Seattle to Florida, women spied on other women's thoughts, feelings, and actions.'[93] Some of those women being used, whom the police described as 'volunteers', would have been recruited from within the targeted groups. Based on the inaccuracy of many of the informers' reports and comments, it seems apparent that the police also infiltrated women into groups and meetings from the outside. Since the trust factor was important from the perspective of the FBI and the RCMP, the handlers or their colleagues would likely have known these women, possibly as girlfriends or siblings. The women supplied regular and detailed reports on meetings. In doing so, they provided blanket coverage, not only by infiltrating feminist groups and in the process covering efforts at 'consciousness raising' through reporting on books being read and personal conversations, but by keeping track of interviews in the media and clipping relevant stories. Many worked as pack rats, gathering any scrap of information that might be remotely of interest to their police handlers. Attendees at conferences would gather up pamphlets and other materials being distributed and turn them over to the police for inclusion in pertinent files.[94] The following was a report submitted from the FBI's New York office that provided intimate details about a gathering of women that only an informer amongst their number would have been privy to:

> On [deleted] [19]69, informant [deleted] who has furnished reliable information in the past, advised that a WLM [Women's Liberation Movement] meeting was held . . . Each woman at this meeting stated why she had come to the meeting and how she felt oppressed, sexually or otherwise. According to this informant, these women are mostly concerned with liberating women from this 'oppressive society'. They are mostly against marriage, children and other states of oppression caused by men. . . . [95]

Reflecting a gendered and homophobic view, the reports of informers, like this one in the RCMP's files about a 1972 gathering of Canadian feminist groups, often commented on the appearance of women or their involvement in activities that transgressed traditional societal norms:

> This was described as consisting of about one hundred sweating uncombed women standing around in the middle of the floor with their arms around each other crying sisterhood and dancing. The church had banned the 'wine and cheese' part of the party so they all got bombed on vodka. Two dykes had been imported from the US to show every-one how it was done which they proceeded to do in the middle of the floor.[96]

The ultimate impact of the snitching, according to Rosen, resembled the model found among radical groups elsewhere: 'For feminists, it was next to impossible to distinguish between informers and ordin-ary women who behaved oddly, suggested weird actions, held rigid positions, had poor judgment, or created dissension every time they opened their mouths'.[97] Ultimately, she notes, this had, perhaps as it was intended to, a devastating impact on the movement:

The FBI's impact, in my view, was that it exacerbated the movement's growing tendency to judge other women by examining the smallest details of their private lives. Fear of provocateurs paralyzed some protestors. Fear of agents and informers eroded trust. Given the widespread assumption of infiltration, feminists sometimes found it easier to accuse one another of being informers than to accept the inevitable differences among them that, even without the FBI, would naturally result in different feminist perspectives and different ideas of sisterhood.[98]

Ironically, factionalism among women and other progressive groups that informing exacerbated, simultaneously aided state security by allowing them to recruit from one faction to spy on another.

Although the FBI viewed devotees to the radical left as the greatest existing threat to the state, its adherents were not the only target of organized informer campaigns. Viewed by the Bureau as misguided patriots, the Ku Klux Klan (KKK) used terrorism through widespread violence and intimidation in the American South against the Civil Rights movement. At the urging of President Lyndon Johnson, the FBI sought to tackle the Klan. The model for their effort was suggested by Attorney General Robert Kennedy: 'The techniques followed in the use of specially trained, special assignment agents in the infiltration of Communist groups should be of value.' Already, an informer, who received $25,000 in return for his assistance, had provided a crucial breakthrough in the case of the 1964 murders of three civil rights workers in Philadelphia, Mississippi.[99]

In the mid-1960s, America's national police force used informers to undermine the Klan through the Counter Intelligence Program against White Hate Groups (COINTELPRO-White Hate Groups). Again, as with other groups, there was a movement away from passive surveillance to actively seeking to disrupt the Klan. Plans adopted deliberately fuelled divisions by having informers spread rumours about infidelity and homosexuality involving Klan leaders or even engaging in sexual relations with the wives of Klan members to encourage further conflict.[100] Another method involved setting up informer-led KKK branches to draw away members from legitimate ones. Nor were such activities performed on an insignificant scale.

In 1965, the FBI deployed over 2,000 people in various capacities, almost half of them recruited over the previous year, to gather information against the Klan. This translated in the second half of the decade into the FBI having, as it had in the past with the Communist Party of the USA, a considerable presence among the members of Klaverns. Frank Church's famous committee, focusing on informers recruited by the FBI and not walk-ins, suggested that in 1965, as many as 6 per cent of Klan members were informers. This figure probably translated into as many as 300 full-time snitches among the Klan's ranks. One became the speechwriter for a national KKK leader and in that capacity influenced the latter's pronouncements. The saturation level finally reached the point that the FBI saw no point in shutting down the Klan since to do so would deprive it of access to the organization's complete plans. The KKK's leadership, aware of the extent of police infiltration, launched an effort to ferret out the snitches in its ranks. But then that was one of the points of using informers — creating the knowledge that they were present in the targeted organization aided the FBI in its efforts at disruption. Former Attorney General Nicholas Katzenbach later acknowledged this fact to the Church Committee: 'It is true that the FBI program with respect to the Klan made extensive use of informers . . . It is true that these techniques did in fact disrupt Klan activities, sowed deep mistrust among the Klan members, and made Klan members aware of the extensive informant system of the FBI and the fact that they were under constant observation.'[101] At one point, J. Edgar Hoover ordered the FBI office in Birmingham, Alabama to act as if they had an informer in the ranks of the local branch of the KKK even though they did not at the time.[102]

Until the 1970s, the FBI leadership did not encourage its members to enforce guidelines governing the activities of its intelligence informers.[103] The lack of control occasionally led the Bureau to suffer 'blowback' from those recruited, such as in the case of Sara Jane Moore, the failed 1975 assassin of President Gerald Ford.[104] Within the targeted groups, some informers became *agents provocateurs*, sometimes directly encouraging violence. An FBI informer who belonged to a New Jersey group opposed to the war in Vietnam took a lead role in a course of action that led the group to burglarize a draft board office in Camden, New Jersey:

> Everything they learned about breaking into a building or climbing a wall or cutting glass or destroying lockers, I taught them. I got sample equipment, the type of windows that we would go through, I picked up off the job and taught them how to cut the glass, how to drill holes in the glass so you cannot hear it and stuff like that, and the FBI supplied me with the equipment needed. The stuff I did not have, the [FBI] got off their own agents.[105]

In the late 1960s, another FBI informer, this one involved with a far right paramilitary organization in California, participated in repeated acts of violence. Although he was under the control of an FBI handler, agents interviewed by the Church Committee admitted that little was done beyond verbal warnings to prevent him from committing crimes. One agent essentially washed his hands of the matters:

> Well, I remember almost on a daily basis, this matter would come up. What can I do such and such. And I've said, well obviously you can't do that. Stay with them as long as you can and then find some logical excuse to bow out at the last minute. But he was never asked by me to participate in anything that I would consider illegal or that I think that he would consider illegal and to the best of my recollection, during our association. I can't recall anything specific . . .[106]

Although such activities were not new, the issue of informers being involved as *agents provocateurs* and even openly participating in violence would become a pressing government concern in the 1970s in the aftermath of the Church Committee's investigations.[107] President Jimmy Carter's administration would bring in new rules to govern the use and handling of informers.[108] With the scandals of the 1970s, the FBI began to wind down its domestic informer operations that had gone after non-criminal targets. Nevertheless, it was still employing around 1,200 domestic intelligence informers by the end of June 1975 and the FBI's budget for 1976 allotted more than double the amount of money to cover the operations of its intelligence informers in comparison to those aimed at organized crime.[109] For informers in the mid-1970s there was $3.8 million in a year, while other government departments budgeted another $8 million. At the time, the Bureau paid about $50 a week to a regular informer. Notoriety over their use continued and, to an extent, the Bureau conducted a shell game by re-labelling informers. In the 1980s, America's national police force emphasized counter-terrorism as a motivation for conducting intelligence investigations of political targets, such as the Committee in Solidarity with the People of El Salvador (CISPES).[110]

The utilization of informers remains contentious in the US into the twenty-first century. In the final decade of the twentieth century, several scandals involving informers prompted the Department of Justice to reform guidelines for their use, which the FBI subsequently had trouble following. The CIA also applied new rules to its human sources after an Agency informer in Guatemala was connected to the murder of an American citizen and the spouse of an American citizen. After 9/11, the Bush administration removed these restrictions.[111]

Like the US, the UK also made extensive use of informers. The leading UK example was Northern Ireland. The informers came in assorted forms — from a tip randomly offered by someone, often on a one-time basis, to longer-term informers, either signed up from within a targeted organization or injected into it from outside. Recruiting them from within a hostile community represented a victory of sorts, as the British military recognized.[112] Human intelligence would be crucial to the British campaign against the Irish Republican Army (IRA). Whereas terrorists could take various countermeasures to avoid electronic surveillance, it was more difficult, although not impossible, to avoid the surveillance that came in the form of a human participating in the activity. The IRA came to recognize its vulnerability to penetration. In response, the group enacted defensive tactics, such as moving to an organization based on cells instead of a wider hierarchy, to reduce penetration and exposure and improve internal security.[113]

Informers occupied a central role in the counter-terrorist effort. First, there was the obvious reason: they provided intimate details regarding operations, future plans, personnel, organization, and even information on personalities, such as feuds. 'Sources are the lifeblood of intelligence and it all stems from there', 'Mike' from Special Branch told a journalist. 'You're fighting against a secret organization that wants to keep its secrets and you want them to impart those secrets to you. Terrorist organizations don't advertise their working parts so it's up to us to penetrate them.'[114]

Informers acting as *agents provocateurs* steered the IRA in certain preferred directions, sabotaged operations and sowed dissent, suspicion and outright paranoia within the terrorist ranks. The IRA, which would later offer immunity to those who willingly admitted having assisted British security, killed more of its own members between 1979 and 1981 than did the police and military. It later emerged that Freddie Scappaticci, allegedly one of the key figures in the group's internal security body, nicknamed the 'Nutting Squad', was an informer for British intelligence codenamed 'Stakeknife'. He may have participated, with the knowledge of his handlers, in the murder of other informers in order to protect his own treachery.[115]

Those recruiting informers, and one of these was Jonathan Evans, who in 2007 would become the new head of MI5, had a crucial aspect to their job. This was how to convince an individual to betray his or her organization, comrades and cause. Various motivations existed. Some walked in of their own accord, but these were frequently greeted with suspicion since their ultimate inspiration for doing so was difficult to determine.[116] For others in Northern Ireland, money served as an obvious enticement but not as significantly as it was in criminal investigations. Payments could be as little as £5 but rose depending on the significance and accuracy of the information supplied. Others received a weekly stipend ranging from £10 to £20 plus bonuses of several hundred pounds for especially valuable information.[117] A number of other motivations came into play, such as the excitement of being involved in betrayal, personal grievances and grudges, disillusionment over operations that had gone badly and compromise, often in the form of blackmail. The latter often occurred after an arrest, when a deal would be offered, allowing the potential informer to avoid jail time. This became such a widely recognized recruitment practice that those released from custody immediately fell under suspicion, prompting some to admit that efforts had been made to get them to inform. Coercion could take other forms. A threat to spread the word in the Republican community that an individual was serving as an informer even if he or she had refused an offer was an example of a particularly strong form of intimidation.[118] At times, the pressure related to personal issues.[119]

Informers provided British security with the upper hand in its campaign against the IRA.[120] By the 1990s, one estimate suggests, 80 per cent of IRA operations, including attacks and weapons smuggling, were disrupted before they could be carried out.[121] The IRA and the British had begun peace talks by then, in part because of a realization on the part of the Irish Republicans that they could not win militarily. Informers alone had not caused this shift, but their work had clearly been of incalculable value to counterterrorist efforts.

Whether in Northern Ireland in the 1980s, the coal mines of Pennsylvania in the 1890s, Communist Party gatherings in the 1930s or in Klan meeting halls in the 1960s, informers performed at the behest of the state. They existed in these different places and times because they were effective. In these contexts, informers served as a crucial tool of information collection in that specific details could be generated from targets that were not possible using other forms of surveillance. Far from being a reactive type of surveillance, informers were proactive. This point went deeper though because informers, in whatever version they exist, had an impact. The simple possibility of their presence caused a reaction. Equally, however, they could have an impact by encouraging splits within a particular group or by undermining individuals in leadership roles. Informers, some of whom would become famous because of their controversial work, served as a critical tool for the state in its efforts against real and imagined enemies. This usefulness has not declined in the present.

CHAPTER 4

Famous Informers

Informers are not born; they are made. The practice they engage in is one almost universally detested throughout history. People do not like those who inform because by definition the act involves betrayal. In the modern era, the state often portrays informing as a citizen's duty. Yet, for many, there are loyalties that trump the devotion pledged to the state. There is the superior allegiance to one's ideology, to one's ethnic group, to one's religion or to one's community in whatever form that takes. Of course, there are also individual loyalties, as E.M. Forster acknowledged in his famous aphorism: 'If I had to choose between betraying my country and betraying my friend, I hope I should have the guts to betray my country.' To transgress these fundamental connections by informing for the state has consistently invited reprisal, ranging from ridicule to violence.

The negativity surrounding informing is not just about retribution, however. It is rare to find anyone, particularly someone prominent, who embraces their previously secret life as an informer. The opposite is true; people run from the designation. An effective way of discrediting a political opponent, or anyone for that matter, particularly in the now defunct informer states of Eastern Europe, has been to raise allegations of prior formalized snitching, sometimes on behalf of past regimes or former colonial masters. The situation is complicated even more by the nature of the business, especially the all-encompassing secrecy. This veil, sometimes coupled with the privilege of controlling access to relevant documents that would reveal (or not) previous involvement with informing, confuses the matter further. There is potential for forging records, inaccurately tying individuals to informing.[1] In addition, the legitimate documentary evidence itself is often problematic because of its frequently one-sided nature. It is those doing the recruiting and handling who compile the documentary account of the liaison. Imagine any other relationship where the perspective of only one partner represents the partnership as a whole. Informing relationships contain the potential for exaggeration by those having to meet a recruitment quota or seeking promotion through the acquisition of an especially prominent informer. The documents are certainly not neutral and their 'revelations' need to be judged accordingly. In their defence, many of the records of the past were prepared without expectation that they would suddenly be accessible by outsiders operating under a variety of motives.

Whatever the stimulus, a number of prominent individuals have faced accusations of past informing. Katarina Witt, the former German Democratic Republic figure skater and Olympic star, is one such example. Although she clearly enjoyed a close relationship with state security in the form of the *Ministerium für Staatssicherheit* (Stasi), which will be discussed in the next chapter, she does not appear to have been an informer. Former Polish president and Solidarity hero Lech Walesa faced similar allegations and eventually cleared his name through the Polish parliament. Ironically, in the case of the Solidarity leader, Poland's Communist secret police sought to discredit him by falsely portraying him as an informer for Poland's Communist secret police; it created the phoney records that later emerged only after the fall of communism.[2] Martin McGuinness, a leading figure in Sinn Féin, has experienced repeated claims that he has worked, or continues to work, for British intelligence.[3] In 2006, papers emerged suggesting that the president of Romania, Traian Băsescu, had been an informer years earlier, while a student.[4] Former Iraqi interim Prime Minister, Ayad Allawi, was allegedly a long-term American intelligence source while active among anti-Saddam Hussein opposition groups.[5] His political opponents accused a past Indian Prime Minister, Atal Bihari Vajpayee, of having been an informer for the British during the 1942 Quit India Movement. No evidence of his role emerged. His response: 'Would I have been able to face you had I committed the shameful act? I would have renounced everything and left' illustrated why his enemies had raised the smear in the first place.[6]

While some face inaccurate allegations of being informers, others have willingly or begrudgingly participated in such activities. The question then remains, carrying on from the previous chapters, why would someone, especially the prominent, partake in an activity that carries the opprobrium of society and which is potentially fatal? In a police state, the motivation for participating seems more readily apparent: coercion can be brought to bear by the state in order to ensure compliance. It thus becomes more understandable why Malgorzata Niezabitowska, who became well-known in Poland with the fall of communism as a spokeswoman for Solidarity, might have been, as records suggest, an informer in the 1980s because of information the secret police held about her.[7] Or why an individual such as Laszlo Toekes, the ethnic Hungarian Protestant Bishop of Oradea, Transylvania in Romania, who worked tirelessly against the dictatorship of Nicolai Ceauşescu, helping to spark the 1989 overthrow, could be pressured to write out the following:

> I, the undersigned Laszlo Toekes, born on 1 April 1952 in the city of Cluj-Napoca, of Hungarian nationality, Romanian citizenship, politically not committed, military service not completed, unmarried, with a clean criminal record, permanently residing at 37, Lenin Boulevard, Cluj-Napoca, temporarily residing in 3, Scinteii Street, Brasov Municipality,
>
> Pledge to cooperate with the Securitate bodies of the Ministry of Interior, to supply information about the concepts, behaviour and actions of persons with whom I am in contact and who are specifically

important to the work of those bodies. I also pledge to supply information about the behaviour and activities of citizens of other states visiting our country and under such cover carrying out hostile actions against our country.

I will supply the information in writing, in the form of notes, which I will sign with the pseudonym 'Laszlo Kolozsvari' rather than my real name.

I received today 20,000 lei — that is, twenty thousand lei. Thank you from my heart. May God bless you as long as you live. [Dated] 20th October 1989. Signed: L. Toekes.[8]

Although many did resist, and Toekes himself denied he had supplied any information to his secret employers, the police state has ultimate power over its citizens when it comes to compelling them to cooperate and the ability to make their lives difficult if they do not.[9] A similar reality applies to police forces recruiting informers from among criminals. Coercion can be applied, such as a promise to reduce a sentence or a threat to increase it.[10] But how does this relate to an individual, particularly a prominent one, assisting in the political investigations of an intelligence service or police force within a democratic state? There are, as has been outlined elsewhere in this book, various inspirations, some of them overlapping. But how do these influences play out in individual cases? What is the nature of the relationship between the informer and his or her handler? What precisely does the informer do and why?

Some of these questions will be explored by focusing on famous informers through a series of vignettes. The most famous informer, of course, at least within the cultural memory of Christian-based societies, is Judas. The very name itself has become synonymous with betrayal of the most extreme kind. That some of the accounts of Judas' life have him committing suicide out of remorse for his sense of betrayal is indicative of the strong emotions associated with what the informer did on behalf of Rome. Since then, there have been others. They already may have been prominent when they served as an informer, or they might be individuals who later became famous for reasons unconnected to their informing. Finally, there were those individuals who became well-known solely because of their informing.

The 'twentieth-century Judas' to some was a Russian: Evno Filipovich Azef. He was and remains a controversial individual. In a locale where the average informer's career lasted no more than two to three years, Azef went five times the latter figure before his treachery against his revolutionary comrades on behalf of the Russian state burst into the public domain. His chief motivation for informing was a simple one: money. Although, in common with many informers, he enjoyed exhilaration or a thrill from the secret work, a version of what famed sociologist Georg Simmel called the 'fascination of betrayal'.[11]

Azef initially wrote to the Russian police in 1891 while living abroad to offer his services. He was soon hired at 50 rubles a month, a not inconsiderable sum of money, with financial bonuses paid at the end of each year. By the end of his informer career his salary had reached an annual sum of 14,000 rubles. Keen to protect his secret double identity, he withheld this money from his long-suffering wife, forcing her to repeatedly borrow money to keep from disappearing into a bog of financial despair.[12] His high level of recompense was due to his radical prominence: he became the leader of a combat unit of the Socialist Revolutionary Party. This eminence delayed his ultimate exposure, since colleagues could not accept the possibility that a senior leader helping to plan revolutionary operations could be a turncoat. 'If Azef is a provocateur,' observed one, 'we are all provocateurs.'[13]

After the exposure of his treachery in 1909, Azef's former colleagues portrayed him as having been heavily involved in violent activity, principally the murder of a Russian minister in 1904 and the Tsar Nicholas II's uncle in 1905. Azef's biographer argues that while he did indeed hold back information out of self-preservation — rightly so, as it would be leaks from the police that would eventually expose him as an informer — his connections to the murders were deliberately exaggerated by his former radical comrades in an effort to discredit him.[14] Whatever the case, the Azef example demonstrates the fundamental damage that a highly placed informer can cause as organizations they infiltrate are forced to re-evaluate their previously sacrosanct history, and commit scarce resources in the pursuit of other informers within their ranks.

If Azef gained notoriety because of informing, an American later in the same century would have his earlier double dealing emerge during the highest point of his fame and power. In 1985, the *San Jose Mercury News* broke the story that both President Ronald Reagan and his first wife, actress Jane Wyman, star of *The Lost Weekend*, had worked as informers for the Federal Bureau of Investigation (FBI) in the 1940s and 1950s.[15] The aftermath of World War II was the era of blanket surveillance of communism in the US by the FBI and one particularly vulnerable area, so went the logic, was Hollywood. From here existed the potential for influencing Americans through popular film. Consequently, the Bureau collected thousands of pages of documents about the movie industry, including files on actors and directors and descriptions of movies. An entire secret history of Hollywood could be written solely based on the FBI's records. Reagan was not the only actor to serve as an informer. However, his rise to the presidency and the governorship of California before that, certainly make him the most powerful ex-informer in history.

For the FBI, the Cold War really began at the end of World War I. It was during this period that it began extensive surveillance of the radical left in the US, culminating in its work against the Communist Party of the United States of America (CPUSA). Naturally, this type of intelligence collection featured informers, be they academics at universities, members of labour unions, or actors in Hollywood. The only minor disruption to this pattern of attention occurred during World War II, when the Soviet Union officially became America's ally in the war against fascism. Americans established bodies supportive of the Soviet Union. With the end of the war, and the rise of the Cold War, dynamics quickly changed. As tensions grew between the Soviet Union and the US, a concomitant fear of an 'enemy within' arose. Those previously sympathetic toward the Soviet Union became obvious targets of suspicion. Anything or anyone remotely connected not just to the Soviet Union or to communism but even to progressive causes would garner attention from the American state through the

FBI. The entertainment industry became an easy target on a number of levels. Prominent Hollywood people had been involved in pro-Soviet groups during the war and some of those were involved in creating movies that embraced progressive causes. There was *Gentleman's Agreement*, which explored anti-Semitism, or various Frank Capra movies that trumpeted the cause of the little man while excoriating vested interests. The connection between pro-Soviet activity or outright communism and the content of several Hollywood movies seemed obvious. Enter the FBI and Ronald Reagan.

Reagan, born in Illinois in 1911, had appeared since 1937 in a series of movies. His politics were liberal in the sense that, like many Americans at the time, he supported Franklin Roosevelt and the New Deal. By 1946, the FBI, in its drive to uncover secret Communists or Communist sympathizers, suspected Reagan of belonging to one of those categories. The suspicion arose from the actor's membership in groups perceived as left-wing, such as the Hollywood Independent Citizens Committee of Arts, Sciences and Professions (HICCASP), originally established as a support group for Roosevelt policies on the part of some within the entertainment industry.[16] The Bureau's concern ended when it approached Reagan directly after a strike by the Conference of Studio Unions (CSU). Reagan later recounted the meeting, heroically portraying himself as someone resistant to 'red-baiting', but who eventually succumbed to the appeal of patriotism. 'It isn't a question of that', came the reply from the FBI agent. 'It's a question of national security. You served with the Air Corps. You know what spies and saboteurs are.'[17] Reagan's brother Neil had already become an FBI informer within HICCASP.[18]

FBI documentary evidence offers an alternative version of the gathering, in which Reagan approached them and not the other way around. At a meeting on 10 April 1947, FBI Special Agents from the Los Angeles Office interviewed not just Reagan but also Jane Wyman. They had come because the couple wished to 'furnish information to this Bureau regarding the activities of some members of the Screen Actors Guild (SAG) who they suspected were carrying on Communist Party work'. Reagan was in a position to have inside knowledge, since at the time he was the president of SAG, the union for Hollywood actors. The future president and Wyman had apparently no hesitation in naming names to the FBI:

> Reagan and his wife advised that for the past several months they had observed during the Guild meetings there were two 'cliques' of members, one headed by Anne Revere and the other by Karen Morley which on all questions of policy confronting the Guild, followed the Communist Party Line. Reagan related that Revere and Morley do not appear to be particularly close, but whenever an occasion arises necessitating the appointment of some member to a committee or to an office, the two cliques invariably either nominate or support the same individual. Reagan and his wife listed the following actors and actresses as supporting Revere and Morley:
>
> Alexander Knox
>
> Hume Cronyn
>
> Howland Chamberlain
>
> Howard DeSilva
>
> Dorothy Tree
>
> Selena Royale

The FBI proceeded to cross reference the names supplied by Reagan and Wyman with those whom they already had listed as known Communists.[19]

The actor, nicknamed 'The Gipper' for his portrayal of the historic Notre Dame University football star George Gipp, was, in the parlance of the business, a 'walk-in'. In volunteering to be a secret spy, his motivation seems obvious. Ideology in the form of anticommunism had driven his actions. In that sense, he was a man of his time, namely the early Cold War period. Reagan, however, was no ordinary informer. He occupied a position of prominence within Hollywood and had access to corners that J. Edgar Hoover's agents could not normally shine a light in.

The FBI listed Reagan as a 'T' informer, specifically working under the codename of T-10. T informers, according to the FBI itself, were '[c]onfidential informants . . . [who] have furnished reliable information in the past unless otherwise indicated'.[20] Reagan's work for the FBI went beyond simply reporting on others in the movie business. In the mid-1950s, while testifying under oath, he confessed to attempting to manipulate HICCASP in ways favourable to his secret employers.[21]

The Gipper, of course, was not alone in his hidden toiling. The FBI actively targeted Hollywood during this period, and informers represented a ready aid for extensive monitoring. A 1958 FBI report recapping assistance over the years referred to T-3 as being 'of unknown reliability' who had 'identified some 28 individuals, practically all of whom were film writers'.[22] There was also T-5 who in 1956 supplied information about activities within Hollywood organizations. Reagan's spouse Wyman joined the exclusive snitch club at their 1947 meeting with the Bureau, providing information as well. While some have speculated that she was T-9, in his study of Ronald Reagan's life, Garry Wills suggests that codename may have belonged to another well-known Hollywood actress, Olivia de Havilland.[23]

The following excerpts from an FBI report from the 1950s summarizing Communist involvement in Hollywood make it clear how significant informers within the industry, such as Reagan, were in helping the Bureau identify alleged Communists and Communist sympathizers, including several entertainment icons. The final passage also demonstrates a traditional intelligence agency tendency to be cautious in dealing with informers who volunteered their services.

Communist Infiltration of the Motion Picture Industry

INTRODUCTORY BACKGROUND

The majority of the information concerning Communist infiltration of the motion picture industry has been supplied by [deleted: name] who is Los Angeles Confidential Informant [deleted: name]. This informant has been associated with the motion picture industry for many years. He is a member of several labor organizations which are active in the industry and is thoroughly familiar with the background of the labor organization in that field. He was a member of the Communist Party or [deleted]. The informant is quite familiar with the Communist key figures in the Hollywood area and is able to obtain information concerning Communist activities in this industry . . .

p. 2
Actors — Five actors and actresses are reported to be known members of the Communist Party in Hollywood. Twenty-four others are members of the Communist Party front groups. Among the known Communist Party members, Gale Sondergaard, Lionel Stander and Lucille Ball are the most prominent. Those belonging to Communist Party front groups include James Cagney, Ida Lupino, Franchot Tone, Walter Huston and John Garfield . . .

p. 3
Screen Actors Guild
This guild has included a number of prominent actors in the Hollywood area. A number of the individuals have supported and taken part in Communist front organizations according to Confidential Informant [deleted] including Helen Gahagan (Helen Gahagan Douglas), Frances Farmer, John Garfield (correct name Jake Garfinkel), Gale Sondergaard, Lionel Stander and Frederic March . . .

p. 5
Screen Actors Guild
[Deleted: name] Los Angeles, California, an informant of the Los Angeles Office, advised that Maurice Howard has continued as business representative for the Screen Cartoonists Guild . . .

P. 9 (November 14, 1946 through February 14, 1947)
[Deleted: name] a confidential informant of the Los Angeles Field Division, compiled a list of motion pictures made by the Hollywood motion picture industry between October 1, 1945, and November 3, 1946, in which there is a possibility of propaganda of a subversive nature. [Deleted: name] indicated that he cannot definitely state there

is Communist propaganda in all the pictures listed below but he has endeavored to list those pictures which have been produced, directed and written by persons whose connections with the Communist movement have been established by reliable and dependable records . . .

p. 10
Lucille Ball, motion picture actress. According to [deleted: name] she is a member of Screen Actors' Guild and to his personal knowledge, she has taken an active part in and supported Communist-controlled fronts in the Hollywood area over a period of six or seven years . . .

p. 11
Joseph Cotton [sic]. According to [deleted: name] Cotton is a member of the Executive Board of the Screen Actors' Guild and is a sympathizer with Communist aims, but is not a member . . .

   Olivia De Havilland. [Deleted: name] has informed that to his personal knowledge, this person began exhibiting sympathy for the Communist cause in Hollywood in 1942, and since that time, has taken an active part in various Communist front activities such as the Hollywood Committee for Writers in Exile and the Free People's Dinner honoring Paul Robeson . . .

p. 12
Cary Grant. [Deleted: name] has advised he knows Grant to be a Communist sympathizer, although he knows of no Communist organization with which Grant has been affiliated . . .

   Walter Houston [sic]. [Deleted: name] informs that information on Houston's membership in the Communist Political Association is lacking but that to his [deleted: name] personal knowledge, Houston has supported Communist and Communist-controlled activities . . .

p. 13
R.K.O. Feature Pictures Containing Communist Propaganda
At the outset, informant [deleted] has stated that the 'western' or 'mystery' type of escapist film are not a suitable vehicle for Communist propaganda and that Communists do not expect that every picture or

even a majority of pictures produced by a studio, be a Communist vehicle. The informant has advised that from his experience in the Communist movement, Communists consider themselves successful even if one of twenty-five motion pictures contain important Communist propaganda. He stated this propaganda may consist of the spoken words, the actions or even the implications in sequences . . .

p. 14

[Deleted]

On May 6, 1947, arrangements were made for [deleted: name] to be interviewed for a brief period in the Los Angeles Office. On this occasion, an attempt was made to consider the possibilities of using [deleted: name] as a source of information on Communist activities in the motion picture industry. This interview was conducted for the most part by Assistant Special Agent in Charge [deleted: name] and Special Agent [deleted: name]. She was also interviewed by Special Agent in Charge R. B. Hood and briefly by Special Agents [deleted: name] . . .

p. 15

In view of [deleted: name] position to get valuable information concerning Communist activities among motion picture actresses and actors in Hollywood, the Los Angeles Office is going to maintain periodic contact with her as a source of information. However, extreme caution is to be exercised in dealing with her in view of her past contacts with persons of known Communist sympathies as well as the manner in which she has suddenly become interested in cooperating with the FBI [deleted] . . . [24]

The last referred to an actress who 'offered her services as a source of information concerning Communist activities in Hollywood and explained her connections with Communist front groups as being due to her curiosity and interest in finding out about these various groups as well as the individuals connected with them'.[25]

Other well-connected informers across Hollywood supplied the Bureau with inside information about top film directors:

pp. 24–5

Screen Directors Guild

Confidential Informant [deleted: name] reported that he and a group of nine other top directors, all members of the Guild, had arranged a confidential meeting on March 12, 1948, for the purpose of deciding on a slate of officers whom they could attempt to elect at the coming Guild elections . . .

The informant expressed the opinion that the Communists and their friends in the Screen Directors Guild had gone underground. He also cited as a change of attitude the fact that a few years previously his influence within the Guild would have been resented but that he now finds various members asking his opinion and advice.

p. 29

Confidential Source [deleted: name] of the William Morris Agency advised that John Huston was the person who contributed the original idea and seemed to be the most closely associated with this group. Huston told his source that it had been his intention to concentrate on his career and retire from politics but that the conduct of the hearings in Washington made it impossible for him to remain on the sidelines.

p. 30

Informant [deleted] continued that Billy Wilder is pro-English and anti-French. Wilder admires the Socialistic experiment in England, and has expressed his antipathy toward the French people of late since the recent elections in which DeGaulle [sic] signified great political strength. Wilder, as has been pointed out above, has been active in the Committee for the First Amendment.[26]

Reagan thus had considerable company in his efforts. His informing continued into the 1950s:

On September 16, 1954, T-10 advised that the IPC's [Independent Productions Corporation] first and only film to date had been the controversial picture 'Salt of the Earth' and that the principal figures behind this film were MICHAEL WILSON, HERBERT BIBERMAN, and PAUL JARRICO, who were, respectively, the writer, director, and co-producer of the film. . . .

On April 18, 1956, [informer T-10] characterized the MCCF as a temporary organization, probably only a paper organization, created for the specific purpose of protesting the hearings by the House Committee and its subpoenaing of certain musicians in Hollywood being backed by the MCCF.[27]

The future president passed along various details, including that Louis B. Mayer, the famous movie mogul, had appointed him to a committee designed to drive Communists out of Hollywood. Occasionally, he turned prescriptive, as when he recommended that Congress outlaw the CPUSA because it was beholden to a foreign power.[28] When Reagan's secret emerged, the White House responded by disparaging the significance of what he did. A White House spokesperson even claimed, inaccurately, that Reagan's designation of T-10 was assigned because the FBI ranked its informers from one through ten with the latter being of lowest significance.[29]

The reaction to Reagan's work as an informer came more from his fame through his political career than from any legacy from his time as an actor. A much bigger Hollywood name from the same era would, similarly, dabble in secret work. Walt Disney had a richer and lengthier secret relationship with the FBI that covered almost a quarter of a century, first as an ordinary informer, and then as a Special Agent in Charge (SAC) contact.[30] The Bureau made several efforts in the 1930s to recruit Disney and even provided him with assistance in an effort to discover his birth parents. By doing so, the federal police force left him in its debt and, in 1940, Disney began to work for Hoover's men as an informer.[31]

He had multiple reasons for the relationship — anti-communism and patriotism during the Cold War were obvious factors. For Disney these conveniently coalesced with naked self-interest: labour disputes at his studios, in particular a nasty strike by his cartoonists in 1941, had frustrated him and led to a convenient stance that portrayed his opponents as Communists. Thus Disney informed the FBI in the mid-1940s that the business agent for the Screen Cartoonists Guild was a

Communist and that he, Disney, believed emphatically that the 'Un-American Committee should continue its hearings until all persons on its list have been exposed'.[32] He proved particularly useful when he travelled to New York in 1943 as a sponsor and guest of honour for an event hosted by the Council for Pan-American Democracy that the FBI believed was connected to subversive activities. Disney filed a report about his experience and soon after this, the organization was designated as subversive by the US Attorney General's office. He played a similar role later in the war when he attended a tribute to cartoonist Art Young that was sponsored by a number of the leading lights of the American left, including Paul Robeson and Carl Sandburg.[33]

The Bureau had no difficulty in recognizing that an informer as prominent as Disney represented several advantages. In 1954, it was even recommended that he be promoted:

> Because of Mr. Disney's position as the foremost producer of cartoon films in the motion picture industry and his prominence and wide acquaintanceship in film production matters, it is believed that he can be of valuable assistance to this office and it therefore is my recommendation that he be approved as an SAC contact.[34]

A SAC contact not only supplied information to the Bureau but was allowed to pass on the reports of other informers as well. Hoover personally was keen to expand Disney's role because of the latter's increasing involvement in television, an embryonic medium that the FBI desired more inside information about.[35]

Unlike his movies, Disney's relationship with the FBI did not have a happy ending. The two had a falling out in the late 1950s over the Mickey Mouse Club and the Bureau became concerned about Disney's depiction of it in the early 1960s. Using additional sources developed around the mouse king, it sought details on a movie project entitled 'Moon Pilot' that it felt did not intend to portray America's national police force in a favourable light. Hoover instructed his Los Angeles office to meet with Disney personally in order to 'point out to him the uncomplimentary manner in which FBI Agents are depicted' and that the Bureau strongly objected to this.[36] Disney promised to forward on the script but, in the end, he did not.[37] In 1963, Disney informed his handlers that he had obtained the rights to a story called *That Damned Cat* and that as part of the film the Bureau would receive a fair depiction. It would later appear as *That Darn Cat!* after Disney changed bumbling FBI agents to generic government agents. By then the Bureau had struck back. In 1959, the Dwight D. Eisenhower Administration considered appointing Disney to the Advisory Committee on the Arts, National Cultural Center. It contacted the Bureau to do a background check on him. The FBI reported it had a file and that the cartoon mogul had been involved in two left-wing events during the war, neglecting to mention that he had supplied information on them to the Bureau at the time. He was not appointed to the Committee. Already, he had stopped informing and, although he had occasional contact with Hoover's organization, his days of performing such work were finished. He died in 1965.[38]

Another prominent FBI informer coincided with Disney's efforts. He was Joseph P. Kennedy, the scion of America's most famous political family. The contact between the FBI and Kennedy stretched back to his time in London when he was ambassador and offered a warm welcome in 1938 to a visiting FBI agent. The formal recruitment of Kennedy as a 'Special Service contact' occurred five years later in the fall of 1943. It began when an FBI Special Agent reported to headquarters on one of his friendships:

JOSEPH P. KENNEDY, former Ambassador to London, . . . has indicated that he would be glad to assist the Bureau in any way possible should his services be needed. Mr. KENNEDY speaks very highly of the Bureau and the Director, and has indicated that if he were ever in a position to make any official recommendations there would be one Federal investigative unit and that would be headed by J. Edger Hoover. He considers the Naval and Army Intelligence Services 'amateurish' in comparison to the Bureau and regrets that they have often meddled in investigations coming within the jurisdiction of the Bureau. However, no attempt will be made to develop Mr. Kennedy as a Special Service contact unless the Bureau so instructs.[39]

Kennedy's flattery toward the notoriously thin-skinned Hoover elicited a response. The following month, the director ordered the Boston office to recruit Kennedy as a 'Special Service contact'. As part of this process, a biographical sketch of Kennedy was prepared, including a list of what he could offer to the Bureau:

> Mr Kennedy is a devout Catholic and is very well versed on communism and what it might possibly mean to the United States. He has said that he has many Jewish friends in the moving picture industry who would furnish him, upon request, with any information in their possession pertaining to Communist infiltration in the moving picture industry. He feels also that he is in a position to secure any information the Bureau may desire from his contacts in the industry with reference to any individuals who have Communistic sympathies.[40]

A 'Special Service contact' was not a normal informer but a member of the elite of informers. Hoover encouraged the Boston office to take full advantage of a prominent individual like Kennedy and not restrict itself to cases currently under investigation: 'There is no objection to asking these individuals to secure information regarding any matters which you feel would be of interest to your office either currently or for reference purposes in the future.'[41] Kennedy supplied information but, by the end of 1945, apparently nothing of sufficient quality for the Bureau to award him its 'meritorious service award' for which he had been under consideration.[42]

The program ended after the war but reappeared in 1950, when the Boston office again recruited Kennedy. He became one of 180 Special Service contacts nationwide. According to the FBI, when approached directly in September 1950, Kennedy assured them that he was 'entirely willing to avail his services for any advantage the Bureau might desire'.[43] Nearly three years later, the FBI praised the former diplomat for being 'extremely cooperative' in providing information for a specific investigation and in other areas.[44] Kennedy commended Hoover, who responded with a letter of adulation of his own.[45] Within a few months, they were 'Edgar' and 'Joe' to each other and the familiarity led Kennedy to offer an invitation to his daughter

Eunice's marriage to Sargent Shriver.[46] The amount of information supplied by Hoover's new friend was never extensive, but it did provide him with the opportunity of ingratiating himself with the FBI. He went so far as to express his belief to his handlers that a newspaper columnist critical of the Bureau apparently was so in an effort to angle 'his columns at the Jews, Negroes and the Communist element behind the Civil Liberties outfit, as well as the NAACP'.[47]

The FBI signed up other prominent individuals during the Cold War, with patriotism a particularly effective recruiting tool when the target of surveillance was communism or fascism. There was German writer Erika Mann, author of the 1938 *School for Barbarians: Education under the Nazis* and the 1939 *Escape to Life*, co-written with her brother Klaus. As part of the exile community in New York and Los Angeles, she sought out the FBI, perhaps out of concern about her own status in the country, to provide information on members of her expatriate community. The informing, which also included introducing the Bureau to another willing assistant, went on for over ten years until she returned to Europe. To encourage her cooperation, the agents involved scrupulously avoided investigating her father, novelist and Nobel laureate Thomas Mann. The FBI even sought her out for tips on the whereabouts of Guy Burgess and Donald Maclean, who defected to the Soviet Union in 1951, since she knew individuals who socialized with the two spies.[48] Also toiling for the FBI was Abe Fortas. He met with and supplied information to the Bureau while serving as a Justice on the Supreme Court of the United States.[49]

The Ivy League yielded its own set of famous informers. At Harvard University, Henry Kissinger, an academic and future senior official in two presidential administrations, contacted the Bureau in July 1953 to report on a summer seminar series at his university. William Yandell Elliott, another academic and Kissinger's mentor, snitched to the police about colleagues and Senator William Fulbright, and was even approached by a senior member of the Bureau, William C. Sullivan, and asked to write an article in praise of the FBI and informers.[50] At Harvard's great rival, Yale University, a student by the name of William F. Buckley, later to become one of the intellectual cornerstones of the modern American conservative movement, supplied to the FBI copies of correspondence and details of telephone conversations.[51]

The FBI was not the only agency relying on writers for information about others. On the other side of the Atlantic, as he lay sick and dying in May 1949, Eric Blair, better known by his writing name of George Orwell, found time to snitch on the prominent, including film star Charlie Chaplin, historian E.H. Carr and novelist J.B. Priestley, whom be believed might be 'crypto-communists, fellow-travellers or inclined that way and should not be trusted as propagandists'. He dispatched a list containing 38 names (divided into three columns: 'Name', 'Job', and 'Remarks') to a friend who worked in the Information Research Department (IRD) of the British government's Foreign Office. Controversy surrounded Orwell's list when it became public decades later. Despite efforts by his sympathizers to offer multiple excuses for his action, what Orwell did represents the classic characteristics of a state informer. That nothing adverse appears to have happened to those he named does not exonerate him from having informed in the first place.[52]

While individuals like Reagan, Disney, Buckley and Orwell were famous in their own right, in the early Cold War an individual could become a celebrity simply by informing. Thanks to their notoriety, some American informers published books and had television programs and movies made about their exploits. Herb Philbrick was the archetype of this type of informer: an individual who rose from obscurity to public prominence in the US because of his efforts as a snitch for the FBI. An advertising executive, Philbrick approached the Bureau and provided information while a member of the Cambridge Youth Council, a Communist-associated organization in Massachusetts. Then the fledgling informer, who went on to write an autobiography of his adventures, *I Led 3 Lives*, which was later turned into a movie followed by a television series, was asked by his comrades to join the Young Communist League (YCL). The FBI encouraged him to do so and to become a full-time informer. Hesitant to take these next steps, he described in a highly dramatized way an exchange between him and his FBI handler that encapsulates several traditional aspects of informing:

'The Bureau would like to have you stay. We know your work. We think that you have what it takes. The Young Communist League is simply the preparatory academy for the Communist party. You will go from one to the other, in all likelihood. We have good reason to believe that information — accurate, inside information — concerning the activities of these organizations is very important to the American people, and to the future of America. You know something of what they are doing. You are in a position to learn more.'

It was not an easy decision to make, although I already suspected, deep down, what the answer had to be. 'Hal, I haven't any doubt what you say is true. I have already seen enough to convince me. It's just that I don't like the idea of being a-a spy, even for the FBI. I'm not the type.'

Hal brushed aside my objection. 'I can appreciate your feeling', he said. 'But the role must be played by someone, because it is the only way through which the whole story can be learned, and learned in time. Normal methods of detection, where crime is involved, are important, but the detective gets the facts after the crime is committed. The counterspy gets them before the crime takes place. It has to be done, like it or not, where we have reason to suspect that crimes against society and the state are in the making.' . . .

'Before you give an answer, let me finish. You would perform an important service, yes. But you would have to make tremendous sacrifices to do it, and your return may be nothing, or worse than nothing. We would want you to go as deep into the party as you could, give up much of your home life and many of your friends. I'm laying it on the line to you, Philbrick, because we don't want it otherwise. There would be an element of danger in it, physical danger. If you are identified as an FBI connection, you might suffer for it. If you are exposed publicly as a Communist party member you may lose your job, and you cannot claim the FBI to justify your position. It may never be learned that you worked with us. Certainly it can never come from you. If you are arrested in your Communist activities, you must expect no assistance from us whatever. We never heard of you. You are on your own. If you join, not even your wife must know what you are doing. Nobody will know. Not even most of the agents in the Bureau will know. You will be a code number. You must never appear in or near our office, nor be observed in conversation with us. Your operations must be thoroughly secret. You will send us regular reports, facts about the party, its members and their activities. Facts only. We will pay any necessary expenses that this entails. You will, of course, keep on with your regular job.'

He stopped and waited, and I stared ahead through the windshield.

'I know you can't make up your mind on the spur of the moment. I don't expect you to. But you must give me a decision as soon as possible. Tomorrow, if you can. You mustn't keep the League waiting.'[53]

The next day, Philbrick accepted the FBI offer and began to supply detailed information, including once typing up a 20-page list of names of members of the Young Communist League. He would later testify in court against some of his former comrades.[54]

In his informing, testifying, and gaining fame for his double life, Philbrick had considerable company. Elizabeth Bentley was another of his cohort. In her situation, she became an informer out of disillusionment with the Communist Party and after the death of her partner, who was involved in Soviet espionage. As first a spy for the Soviet Union, and then as an informer for the FBI, she faced the double burden of being a woman having to negotiate an all-male intelligence system and the wider expectations of American society. Both were replete with pervasive gender stereotypes.[55] Thus, Bentley became, in the words of her biographer, 'either a sex-starved, man-eating temptress or a sexually repressed, man-hating spinster'.[56]

Then there was Harvey Matusow. Originally a dedicated Communist, Matusow became increasingly disillusioned with the Party and began to snitch about friends, primarily in pursuit of money, on behalf of the FBI. The Bureau, suspicious of his motivation, initially treated him with caution, often seeking to double check the details he supplied them.[57] The CPUSA eventually expelled him and he went on to write a book about his adventures, *False Witness*, in which he declared that the informer had become a 'hero' for the 'first time' in American history.[58] In the case of Matusow, he was not finished with betrayals. Angered by his treatment in general, he later embarrassed the FBI when he recanted much of his testimony.[59]

In response, the *New York Times* observed editorially: 'Informers undoubtedly do have value in uncovering elements of the Communist conspiracy; but a corollary of their use is the clear obligation of the Government to crack down on them . . . the moment it appears they are not telling the truth.'[60]

One more famous American informer in this period was Matt Cvetic. Born in 1909 to Slovenian immigrants, he found a career as a low-level government worker in Pittsburgh. Two years after becoming an FBI informer in 1941, apparently out of a patriotic sense of duty, he joined the Communist Party. Cvetic later boasted of having supplied the Bureau with the names of close to a thousand Party members, along with thousands of pages of CPUSA documents, all despite being an obscure Party member. Ironically, his energetic work in the CPUSA later cost him his government job, forcing him to rely heavily on the FBI's $85 per week informer payments that eventually reached $100. By the late 1940s, the FBI ended his employment after he became increasingly undependable, in part because of excessive alcohol consumption. After testifying to the House Committee on Un-American Activities (HUAC), Cvetic capitalized on his fame by selling his admittedly embellished story to the *Saturday Evening Post* for $5,000. He then sold his tale for $12,500 to Warner Brothers, which made it into a 1951 film called *I Was a Communist for the FBI*.[61] Radio and television series followed. As for Cvetic, an effort to become a Republican congressman failed and he drifted much further right, ending up active with the fanatically anti-Communist John Birch Society at the time of his death in 1962.[62]

By the 1960s and 1970s, informers gained fame for work against left-wing groups outside of the traditional Communist circles. Two such individuals were Larry Grathwohl and William Tulio Divale, both of whom infiltrated New Left organizations on behalf of the FBI. The FBI recruited Divale in 1965 while he was a student at Pasadena City College, having done a complete background check on him before making the pitch. Divale accepted, signed a contract, and for four years became a prolific informer. He eventually produced almost 800 verbal, written and recorded reports related to his energetic activities often involving leadership in a variety of radical organizations, including the Students for a Democratic Society (SDS). All of the reports were expected to include his real name at some point in the text, although he signed off at the end each time with a codename. He also regularly identified individuals in surveillance photos for his FBI handler. He did all of this for a regular monthly salary of $125. At times, to cover expenses, the figure would be increased to as high as $350 a month. His informing career concluded in 1968, when he testified against his former comrades before the Federal Subversive Activities Control Board (SACB).[63] Divale, who would go on to a career as an academic, had told the FBI their relationship had to end because:

> I felt dirty inside. For more than four years I'd been living a lie. I'd slept with the Movement, taken to my bed its most fervent philosophy and some of its most passionate women, and when the encounters were concluded, I had been guilty of betrayal. Like an addict going for the needle, I had reached for the Bureau's tape recorder, inserted one of the Bureau's tapes and told all. It was as tawdry as an errant husband recounting the details of an affair just concluded with his mistress, five minutes after sneaking home and climbing into his own connubial bed. My mistress — the Movement — had become my wife. I was wedded to it spiritually and psychologically. I wanted a divorce — from the FBI.[64]

Larry Grathwohl came to informing after Divale had already left the secret employment of the FBI. A Vietnam War veteran, the 21-year-old Grathwohl first began supplying information to the Cincinnati police force about radical activity at the University of Cincinnati. A few weeks later, he approached the FBI with more details about campus radicals and, in turn, the Bureau asked him to attend a meeting of the local branch of the Weathermen, later known as the Weather Underground, a radical left-wing group that had emerged from a split in SDS.[65] From that point, he would become intimately involved with the Weathermen, going underground with his new comrades, meeting senior leaders, having multiple sexual relationships and a girlfriend and possibly playing the role of an *agent provocateur*.[66] The fact that he had penetrated an underground organization engaged in violent activity increased his value to the Bureau, which offered him $600 a month plus up to $500 to cover expenses. In the end, however, it was his employers who exposed his treachery. An arrest of a radical colleague of Grathwohl's that the FBI ordered him to facilitate, inadvertently led to the growing suspicions of his Weather Underground colleagues being confirmed.[67] Following in the footsteps of informers of the 1950s, both Divale and Grathwohl published memoirs about their secret work. Long after the events he informed on, Grathwohl found himself in demand by the media during the 2008 US presidential election. He offered commentaries on the former Weather Underground leader Bill Ayers because Ayers had an association with Democratic Party nominee and eventual victor, Barack Obama.[68]

Although the predominant target for informers employed by domestic intelligence agencies in western countries during the Cold War was the political left, the far right did not escape surveillance, as examined in the previous chapter. In the 1960s, the activities of the Ku Klux Klan (KKK) drew increasing attention, particularly its use of violence against civil rights protestors. The FBI targeted the Klan through large numbers of informers, including one, Gary Thomas Rowe, who later became well known because of his work. A Klan member from 1959 to 1965 in Birmingham, Alabama, Rowe engaged in 'total reporting', simultaneously feeding intelligence concerning Klan operations to the Bureau along with general and intimate information on Klan members and their activities that did not necessarily involve criminality. More controversially, Rowe participated in KKK terrorism, with the goal of putting himself beyond suspicion, but additionally to be in a position to report regarding violence planned and carried out. He famously turned up in 1961 in a photo on the front page of a Birmingham newspaper holding down an African-American man as two Klan members beat him. Although the FBI formally and repeatedly warned him not to actively partake in the violence, Rowe's handler admitted that 'to gather information [on violence] you have to be there'.[69] Hence, he was instructed to join the Klan's 'Action Group' that violently targeted African-Americans and civil rights activists. Only when he took a leadership role in the squad did the FBI draw the line, telling Rowe to either quit the position or cease being an informer. The Bureau distinguished between organizing and leading acts of violence and participating in acts of violence in a supportive capacity.[70] Rowe's KKK work ended in 1965 with the murder of Viola Liuzzo, a civil rights worker and mother of five in Alabama in March of that year. Told by his handler to accompany a group of Klan members looking to attack a civil rights march, the FBI's Klan member became an eyewitness to her murder. He quickly informed the Bureau of what had happened and his testimony in court against his former colleagues would expose his identity.[71] A recent biography of Rowe portrays his successes as inconsistent at best and the actual extent of his involvement with Klan violence as not fully documented.[72]

The Canadian equivalent of Rowe was Grant Bristow, who infiltrated that country's racist right from 1988 until 1994 when his informing was exposed by the media. Bristow, originally a private investigator in Toronto, had approached the Canadian equivalent of MI5 and the FBI, the Canadian Security Intelligence Service (CSIS) after an apartheid-era South African diplomat tried to hire him to spy on anti-apartheid activists. CSIS soon employed Bristow as an informer or 'asset' in the lexicon of his employer, and he set about infiltrating the Canadian extreme right. Bristow shortly became part of the inner circle of the Heritage Front, a far-right group. Controversy would erupt with his exposure in 1994, including over how active he had personally been in organizing racist activity and whether he had been an *agent provocateur*. A subsequent investigation largely cleared him of the allegations.[73]

However, the two most famous informers in Canadian history overshadowed Bristow's work. One gained fame because of her undercover work, while the other was an already well-known provincial politician. The latter, Claude Morin, belonged to the senior ranks of the Parti Québécois (PQ), a separatist party that sought the eventual independence of the province of Quebec. The Royal Canadian Mounted Police (RCMP) recruited him in 1974 by his own account, and much earlier according to other sources. From then until 1977, even after he became a cabinet minister in the new PQ provincial government of Quebec, Morin met with RCMP handlers, receiving several hundred dollars for each meeting, which occurred roughly six weeks apart. At one point, the RCMP allegedly secretly filmed Morin receiving his payment, apparently in an effort to provide leverage over their prized snitch should he seek to terminate their illicit relationship. When Morin's informing emerged, shock erupted throughout the Canadian political world, especially amongst Morin's former colleagues, who felt a strong sense of betrayal, since he had played a key role in planning the course toward independence for Quebec. Former Premier René Lévesque, Morin's boss while he served in government, reputedly suffered a mild heart attack upon hearing of his fellow separatist's treachery.[74]

A parallel informer to Morin was Carole de Vault, a 25-year-old Montreal university student who was approached to join the *Front de libération du Québec* (FLQ). The FLQ was a small terrorist group seeking the independence of the province of Quebec through violence. In October 1970, a period that would become known as the 'October Crisis', members of one FLQ cell kidnapped the British Trade Commissioner, James Cross (he would be freed a few months later). Another cell snatched a provincial cabinet minister, Pierre Laporte and, after the Canadian government declared martial law, murdered him. Repulsed by the tactics and their potential impact on the peaceful pursuit of independence, which she supported, in early November 1970 de Vault walked into a Montreal police station and offered information about the FLQ. Initially treated with scepticism, undoubtedly because of the general dislike police forces and intelligence services have toward 'walk-ins', the Montreal city police employed her as an informer. She met with her handler in a restaurant. Unbeknownst to her, he recorded their five-hour conversation, which became the basis of the following report:

November 14, 1970

Re: Extra-secret source 945-171

1 This day November 14 1970 about 01:00 hours I met the above-mentioned source who informs me of these facts:

   A That two communiqués of the FLQ will appear this day of

November 14 1970 and more particularly Communiqué Number 2 'Viger Information Cell'.

B These two communiqués will be hand-written by two different persons in square letters with a ballpoint pen and will relate the correct circumstances surrounding the arrest of Bernard Lortie and will speak of police guns left behind on the premises by the police on November 7 1970 about 18:30 hours. . . .

2 To show his [the handler's use of the masculine undoubtedly was to protect de Vault's identity] good faith, the source gave us the opportunity to photocopy the drafts and the original copies of Communiqué Number 2 of the Viger Information Cell (see copies herewith obtained at about 02:00 hours on 14/11/70.)

3 The source informs us that, according to his information, the wife of "X" (a minister in the Quebec government) is the sister of "Y" and one of the FLQ has this wife as a mistress.

4 The source informs us that a member of the FLQ, Luc Gosselin lives with the daughter of a chief of police. . . .[75]

She would be given the codename 'Poupette', the file number 945–171, and would receive $30 (Canadian) each time she met her handler, usually twice a week. At one point, she received a lump sum payment of $15,000, a sign of her significance to the police. Her informing, which she performed unbeknownst to her then husband, continued until the end of 1974, by when the FLQ had effectively ceased to be a threat. Her last contact with her handler was in the form of a farewell dinner.[76]

As in the cases just profiled, those who inform continue to draw considerable public attention. The interest emanates from the secrecy associated with informing, but additionally, there is the power of betrayal that is inherent in much of what informers do. These forces, coupled with the involvement of the prominent, encourage an escalation of coverage. Thus, headlines about the interaction of the famous and informing abound: Henri Paul, the driver of the car in which Princess Diana crashed, was an informer for French intelligence; a Spanish Nobel laureate, Camilo Jose Cel, informed on behalf of the regime of Francisco Franco; a former mayor of

Jerusalem, Teddy Kollek, secretly supplied information to MI5 about the Menachem Begin-led Jewish terrorist group Irgun; LSD guru Timothy Leary groused to the FBI on a number of friends in order to get out of prison.[77] Informing, a centuries old practice, remains both a controversial and a continuing relevant practice, whether the informer emerges from the prominent, from the anonymous or from police states.

CHAPTER 5

The Informer State

The family could not actually be abolished, and, indeed, people were encouraged to be fond of their children, in almost the old-fashioned way. The children, on the other hand, were systematically turned against their parents and taught to spy on them and report their deviations. The family had become in effect an extension of the Thought Police. It was a device by means of which everyone could be surrounded night and day by informers who knew him intimately.
— George Orwell, *1984*

If in liberal-democratic states, informers frequently represent a more precise type of surveillance in comparison to technological collection, the situation has been and is different in other polities. There informing on behalf of the state can represent an activity more widely participated in. Sociologist Malin Åkerström recognizes that the nature of the state may lead to different requirements of its populace:

Some societies make, create, or produce more betrayers than others because of the way their social control is arranged. All societies demand that citizens report on each other to a certain extent. How much and the range of behavior expected to be reported varies between countries. In some countries only strictly illegal behaviour should be reported. In others, information concerning a much broader range of behaviour is not considered private; on the contrary, it should be revealed to different authorities. . . . . The more totalitarian and the more interested their leaders are in suppressing criticism, the more such informer systems will be used. An informer system is not only a means of collecting information, but its most effective social function perhaps is the general fear it produces.[1]

Arguably, even where there is such widespread participation, the legitimacy of informing is no greater as a result. This remains difficult to ascertain, however, since it has been retroactively, in places such as former Communist countries, that people have turned against informing. These were informer states where large numbers of citizens from all backgrounds participated in supplying information on the activities of others. As in George Orwell's dystopian world of *1984*, this could involve informing on close family members. This is not to suggest that democratic states never have taken on the elements of an informer-state. In times of crisis through war, civil unrest and terrorism, their security agencies have expanded the number of informers in their employ, although generally it is those on the margins who experience these tactics.

In informer states, the activities of those supplying information, or even simply the feared possibility of informer activity, in some ways parallels the blanket effect of technological surveillance in liberal-democratic states. The presence of a camera on a pole or through a mobile Closed Circuit Television (CCTV) unit parked in the middle of a public location, for example, could influence behaviour even if it was an empty shell, since no one would know whether it was recording or not; its presence alone affects behaviour. Thus it is with informers in authoritarian and totalitarian states and in marginalized communities in democratic states, except that the impact emerges not from an impersonal technology but from a very real person.

But the situation is more complicated than this. The public in these places would have been aware of the presence of informers. Indeed, the Soviet Union celebrated the activities of informers as a civic virtue and a key component of citizenship. Nonetheless, the extent of their activity and the sheer numbers of those informing would not have been evident until after the collapse of the political systems in these countries. This occurred principally after 1989, when relevant records emerged. In general, there would have been recognition in the German Democratic Republic, for example, that informers hovered in the public sphere, and that aspect alone would have affected behaviour. The true extent of their numbers, however, and the reality that they also operated in the private domestic sphere would have surprised many.[2] Otherwise, in these authoritarian states, secrecy governed the activities of domestic intelligence agencies even more so than in democratic states. This lack of full knowledge helps explain the powerful reaction, including retribution, on the part of the publics across Eastern Europe since 1989.[3]

In that sense, the extent of surveillance afforded by informers in these states closely represented the Panopticon as discussed in Chapter 2. The complexities of reality, however, render many generalizations problematic. For Michel Foucault, such technology represents 'disciplinary power' that is 'bi-directional' in its impact. William Staples, who writes about 'the culture of surveillance' in a 1997 book of that name, warns that such a model represents 'post-modern social control . . . that tends to be systematic, methodical and automatic in operation'. He adds that it is usually 'impersonal' because the watcher is 'rarely' observed.[4] Although warning about the impact of technology in the present, his model does apply to informer states, in that those being observed would normally have been unaware of who was doing the observing. In some respects, that system has even less of an impact than a technologically based approach, since the latter tends to be a visible form of surveillance, as opposed to a faceless informer in a group of people.

This chapter looks at the evolution of the informer state and provides specific examples of the model in practice. There is no precise definition of what constitutes an informer state, because there is no precise count for the number of informers in these states. It is possible, nevertheless, to describe the broad trappings of such a locale. It is a place where state security employs potentially a large number of informers from the general populace as an important form of human surveillance targeted against specific individuals or groups and against the wider society in general. The necessity for ordinary citizens to be involved in such a system was, according to historian Robert Gellately, a crucial element in the new security state that appeared in the nineteenth century: 'The surveillance societies that emerged over the past two centuries can be distinguished from their predecessors in part on the basis of their new formal policing activities, but particularly because of the role envisaged for citizens, whose duty became to watch, listen, and inform the authorities.'[5]

Before examining some of the more famous examples of informer states, it is important to address why these states turned to this form of surveillance in the first place. One factor may be the lack of technological prowess to conduct surveillance of the type increasingly developed since the end of the Cold War, with cameras, massive databases, sophisticated microphones, voice and facial recognition software and the increased ability to collect material electronically.[6] A reliance on human surveillance for informer states, according to Cyrille Fijnaut and Gary T. Marx, 'offers a reminder that repressive regimes are not caused by high technology, nor is the latter necessary for them. Yet as the technology becomes more available, cheaper and easier to use, it will become more commonplace and enhance the surveillance capability of the state, without necessarily reducing reliance on humans.'[7] In part, that is because informers can do things that technology cannot. As illustrated in Chapter 2, he or she, through the coaching of a handler, can ascertain specific plans and, if necessary, shift into the role of a direct *agent provocateur* and actively work to undermine said plans although, arguably, the mere possibility of the presence of an informer influences behaviour. Finally, enlisting large numbers of citizens as informers makes them directly complicit in the operations of a security state and, in the process, provides greater legitimacy to it.

State security agencies, going back to their initial development in the nineteenth century, recognized the power of informers. Their irregular use occurred in the Austro-Hungarian Empire of Prince Klemens Metternich, in Emperor Napoleon III's France and in Prussia under Friedrich Wilhelm IV.[8] Informer states only came into existence in the twentieth century, however, with the creation of modern intelligence and police services, along with concomitant bureaucracies and filing systems, which allowed for the sustained and systematic monitoring of individuals. The most famous example of an informer state would undoubtedly be the former German Democratic Republic (GDR). Nevertheless, before the GDR, there was Nazi Germany and before Nazi Germany there was the Soviet Union and before that there was Russia. Indeed, it was in the latter where the first widespread use of informers in the modern era was made against targeted groups, specifically those actively working through violence to overthrow Russian autocracy.

In Russia, informers became 'the cornerstone of the political police work'[9] in the late nineteenth century as the Russian secret police, the Okhrana, worked against revolutionaries. The assassination of Tsar Alexander II in 1881 demonstrated the potential risk involved and the necessity of greater coverage of the Russian radical world.[10] Estimates have put a figure at anywhere from 10,000 to 26,000 for the number of informers tasked on behalf of the Russian state with infiltrating radical organizations between the 1870s and the 1917 Russian Revolution, although these figures appear to have represented all informers who aided the Russian state, not just long-term penetration agents.[11] The number of enduring informers who infiltrated radical organizations like the Socialist Revolutionary Party (SRs), Social Democrats (SDs) and Anarchists was a few hundred.[12] One senior member of the Okhrana, estimated that it never had more than a thousand agents.[13] By this they meant longer-term agents and not anyone who assisted the state by secretly supplying information.

Indeed, the Russian secret police made a systematic effort to pursue political radicals through infiltration of 'secret collaborators' (*sekretnye sotrudniki*) or through the signing up of those already members of targeted organizations, the latter being known as 'informers' (*osvedomiteli*).[14] Those who the police enlisted came either from within or outside. With the former, an effective tool of recruitment came through arrests that then provided an advantage over the potential collaborator. Still, the coercive measures could only go so far. The person doing the recruiting 'had to be positive that the converted revolutionary honestly and wholly possessed a desire to serve the Department of Police'[15] since otherwise the risk of poor information or betrayal would be that much greater. According to historian Nurit Schleifman, the Russian 'police were well aware of the connection between the manner in which an agent was recruited and the quality of the service he subsequently provided'.[16] Those forced to act as informers naturally would do as little as possible on behalf of those applying the pressure. Another danger recognized by the police was that coerced individuals might actually feed them disinformation or even engage in 'counter-provocation'. Indeed, some exposed informers would retroactively declare their work for the police had really been performed on behalf of the radicals in order to discover what the police were up to or even to damage the latter's operations. The police would increasingly move away from using coerced informers or those who volunteered for no apparent reason. The best informer was the willing informer.

One study of the SRs found three distinctive categories of informer. Some were not members but supplied information about the Party nonetheless. Then came those who belonged to the party and assisted the police for financial remuneration. Lastly, outside agents migrated into the party.[17] In the example of those infiltrated into targeted organizations from the outside, the Russian secret police sought credible political radicals so naturally it looked for educated individuals at universities who could convincingly demonstrate their revolutionary credentials. Coercion, namely involving the police arresting and, more commonly to crime-related informers, offering leniency if they cooperated, proved a useful enlistment tool but did not predominate.[18] For those recruited, what followed was a life of continual stress, particularly in personal relationships — disputes with partners often led to their disgruntled other halves exposing their secret identities. The pressure emerged from the secrecy, risk, (including the possibility of being murdered if exposure occurred) and the need to advance upward: the level of a monthly salary was frequently based on how prominent the informer became in the targeted group. Some informers became adept at milking as much as possible out of their secret employer by parcelling out information in an effort to generate more revenue.[19] All of those who informed on a significant and regular basis invariably received a salary once having put their name on a contract. Payment, in any form, was preferred since it provided the handlers with leverage over the informer.

The vast majority of those who informed were men like Evno Filipovich Azef, profiled in the previous chapter, but occasionally women did make it into the ranks. Anna Egorovna Serebriakova was a revolutionary whom the police recruited after her arrest. She continued to be a credible radical, even having revolutionaries as guests in her home, while supplying information to the state all the way from the 1880s until her retirement in 1905.[20] A parallel was Zinaida Zhuchenko, active in the SRs for years after becoming an informer in 1894 for ideological purposes, in particular her support of the Tsarist Russian state. After being abroad for a number of years, she returned in 1905 at the request of her hidden employers. She quickly became involved in SRs violence, all the while supplying information about these activities. In 1906, this information possibly saved the life of the governor of Minsk, an intended target for assassination. Zhuchenko allowed the police access to the means of his death — explosives — which they rendered harmless.[21]

For the handlers, running informers served as a developing science. As late as 1906, they met with their informers in St Petersburg at the police station. Eventually, the police established a system of codes to protect the identity of the informers from the prying eyes of others. In advising his charges on the absolute necessity for secrecy, one police officer compared the relationship between a handler and his or her informer to an illicit love affair: '. . . [you] must look at *sotrudniki* as a beautiful woman with whom you are maintaining a secret liaison. Be careful with her as [if she] is the apple of your eye. One careless step and you disgrace her.'[22] Prestige went to the handlers with the greater number of informers; an obvious inducement to recruit more.[23] In an era before modern technological surveillance, informers clearly were crucial to police operations against radicals, and a rise in radical activity as the war and the revolution neared led to a concomitant climb in the enlisting of informers.[24]

Although the exposure of spies within radical ranks harmed police operations, the revelations, nevertheless, aided their side. This was because simply the awareness of the possibility of informers in their midst (the overall number was in fact exaggerated by those being watched) inspired even greater suspicion and paranoia among the targets of surveillance. Those spied on responded with increased secrecy through codewords, less sharing of information, and denunciations of suspected informers. These usually turned out to be innocent, since a majority of the real ones remained undiscovered.[25] The more inward-looking and focused on internal security groups became, the less effective they were at carrying out operations. E.P. Thompson noted a similar impact of informers in the English milieu: 'a convincing history of English Jacobinism and popular Radicalism could be written solely in terms of the impact of espionage upon the movement'.[26] Be they radicals in England or Russia, the impact, not of the informers themselves but the knowledge of their informing created, in the words of Michel Foucault, 'a state of conscious and permanent visibility that assures the automatic functioning of power. So to arrange things that the surveillance is permanent in its effects, even if it is discontinuous in its action'. Certainly the parallel with the Panopticon was not exact but the 'unverifiable' element remained, since those targeted while being unsure of when they were being observed by an informer 'must be sure that he may always be so'.[27] And, instead of being observed by a camera on a pole or an unseen prison guard through a peephole, the watcher might well be a close friend or a family member.

It was this Russian security environment that the Bolsheviks inherited and expanded on, first during the Russian Revolution and Civil War, and then in the party's consolidation of power in the interwar period. The internal security system they created made the previous one appear almost amateurish in comparison. As a point of comparison, there were the two informers most widely associated with the respective eras. There was the notorious Azef of pre-revolutionary days. By the time of Stalin, however, informing on behalf of the revolutionary state was considered to be a positive mark of citizenship. Pavel Morozov, a boy of 13, became a celebrated figure in Stalin's Soviet Union when in 1932 his family murdered him, allegedly after he had turned in his father in to the state because of corruption.[28] The informer had become a state hero.

In contrast to liberal-democratic polities, where generally more targeted uses of human surveillance occur, the Soviet Union relied on the assistance of countless individuals to serve as its daily eyes and ears.[29] One estimate puts the number of Soviets serving as informers in the 1930s as high as 10 per cent. The same source argues that the percentage who in some fashion cooperated with the secret police could be much higher.[30] In the 1930s, the Soviet domestic security, in the form of the NKVD [*Narodnyi Komissariat Vnutrennikh Del*] separated informers into those who aided in criminal cases versus those who supplied information connected to political policing. The NKVD eventually developed a handbook for its members that made recruiting structured and hierarchical, with permission from above required when an effort to enlist someone was made. When coercion needed to be employed, blackmail was the chosen method.[31] Payment was not regularly offered in this era. Beginning in 1927, Soviet security adopted practices that would become standard in much of Soviet-dominated Eastern Europe: informers were required to sign contracts, sworn to secrecy and received codenames. Recruiters shunned some, such as young people, due to their perceived unreliability, and party members, because their recruitment was politically controversial.[32] The system became even more formalized in the later years of the Soviet Union and, by its end, members of the NKVD's successor, the KGB [*Komitet Gosudarstvennoy Bezopasnosti*], similar to intelligence services in Eastern Europe, received informer quotas — two being the minimum for a year — along with bonuses. The KGB would eventually develop three types of informers, drawn from those 18–60 years in age: its own members, who went undercover to inform; 'trusted persons', such as academics or telephone switchboard operators who did not work directly for the police but supplied information at times;[33] and the largest group, the more formal informers, who served as observers but also in some cases as 'agents of influence'.[34]

Not all Soviet informing occurred in complete secrecy. As with Pavel Morozov, some made voluntary denunciations — what Robert Gellately labels as a 'variety of popular informing'[35] — both publicly and privately. Around Leningrad, for instance, less than 0.01 per cent of letters sent to denounce another were submitted anonymously; the number was higher elsewhere. Still, the majority who made denunciations, in keeping with the characteristics of an informer, wished for their identity to be kept private. Only the state would know who they really were. In some cases, the NKVD tried to recruit letter writers, particularly those who participated in the first place out of a desire to be an informer.[36] The motivations varied with individuals but, in general, some sought to promote egalitarianism by denouncing those who had seemingly grown too powerful. Denouncing then, similarly to a form of gossip, served as a societal leveller. It had a major impact, as Sheila Fitzpatrick notes:

> The surveillance function of denunciation has to do with the disciplining of citizens — the exertion of state or collective power to enforce conformity to certain socially accepted norms. The primary motivation associated with performing the surveillance function is duty, expressed either as 'my duty as a Communist' or 'my duty as a Soviet citizen'.[37]

As two scholars point out, a discourse developed around denouncing/informing in which if others did it they were considered 'informers', while individuals perceived themselves as performing a public service.[38] This conceivably explains the complex nature of the Russian relationship to informing, both during and after the fall of communism. If apparently done out of selfless motives, the perception of the activity was positive because it challenged the negativity surrounding informing. Additionally, this surveillance system seemed to offer domestic stability and security. Perhaps it was for this reason that some Russians, including, not surprisingly, KGB veterans, began to advocate for the restoration of the *seksoty* (a shortened version of the Russian words for 'secret collaborators') in the wake of the 2004 Chechnyan terrorist attack on a school in the Russian town of Beslan that left over 300 people dead, many of them children.[39]

The Stalinist model of the informer state, successful at enforcing state control of a society, would eventually be replicated elsewhere in the Communist bloc. This was true most notably in the former GDR, whose internal security system was created by Germans trained in the Soviet Union.[40] The GDR has become the poster child of informer states, to the point that it is regularly invoked in public discourses in democratic countries over the danger of the development of the police state. Predating the GDR, however, was Nazi Germany, which did not quite fit the pattern as reflected in the Communist bloc. Plainly, it represented a police state like the others, but equally Adolf Hitler's regime was different, according to those who have looked into the question in depth. One significant divergence is that it did not rely on large numbers of security agents as the GDR later would. Various statistics, which are difficult to verify in terms of their accuracy, show the Gestapo having 1 regular member per 4,800 citizens in 1938 compared to the Soviet Union with the KGB's 1 per 5,830 in the late 1930s. The GDR came in at one *Ministerium für Staatssicherheit* (Stasi) member per 180 citizens. If informers are factored in, the GDR security presence was as low as 1 for every 70 citizens.[41] Despite perceptions of Gestapo eyes and ears being everywhere, the secret police in Nazi Germany had limited resources for spying. What made up for this was the participation of ordinary citizens through informing activities and denunciations.[42] Whatever the label, the activity was meant to be secret between citizens and the state and thus represents informing.

There were two general categories of informers in Nazi Germany. First, there were those who had a more formal relationship with the Gestapo and often had connections to the activity they were informing on.[43] The state often paid this type of individual, the most important of whom were known as *Vertrauensleute*, or V-persons, like one person in the German city of Wurzburg, who established a secret Communist organization as a way of luring Reds into the Nazi web.[44]

Many of those who have studied this more formal version of informers appear surprised that coercion does not appear to have been a key recruitment tool for people including Catholic priests, non-Germans, Communists, Jews and some opposed to the Nazi state, who worked as Gestapo informers.[45] These numbers appear to have been rather small. In Nuremberg in 1943 and 1944, for example, there were approximately 80–100 paid informers, at a ratio of 1 informer per Gestapo agent covering a population of 2.75 million people.[46] Other micro studies, including one of Gestapo files in Frankfurt at the end of the World War II, found that not all informers were paid. Some may have been subjected to low-level coercion to aid the secret police, although this is far from conclusive.[47] Indeed, compulsion as a sole tool of recruitment appears to have been unlikely, for the practical reason, as suggested elsewhere in the book, that coerced individuals are not so effective as informers who do it willingly. Several did resist efforts to engage them as informers.[48]

The numbers of those formally enlisted, however, paled in comparison to the second major category: volunteers who came forward to inform on or denounce an acquaintance or neighbour or even a spouse or child, to the Gestapo. These did so through letters, both anonymous and signed, tips and even visits to the local Gestapo office.[49] Gellately offers an explanation for the prevalence of denunciations over more formalized informing:

> The widespread use of denunciations has to be seen in the cultural and social context of an interventionist system that fostered instrumental relations between citizens and regime. The Nazi system of party and state was certainly repressive and highly invasive, but it was almost immediately 'normalized' by many people as they began to accept it as part of the structure of everyday life.[50]

There was, for example, a woman in Düsseldorf who wrote to authorities to report that her 66-year-old neighbour was listening to forbidden radio broadcasts and even offered her flat to the Gestapo in order to catch her neighbour in this subversive act.[51]

Because of this type of denunciation/informing, those most

targeted were within the informers' social milieu. The motivations for informing, the vast majority of which was done by men, varied but included the traditional ones of jealousy, revenge, racism and, although seemingly lower down the list of possible motivations, ideology, in the form of loyalty to the state or the Nazi party.[57] Gellately memorably describes the denunciation system this way: 'self-interest fuelled the self-policing system.'[53] This was crucial to the ability of the Gestapo to do its job. One localized study of the German city of Würzburg, replicated in parallel studies of other German locales, found that concerned citizens initiated 57 per cent of cases related to the enforcement of laws separating Jews from other Germans in terms of friendship and sex. They acted as amateur informers.[54]

Whatever the reason, there was a strong element of volunteerism to Nazi informing that differed from other police states.[55] It certainly deviated from the most famous informer state, the GDR.[56] Numerous comparisons have been made between the two, and yet, in many ways, it is an exercise in apple-orange comparison. The model for the GDR's security system, that would see the rise of its famous network of informers, came from the Soviet Union of Stalin, not Hitler's Germany. The secret police of the GDR eventually grew and expanded, leading to its representing a high percentage of staff to general population compared to either Nazi Germany or the Soviet Union.[57] Having a large number of secret police members, in turn, undoubtedly contributed to a proportionately high number of informers.

It was in the GDR that the informer state became a science, mirroring the state's wider state socialism in the way it was organized, as informing became 'institutionalized'.[58] The numbers are remarkable. Various categories of informers existed, but most belonged to a single category, albeit with subdivisions within that grouping.[59] Anywhere from 100,000 to 180,000 East Germans, or 2–3 per cent of the country's population, have been labelled through the examination of the actual records as full-time informers of the type known as an *Inoffizielle Mitarbeiter* (IM) (unofficial contributor). This was the more neutral term adopted in 1968 to replace *Geheime Informatoren* (secret informer).[60] Nearly 10,000 of that number were drawn from those below the age of 18. The overall total, which may run as high as 500,000, especially since there was roughly a 10 per cent turnover rate per year,[61] does not include others who might have served as part-time informers. One source argues that when these contributors are taken into consideration the number may have been as high as 2 million.[62] Whatever the exact figure, the GDR represented a society where informing became an accepted and normal practice for many of its citizens and an increasingly employed tactic of a police state that found itself under growing domestic pressure from the 1970s on.[63] Gellately aptly describes the informing evolution that occurred in Eastern bloc countries, like the GDR, Poland and Romania:

> The impression that emerges from the literature on the GDR — and other Central European states — is that the longer such regimes lasted, the more revolutionary zeal and improvisation dissipated, with numerous implications for citizen participation in the policing and security systems. Those in charge of the political police had more time to establish and improve the systems and to institutionalize denunciations, and the longer the regimes lasted, the more citizens came to terms with them. Furthermore, the Stasi and other parts of the system of domination (party and state) had more time to sink deeper roots and to spread through society in numerous ways, playing a role not only as repressor and persecutor but also as mediator of conflicts.[64]

Who was the typical Stasi informer? The most common characteristic was gender: 80–90 per cent were men, a reflection of the patriarchal GDR society. This trait applied to the Stasi itself, in which only men functioned as handlers.[65] Sexism was evident in the 1950s, when the Stasi advised its handlers to 'offer female unofficial employees something sweet to eat' as a means of maintaining their loyalty.[66] Besides men, the Stasi sought informers in targeted organizations that tended to be areas considered suspicious by the state, recognizing that it was far easier to recruit informers from within these crucial areas than to infiltrate its own members into them.[67] Thus, fields such as education, culture, religion and politics had a disproportionate number of informers and potentially a disproportionate impact on political protest against the state. Historian Mary Fulbrook raises the possibility that informers may have pushed their constituent organizations into more radical positions so as to provide the authorities with an excuse to crack down on them.[68]

The Stasi searched for these characteristics in potential recruits:

The ability to assess situations

The ability to fully comprehend the political and ideological content and consequences of events

The ability to judge human character and behaviour

The ability to form and preserve relationships based on trust

The ability to observe and take in information on situations and people in a planned and concentrated manner, over a short or long time, as well as the ability to retain and reproduce this information as quickly as possible

The ability to cope with high demands and burdens and to deal with individual doubts and scruples.[69]

One former Stasi member told author Anna Funder that the ideal informer needed to be highly adaptable but also consistent enough to maintain his or her secret career. Finally, and more than slightly ironically, an IM had to be 'honest, faithful and trustworthy' — to the Stasi, not to those he or she spied upon.[70] Despite seeking these qualities, the Stasi never fully trusted its secret contributors. The agency scrutinized the activities and accuracy of its covert helpers by using other IMs to report on them. Precision was all-important since, again reflecting a scientific approach to informing, that which they reported needed to be verifiable for it to have ultimate value. Any suspicious behaviour on the part of an informer, such as unpredictability, untrustworthiness, a lack of cooperation, or anything else deemed mistrustful, was required to be investigated, although often it was not. The dishonesty discovered eventually in nearly 10 per cent of informers emerged through multiple other sources available to the Stasi.[71]

The recruiting of informers by the Stasi occurred, in theory, in a systematic and organized way with detailed study of the potential candidate and their family taking place before the approach.[72] That appeal was then made, sometimes at home or at work, in person or by letter or via the telephone.[73] Once the candidate agreed, he or she had to sign a written document attesting to their secret relationship although some, particularly those in the religious community, received an exemption from this requirement if the Stasi felt it would aid in their recruitment.[74] A codename for the new employee was then issued and a file opened. Of course, there was no guarantee that even a measured approach would be successful. The recruiting success rate in the 1960s and 1970s may only have been one-quarter to one-third.[75]

Two related questions exist when it comes to those who were recruited. What enticements did the Stasi offer and why did those who signed up agree to do it? First, the key idea is that the secret police selected whom it wanted. They did not fully trust those who volunteered. The 1952 Stasi handler manual warned that '[p]articular care should be taken with those individuals who voluntarily offer their services'.[76] Certainly, compulsion played a role and, in the aftermath of the fall of the Berlin Wall, former IMs emphasized this as the reason for their collaboration. In other words, they had no choice, especially in a police state. Some evidence of coercion exists, and the Stasi's own research suggested that nearly 8 per cent of informers had been recruited through the use of 'compromising material', such as evidence of adulterous activities. This figure is conceivably on the low side, because of Stasi instructions to use blackmail only as a last resort.[77] Coercion could appear in different forms. People in prison or under arrest, for example, were offered early release in return for assistance to the Stasi. Still, the role of duress appears to have dissipated over time, as the Stasi became more skilled at recruitment and recognized the drawbacks of the use of compulsion. The best evidence those approached had a choice is that some refused to become IMs and suffered few apparent hardships as a result. Several refused to participate directly. Others did so more surreptitiously, like the factory worker who, after being visited by the Stasi, told others of the offer, thus rendering himself useless to the secret police. Even a number of those enrolled resisted, by supplying poor information or revealing their identity to those they were spying on, becoming what the Stasi called 'a drop-out'.[78]

Why did those who informed do it and how? In his study of the Stasi, Mike Dennis lists five general motivational categories: 'political and ideological conviction; coercion and fear; personal advantage; emotional needs; and a desire to influence official policy.'[79] Certainly, the traditional reasons were also present, such as greed, ideology and, in an echo of Åkerström, notions of power and the allure of the sexiness of secrecy. Some rationalized their secret work by invoking what Åkerström calls the 'denial of injury, that is, a denial of the causal efficacy of the action'.[80] To put it simply, the information they supplied did not hurt anyone. Certainly, the informers would usually not have witnessed first hand the impact of their information on those about whom they supplied it.[81] Others, argues Mary Fulbrook somewhat dubiously, specifically those who served in higher positions in targeted organizations, may not have realized that they were working as IMs. Instead, they would have viewed their participation as an effort to influence the state.[82] Some genuinely believed in the cause and saw it as their duty to assist the state in any way possible. One study of recruitment in Karl-Marx Stadt found that 81 per cent of informers signed up out of political beliefs; a number potentially inflated by self-rationalization.[83] In another survey, of informers run out of its Potsdam office, conducted by the Stasi itself in the 1960s, 60.5 per cent indicated that 'recognition of societal needs' motivated their involvement, versus 27.4 per cent who listed 'personal advantages'.[84] Still others argued *post facto* that they were attempting to engage in a dialogue with the state or even to change it by pointing out deficiencies within GDR society and thus, hopefully, sparking reform.[85]

For the handlers there was a detailed set of rules that reflected the Stasi's scientific approach to informing.[86] Three sets were issued in the 1950s; another came out in 1968; the final one emerged in 1979.[87] The 1952 guidelines singled out those who could function in targeted groups as the best type of informers. In 1958 and 1968, the guidelines emphasized ideology, perhaps deeming it an important skill to allow an informer to be as inconspicuous as possible within those groups considered in some way subversive. In theory, these criteria would have pushed the secret police away from recruiting Communist Party members, but, in reality they did not, as this represented a pool of loyal informers readily at hand.[88] The 1979 guidelines offered instructions to Stasi handlers on how to direct those who signed up out of genuine belief: 'Recruitments based on the positive political stance of the candidate should build upon the candidate's outlook on life as well as on their moral and political convictions, thus developing their willingness to work with the [Stasi].'[89]

Similarly to elsewhere, for individual members, stature went with the number of informers recruited and the correlation was simple: the more informers recruited and controlled, the higher the handler's prestige. The number of informers supervised by an individual could be as high as 30, as was the case at the Stasi's Berlin headquarters.[90] Contrary to promoted Stasi practice as enunciated by its longtime leader, Erich Mielke, this led to the signing up of informers simply for the sake of recruiting informers not because of any valuable information they might have been able to supply to their handlers.[91]

Once signed up, it was the handler's job to keep his secret partner motivated. In that sense, as it did with the initial conversion, the Stasi became increasingly adept at catering to the needs of individual informers.[92] Regular payments, even if just to cover expenses, became one tool for ensuring compliance, although not everyone was paid and other perks, such as a job, accommodation or a car, were more highly sought after.[93] Those who did receive money often had the amount determined by the quality of the information or by their significance in the organization that they spied on.[94] Stasi surveys found that whereas only 21.5 per cent of informers said that a 'financial reward' motivated them to work better (as opposed to 38.1 per cent who listed 'praise', presumably from the handler), 58 per cent of handlers listed it as the chief motivator (compared to slightly more than 20 per cent who cited 'praise').[95] Some of these factors appear in individual stories. Lothar Pawliczak, approached while he was still in high school, became a Stasi informer at 18 when he signed a contract. He joined for the excitement, meeting his handler about once a month and receiving 50–100 marks on a regular basis. Monika Haeger, an informer within the dissident organization Women for Peace, was an orphan who found in her Stasi handler the father figure missing from her life.[96]

The Stasi put considerable effort into maintaining control over its informers and keeping them motivated. As a result, handlers habitually developed close relationships with their charges. The secret police went so far as to establish its own psychology unit to explore this and related questions, and its own members produced scholarship that addressed various issues related to motivation.[97] Of course, there was a fundamental inequality in the relationship between handlers and their informers and a pattern of dependency between the two often developed. The Stasi members frequently cultivated this by performing tasks on behalf of informers, even in one case arranging for a divorce. The bonds were so close that several ex-informers after the fall of the GDR expressed a desire to be reunited with their superiors.[98]

The length of an IM's service varied. Some listed on the books, possibly to pad out statistics, never received any attention. Others were released for a variety of reasons, or left of their own accord. Edward Peterson's detailed examination of the Stasi in a particular GDR district offers these statistics on the reasons why the careers of informers ended there in 1983 and 1984.

TABLE 5.1 IMs dismissed, Magdeburg Stasi, 1983–1984[99]

	1983 IM	%	1984 IM	%
Those dismissed	61	100	73	100
Refusal to cooperate	25	41	26	36
Unsuitability	21	34	17	23
Dishonesty	3	5	6	8
Other reasons	12	20	24	33

Despite Stasi guidelines that discouraged the structure of meetings from becoming ritualized, a pattern often set in. There would be regular get-togethers between the handler and informer that occurred away from the latter's home, such as in a park or a safe house. The secret police member ran the meeting and readied for it in advance in order to make it as productive as possible from the perspective of the Stasi. A written and, occasionally, a tape-recorded record of the gathering was created and a copy put on the IM's file. The veracity of the material contained within was also tested, as a means of evaluating the source.[100]

In an archetypal informer state, stories of Stasi informers abound. Recruiting informers became a consistent response to any perceived threat to the state, be it soccer hooligans, political dissidents, punk rockers or skinheads, the latter being a focus of the 1980s in the years before the Berlin Wall and Eastern European communism collapsed.[101] Because the Stasi focused on specific areas in its hunt for dissent, it was natural that some areas would be overrepresented when it came to informing.[102] This certainly applied to the cultural sector. The Stasi started a unit focused on literature in 1969 and six years later, nearly 400 IMs were active in the field. These numbers would later include 12 of the 19 members of the GDR's Writers' Association, 49 out of 123 members of the executive of the Writers' Union, and famous authors such as Christa 'Mararete' Wolf (active for the Stasi between 1959 and 1961 and then the subject of surveillance by the same agency), Monika 'Mitsu' Maron, Herman Kant and Sacha 'Fritz Müller' Anderson.[103]

Athletics, so important to the international profile projected by the GDR in the 1970s and 1980s, also swarmed with IMs. An estimated 3,000 informers were active in the top sports in these decades, including approximately 20 per cent of the staff of the 'Research Institute for Physical Culture and Sport in Leipzig'.[104] In 1992, a German newspaper revealed that Harald Czudaj, a member of a European champion four-man bobsled team, had been coerced into becoming an informer in 1988 by the Stasi and had subsequently supplied details about his teammates.[105] After the collapse of the GDR, rumours abounded about Katarina Witt, arguably the most famous GDR athlete of the 1980s. She repeatedly denied being an informer, portraying herself instead as a victim of the Stasi and as someone who had rejected its advances. She made these proclamations while simultaneously fighting in the courts to block the release of her secret police dossier. Labelling her as a 'beneficiary of the regime', eventually the German government allowed a 181-page section of her 1,354-page Stasi file to be made public.[106] Despite not being an official informer and being subjected to Stasi surveillance, Witt, perhaps out of self-interest, did have regular contact and a friendly relationship with the Stasi to the point that in 1986 she inquired as to how one would become a Stasi agent. Two years later, she requested a new car from the agency and expressed gratitude when she received it. Referring to it as a 'partner' and as a key contributor to her athletic success, the skater reassured the Stasi that it did not need to open her mail since she informed 'the MfS . . . about everything'.[107]

Religion and education represented other gathering points for IMs. In the case of some synods, nearly 20 per cent were informers. One prominent GDR churchman, Manfred 'Sekretär' Stolpe was later exposed as an IM (a role he denied, noting that he had not signed a contract with the Stasi, as others had done) while serving as premier of the state of Brandenburg in the newly united Germany.[108] Education wise, universities yielded informers the way that institutions of higher education in Russia had once done in the era of the Tsar, as the Stasi sought well-educated young people for recruits. Staff joined in the act as well. Professor Kurt Meier, a historian at the University of Leipzig, became an informer in 1957. At Humboldt University, an estimated 25 per cent of staff worked secretly as IMs.[109]

Politics was another obvious place for informers. There were politicians like Dirk Schneider from the Green Party and a dissident group, Initiative for Peace and Human Rights, in which half of its members were Stasi informers, including prominent activists, Ibrahim Böhme and Wolfgang Schnur.[110] The mother of Werner Fischer, a GDR human rights activist as a member of the 'Swords to Ploughshares' peace group, supplied information on him under the codename 'Ursula' and even received an award from the Stasi for her work. For Vera Wollenberger, another political dissident, it was her husband Knud, under the alias of 'Donald', who was the Stasi spy; their marriage ended as a result of his treachery, although she later forgave him after he wrote a letter explaining his actions.[111]

While the GDR is the world's most famous informer state, it was not the only one active in the post-1945 era. Across Eastern Europe, informer states resembling the Soviet model existed and, in some cases, thrived. All were characterized by the presence of informers seeking out political dissent. In Poland, it was the SB (*Służba Bezpieczeństwa Ministerstwa Spraw Wewnętrznych* — Security Service of the Ministry of Internal Affairs) that employed informers. In the former Czechoslovakia it was the StB (in Czech: *Státní bezpečnost*; in Slovak: *Štátna bezpečnosť*). In Romania it was the Securitate (*Departamentul Securității Statului* — State Security Department)

As elsewhere in Eastern Europe, the StB relied heavily on informers to keep watch on the domestic scene in Czechoslovakia. Beginning in 1954 it kept detailed records that included the informer's name, codename, their history of informing and a signed loyalty oath. Handlers received yearly quotas that ranged from 10 to 15; they ran 8 at any given time. This pressure led to cases of individuals being listed as informers to inflate statistics, including one StB member who had only 1 genuine informer out of 17 appearing in his files. For the authentic ones, the motivations ranged from ideology to fear to blackmail to money, although the latter two did not represent significant factors.[112] A former handler described the situation this way: 'Some agreed out of fear, but the big reason people joined us was that we made them feel appreciated. The personal relationship was always more important than ideology. Very few declined.'[113]

Through the Securitate, Romania had arguably the largest network of informers in Europe, even by the standards of the GDR. By the end of the regime of Nicolae Ceaușescu, anywhere from an estimated 400,000 to 700,000 informers had secretly laboured at some point for the state. These numbers had risen dramatically with the arrival of the Communist state in Bucharest. At its creation in 1948, the Securitate inherited 830 informers from the previous military security agency. By 1951, that number had grown to 42,187.[114] In December 1989, at the time of the downfall of Ceaușescu, the Securitate had 150,000 informers still on the books in a country of 23 million people.[115] The Securitate distinguished between different types of informers. Fully half were classified as *colaboratori* (collaborators). The rest were divided between *gaze* (hosts), *informatory* (informers) and *rezidenti* (residents). Other practices resembled those employed elsewhere in Eastern Europe, specifically pursing motivations such as patriotism or rewards, requesting the new informer recruit to sign a contract and then issuing the individual a codename.[116]

The expectation that clandestine relationships and acts of betrayal would remain hidden ended with the collapse of communism across Eastern Europe. Recriminations for ex-informers would follow the emergence of previously secret records into the public domain. The documentation included materials seized by the Central Intelligence Agency just after the collapse of communism in the GDR and returned to Germany in 2003.[117] A word, *lustration*, based on the Latin for purification, even became associated with the process of publicly exposing the alleged informing activities of citizens.[118]

Some countries administered this difficult period better than others. Germany established a commission, known as the Gauck Authority, after its head, Joachim Gauck, to manage the records. The German government provided it with a large budget, over 3,000 employees and clearly established rules on who was to have access to Stasi records and how they were to do it. By November 1993, nearly 2 million people had applied to see their files.[119] Former IMs, however, faced restrictions in their access. They were only allowed to view the parts of their file that pertained to them and not to those they reported on.[120] Some Germans did not escape retribution for their previously secret work. The Stasi Document Law of December 1991 allowed for the firing of civil servants because of secret contacts with the Stasi, although it did not make it automatic, as was done elsewhere. By February 1997, 42,000 civil servants had lost their jobs because of Stasi connections and more than 13,000 outside of the civil service found themselves unemployed for similar reasons.[121]

Across Eastern Europe, the picture varied. In some places, equal measures of rumour, revenge, chaos and even indifference erupted. Bulgaria escaped some of the turmoil, as over 150,000 secret police files were destroyed after the fall of communism.[122] Controversy erupted in Hungary after a number of prominent politicians, including then Prime Minister Peter Medgyessy, were named as informers in 2002 by a parliamentary committee. The identities of other informers have periodically emerged since.[123] In Romania, the Romanian Information Service ultimately took charge of the Securitate records after the fall of Communism. This led to a variety of leaks, in some cases designed to damage the political careers of prominent politicians.[124] Eventually, the Council for the Study of Securitate Archives (CNSAS) was established to manage access to the documents.[125] In March 2003, 3,000 people protested publicly in a call to have the Securitate files opened to the public. Later that year, the government opened up the documents under restricted access.[126]

Among the prominent Romanians alleged to have been an informer was Bishop Laszlo Toekes, a leading figure in the revolt against Ceauşescu. The Bishop claimed that the Securitate had used coercion to compel him to inform. He subsequently launched a lawsuit against the Associated Press over the allegations; he lost, but in the end, in a sign of the greater sophistication being applied in interpreting the meaning of the records, the agency controlling the records cleared him of being a collaborator because he aided the Securitate under duress.[127] A newspaper later printed Toekes' alleged initial recruitment form, and a signed receipt for a cash payment he apparently received in December 1989 (see Chapter 4 for the text).[128]

Controversy over record revelations exploded in Poland as well, where the number of informers grew in the 1980s. Internal protest fuelled the increase, as handlers had their quota for informers upped from 10 to 25 a year.[129] Initially, the Polish government opted to keep the secret police files closed. Perhaps as a result of this decision, a plethora of stories emerged, naming prominent individuals as former informers for state security agencies. Some, such as accusations against former Polish president Lech Walesa, which began to emerge in 1992, turned out to be false.[130] In 1998, however, the Polish government passed a law requiring public servants, members of the judiciary and politicians to declare whether or not they had been a collaborator with the SB. That declaration was then compared with the existing files and if the individual lied, he or she would face a ban from public office for ten years.[131] After the non-partisan National Remembrance

Institute took control of the files, some clamoured for the release of all of the names listed as informers. Instead, Poland arrived comparably late in allowing access to records. They were only made available in January 2005, when those who thought they had been a victim of the secret police could apply to access their files. Very quickly, and either deliberately or unintentionally, a list of approximately 150,000-plus names appeared on the internet.[132] The material, collectively known as the Wildstein List after Bronislaw Wildstein, the journalist who made the original copy, included those who worked for the secret police, those who had been informers, and even those individuals approached to inform but who refused. The accompanying codes made it difficult to decipher the real identity of individuals, as did the repetition of names such as Jan Kowalski, a common Polish name, which appeared 37 times on the list. Mass controversy and interest ensued. Wildstein lost his job and subsequently the government passed a law to mitigate some of the damage done by the leak.[133] Consequently, Poland began to regulate access to the files and allowed those interested to see why someone had cooperated with the state, such as for money or because of blackmail.[134] Others could go through the courts in an effort to free their names from the taint of informing.[135]

The new access began to have an impact. Implicated as an SB informer codenamed 'Nowak' was Malgorzata Niezabitowska, the main spokeswoman for the Solidarity movement in the early 1980s. Like Walesa, she too claimed that documents in her file were forged. She did admit, however, to meeting with a member of the secret police once, in December 1981, and supplying harmless information about some of her journalist colleagues. One of these eventually obtained his file and made public her clandestine collaboration. Any additional material, she added, resulted from forgeries, a suggestion dismissed by those responsible for the current maintenance of the records. The file, which contained a document with her signature on, referred to 11 reports from Nowak's handler. Its material also suggested that at the time, Niezabitowska apparently justified her informing as an effort to aid in 'avoiding bloodshed'.[136]

It was in the Czech Republic that the most politicized use of files occurred, with individuals frequently being fired if their names turned up as informers, regardless of the context of their involvement. The situation grew worse in June 1992 when a list of supposed StB informers numbering around 160,000 appeared in a magazine, prompting a backlash against some of those named. By the following year, 150 alleged informers faced lawsuits — 70 out of 70 legal decisions found them innocent of the informing accusations.[137] One individual nearly caught up in this net was Vaclav Havel. The secret police approached the famous Czech dissident in 1965 to evaluate his potential as an informer. He was listed as a possible collaborator but later, when his opposition to the government became clear, he became an enemy of the state.[138] Then there were the prominent people who actually had been informers. In Slovakia, for instance, Jozef Banáš, a member of parliament for the governing party, admitted to his StB past although, in typical fashion, rationalized it by arguing his work had not harmed anyone.[139] Former president Rudolf Schuster was an informer, although he denied knowing that he had secretly worked for the StB.[140]

The controversy surrounding informers demonstrated the pain that treachery provokes. Impersonal technological surveillance simply does not inspire such pain. Any anger directed at it is really aimed at the state that deploys such a tool for information collection. Informers are different. In Eastern Europe they represented flesh and blood surveillance, in some cases carried out by someone familiar and even especially close to the person under surveillance. Rage at the informer is, of course, also directed at the state, but much of it centres on the actual spy — not just those who use them.

Thousands of human surveillance tools were active in informer states, particularly after World War II, because they afforded the state access to discussions in lunch rooms, locker rooms, classrooms, church halls, living rooms and even bedrooms. Informers remain an effective tool for less democratic states to monitor the general population. Although the informer states depicted herein have collapsed, others remain. Lingering on as well is the possibility that liberal-democratic countries will use informers to spy on specific communities in the name of security in the same way that police states targeted entire nations.[141]

CHAPTER 6

Informers in the 'War on Terror'

As the twentieth century progressed, technological developments arrived that seemed to begin the writing of the obituary of intelligence informers. First, with the emergence of aircraft equipped with cameras able to take detailed photos from a high altitude, followed by spy satellites capable of doing the same from even higher up, human intelligence (HUMINT) appeared increasingly less relevant to modern intelligence agencies. Informers did remain crucial to domestic investigations but also here technology, initially through more elaborate microphones, then tracking devices and sophisticated cameras able to feed images into databases, seemed to triumph. Even police forces now deploy unmanned drones capable of conducting surveillance over urban centres.[1] These forces of change buffeted the Central Intelligence Agency (CIA) in the late 1970s when President Jimmy Carter's CIA director, Admiral Stansfield Turner, eliminated HUMINT-related jobs and declared electronic surveillance as representing the future.[2] Financially, the US government's present priority is unmistakably in the direction of technological intelligence collection — the budget of the National Security Agency (NSA) is double that of the Central Intelligence Agency.[3]

Additional factors beyond a belief in technology came into play. Information acquired through technological surveillance has an illusion of objectivity that the equivalent supplied by an informer does not. In the UK, the domestic intelligence agency, the Security Service (MI5), has begun to release transcripts of bugged conversations of those convicted in serious terrorism investigations, seemingly a means of further demonstrating their guilt.[4] The testimony of an informer clearly would not have the same influence on public opinion. Technology certainly lacks the taint of betrayal associated with informing. Cameras have never directly killed anyone. Unquestionably, the information such surveillance produces can prove to be fatal, as in the case of CIA missile strikes against suspected al-Qaeda members, but in itself it is an impersonal piece of technology without blood on its lenses. The equivalent cannot be said of informers, some of whom are criminals, terrorists and murderers. They frequently associate with unsavoury characters who they then inform on, and they are subject to human frailties from which machines enjoy an inherent immunity.

Modern terrorism, however, has proven a challenge to technological surveillance. Certain aspects of this form of intelligence gathering were designed not on the micro level of terrorist cells but on a scale involving nation states. Satellites and spy planes have proven to be skilled at determining missile deployments, troop movements and, in the case of terrorism, even discovering training camps, but are largely useless at deciphering the planning of actual operations conducted by small collections of people. In that sense, electronic surveillance is increasingly relevant, but it too is not without limitations. Emails can be encrypted and used in different ways, with coded messages hidden within a digitized picture or messages saved in the draft section of an email account and accessed from there, instead of being sent out through cyberspace. Rooms can be swept for bugs, and terrorists with a desire to continue living, like Osama bin Laden, can and do stop using telephones that are tapped or satellite telephones that reveal their location.[5] Or, if they have to utilize a telephone, they speak in code, with the knowledge that someone somewhere is listening in on the conversation. In liberal-democratic states, rules and regulations govern technological surveillance, often requiring the acquisition of a warrant, which informers do not need. As discussed in Chapter 2, in the US, the 1978 Foreign Intelligence Surveillance Act (FISA) established the Foreign Intelligence Surveillance Court (FISC), the body responsible for authorizing electronic surveillance against foreign intelligence targets — no similar body existed for informers.[6] More resources were and are needed than human intelligence operations require. Around-the-clock surveillance of a single individual without the use of an informer can entail as many as 60 people (up to three surveillance teams consisting of 15–20 personnel per team) over a 24-hour period. The use of technological surveillance can still require the involvement of as many as a dozen personnel.[7] A British parliamentary committee claimed that to keep watch on all of the individuals potentially involved in domestic terrorism after *9/11* would have required that MI5 have 'several hundred thousand officers'.[8]

Finally, specialized technological surveillance is often reactive and thus, limited in its possibilities. A microphone hidden in a wall might yield details on a proposed attack but only if somehow the targets being listened to have come under suspicion in the first place and, of course, have elected to speak in a clearly defined way about a particular operation. As Federal Bureau of Investigation (FBI) Director Robert Mueller suggests, informers represent a proactive counter-terrorism tool:

> Human sources . . . often give us critical intelligence and information we could not obtain in other ways, opening a window into our adversaries' plans and capabilities. [They] can mean the difference between the FBI preventing an act of terrorism or crime, or reacting to an incident after the fact.[9]

When technological surveillance yields results, it often occurs after HUMINT serves as the initial spark drawing the attention of security agencies and police forces in the direction of a target. A 1996 US Congressional report explicitly addressed the limitations of such surveillance:

They [technological surveillance] do not, however, provide sufficient access to targets such as terrorists or drug dealers who undertake their activities in secret or to the plans and intentions of foreign governments that are deliberately concealed from the outside world. Recruiting human sources — as difficult, imperfect, and risky as it is — often provides the only means of such access.[10]

The advantage that informers enjoy over electronic surveillance for spy agencies and police forces runs deeper than the intelligence that they generate. The power of informers as a counter-terrorism tool relates exactly to the lack of neutrality surrounding snitches. Betrayal is and remains a powerful human force. As noted earlier in the book, the presence of informers, either real or imagined, sows division and paranoia and can have a direct impact on operations. It is a force of disruption and discontinuity that divides instead of unites. When senior Sinn Féin member Denis Donaldson was exposed as an informer, a former colleague of his admitted that 'nobody knows who to trust. Wee suspicions about individuals that have festered over the years are now huge'. Another Irish Republican acknowledged 'panic and disillusionment' in the movement.[11]

Practitioners of counter-terrorism also use informers because of the nature of terrorism. By definition, terrorism is an activity of the weak against the powerful; otherwise, terrorists would have no need to employ such tactics. Weakness often equates with some form of marginalization, be it in terms of language, ethnicity or religion, or a combination of all of these factors. In turn, those countering terrorism often do not resemble the terrorists. The increasing problem of Middle Eastern-related terrorism fits into previous patterns of informer use in the western world. Intelligence agencies and police services lack expertise about Muslim communities in general, let alone about small terrorist cells within these groupings. The default position in such a scenario is not to try to penetrate extremist groups with police officers but to recruit members on the inside or to infiltrate others with a cultural and linguistic familiarity into such groups. This is the pattern that has occurred for centuries and that is even more prevalent in the multicultural world of today, especially since

9/11.[12] Indeed, the larger the difference between an investigating agency and those being investigated, the greater the need for informers. This is patently evident when it comes to the current battle with Middle Eastern-related terrorism, but it also applies to other threats, such as environmental or animal rights extremists organized in small cells without overarching connections to each other.[13]

While the attacks of 9/11 in 2001 did not mark the beginning of a search for human intelligence, they did spark a renewed emphasis on HUMINT, including informers, as an effective weapon for tackling terrorism. This new priority contained explicit and implicit criticisms of the heavy reliance on technological surveillance.[14] The then head of the CIA's Directorate of Operations told a public gathering in April 2002 that the one factor that could have prevented the attacks of 9/11 was someone well-entrenched within al-Qaeda providing information to security agencies of the US.[15] In 2003, six former senior members of the intelligence community penned a joint article that highlighted human intelligence as the biggest failure pre-9/11. Specifically, they pointed to the failure to penetrate a foreign conspiracy that would wreak havoc on American soil.[16]

The consensus that human intelligence is crucial for countering terrorism, which emerged after 9/11, has old roots. It developed as part of the counter-insurgency model designed to deal with ethnonationalist insurgencies, which often employed terrorist tactics or outright terrorism. In the latter half of the nineteenth century, British police extensively used informers to infiltrate the Fenian movement, to the point that, in the words of a Special Branch advisor, '[n]o man feels sure that his most intimate friend is not a traitor, and they find it exceedingly difficult to get workers'. The Fenians may even have started carrying out attacks in London because informers had so thoroughly penetrated their units in Ireland and Liverpool.[17] With some counter-insurgency experience in Indochina, the French military in Algeria in the 1950s and 1960s sought detailed intelligence about their *Front de Libération Nationale* (FLN) opponents. The methods used to obtain it included the recruitment of informers, sometimes through torture. Low level informer networks were established, but more important was the French ability, through various levels of pressure, to recruit higher level FLN informers, who became known as *bleus*. Such recruits allowed for the fundamental disruption of FLN operations while also generating suspicion and mistrust in the ranks of the insurgents. The French further fuelled these damaging forces by planting manufactured documents on the bodies of insurgents that falsely portrayed legitimate leaders as *bleus*.[18]

A similar intelligence-led approach to counter-insurgency as the French example was developed by the British after World War II. In Kenya, informers recruited from amongst imprisoned Kikuyu who were participating in the Mau Mau insurgency proved effective not only at supplying information but also at demoralizing camp members, who found it difficult to pursue collective practices out of fear of betrayal. In retaliation, they murdered suspected informers.[19] One British officer particularly skilled at counter-insurgency operations was Brigadier General Frank Kitson. He had experience in such work in Kenya, along with Malaysia, Oman and Cyprus, before arriving in Northern Ireland in the early 1970s.[20] His emphasis was on intelligence as a key element in fighting against an insurgency and, in particular, the recruiting of informers from the ranks of the enemy and using them against their comrades.[21]

The British applied Kitson's approach in Northern Ireland, where informers played a crucial role in British efforts to defeat the Irish Republican Army (IRA). Multiple agencies, including MI5, Special Branch, and the British Army, ran informers; they noticeably had an effect, prompting the IRA to move into cells to frustrate intelligence-gathering efforts. It also established an internal security agency, nicknamed the 'Nutting Squad', which executed dozens of suspected informers, often after torturing them first.[22] The British ability to recruit what Steven Greer calls 'multi-event' informers grew in the 1970s and 1980s. Several of the names have become well known because of media coverage or memoirs: Freddie Scappaticci, the head of the 'Nutting Squad'; Sean O'Callaghan, who would write about his snitching in *The Informer*; Denis Donaldson, a senior Sinn Féin member later murdered for his treachery; Kevin Fulton, a member of the British military, who infiltrated the IRA.[23] A different type of informer, and one outside of the remit of this study, would emerge in

Northern Ireland in the early 1980s with the so-called 'supergrasses', a term borrowed from prominent criminal cases against organized crime in England in the 1970s. These individuals were terrorists who turned against their former comrades and testified in court against them. Between 1982 and 1986, 11 of these trials occurred, leading to over 100 convictions and a cost to British taxpayers of over £1.5 million spent resettling those testifying under new identities. The practice was eventually shelved over concerns about the accuracy of the testimony being presented.[24]

As the British forces realized, the ultimate impact of informers went well beyond nuggets of information they could supply the authorities. There was an important symbolism to recruiting informers, which spoke to the capacity to win over 'hearts and minds', and thus the wider viability of a campaign against Ireland-related terrorism. 'The crucial line to be crossed is one where a passive acceptance in the Catholic community moves to a readiness to betray', was how a senior British military commander put it.[25] Ironically, in his profile of informer Kevin Fulton, journalist Mathew Teague asked Denis Donaldson, not yet exposed as an informer, about IRA informers like Freddie Scappaticci and Kevin Fulton: 'Donaldson's shoulders slumped. "I still can't believe it," he said, shaking his head. "My God." His face seemed thin and gray, the face of a man who senses an end looming.'[26]

Israel and the Occupied Territories also demonstrate the significance of informing in counter-terrorism efforts. One estimate from June 2003 suggested that as many as 80 per cent of potential terrorist attacks against Israel by Palestinians were being foiled through intelligence. Indeed, one of the arguments for the Israeli Defence Force's continued occupation of the West Bank is to ensure ongoing access to those supplying information.[27]

For the British and the Israelis, recruiting informers in Northern Ireland or in the Occupied Territories has proven easier than American efforts against their current chief counter-terrorism target. Immediately after 9/11, allegations arose that the US had placed too many restrictions on recruiting informers with unsavoury backgrounds. The matter began with a CIA informer in Guatemala's military connected in the early 1990s to the murder of an American citizen and an American citizen's spouse. Subsequently, members of Congress did not receive the full picture in CIA briefings about the informer's involvement in the two deaths.[28] When the truth finally emerged, the then Director of Central Intelligence, John Deutch, fired two officers and punished several others for their role in the cover-up. He also issued a so-called 'scrub order' or the 'Deutch Rules', that required CIA members recruiting anyone with a dodgy human rights or criminal record to seek approval from a committee at Langley. This led to the removal of hundreds of sources from the ranks of CIA informers.[29]

This new rule held until the aftermath of *9/11*, when it was quickly portrayed as an impractical constraint on American intelligence in its pursuit of terrorists. The simple refrain became that if you want informers to infiltrate terrorist organizations then they have to be credible or, as Deutch's predecessor James Woolsey put it:

> To deter CIA officers who are trying to penetrate terrorist groups from recruiting people with violence in their past is like telling FBI agents that they should penetrate the mafia, but try not to put actual crooks on the payroll. There's nobody in the mafia but crooks, and there's nobody in terrorist organizations but terrorists.[30]

The blame peaked in July 2002 with a House Intelligence subcommittee report, which stated that one of the CIA's central failings before *9/11* was its inability to penetrate al-Qaeda adequately.[31]

Some questioned the significance of the 'scrub order' when it came to informer recruitment. Paul Pillar, who served as the head of the CIA's Near East Division from 2000 to 2005, wrote that its impact had been overstated: 'In practice, virtually all proposals submitted to headquarters to recruit sources — even ones with blood on their hands — who have at least a reasonable chance of providing useful intelligence on terrorism are approved.'[32] Indeed, at the time of the criticism of the House Intelligence Committee report, an unnamed CIA source said that headquarters had never turned down the recruitment of a source with a questionable background.[33]

These rebuttals suggest the need for a deeper examination of the issues connected to informing and terrorism. Missing in all of the criticism was one significant point: seeking more human intelligence is not the same as acquiring it. Questions left unasked in the politicized debate and finger pointing that emerged after 9/11 included the difficulties involved in recruiting informers from within, or penetrating from the outside, small terrorist cells consisting of ideologically committed individuals.[34] As two former CIA members point out, the individuals with the most knowledge of al-Qaeda plans are both those highest up in the organization and the most committed to the cause.[35]

A central issue largely ignored in the discussion of the impact of Deutch's 'scrub order' pertains to the CIA's level of expertise. Robert Baer, an Agency member, was surprised in the mid-1990s by the radical nature of publications that he encountered in Arabic bookstores in London. However, his UK-based colleagues remained untroubled, primarily because they lacked any proficiency in Arabic.[36] Between 1990 and 1996, the CIA had reduced 'core humint collectors', who produce informers, by nearly one-third.[37] Research after 9/11 found the CIA suffering from a 'deteriorated human-intelligence capability that made it almost impossible to penetrate key targets such as terrorist organizations, crippling US efforts to detect and prevent attacks'.[38] The 9/11 Commission report recommended that the CIA achieve greater diversity, arguably as an assist in the recruitment of informers.[39]

Domestically in the United States, the situation was not much better.[40] Before 9/11, the FBI had already encountered Middle Eastern-related terrorism on American soil, with the 1993 bombing of the World Trade Center. In its aftermath, some efforts were made to develop sources within American Muslim communities. An informer named Emad Salem, whom the Bureau let go before the 1993 bombing, was hastily rehired to spy on the 'blind sheik' (Sheikh Omar Abdel Rahman) and his followers. Salem's efforts, for which he received over $1 million, helped convict Rahman and 11 others.[41] In San Diego, a prominent American Muslim, Abdussattar Shaikh, became an FBI informer in the 1990s and even met two of the eventual 9/11

hijackers.[42] At the time of the attacks, the FBI had 70 Arabic transla-
tors, a number that had grown to 269 by July 2006. Even then, only
129 FBI agents out of a force of 12,000 enjoyed any basic skills in
Arabic, defined as the ability to recognize a few words in Arabic.[43]

Beyond the limitations of expertise, questions left unasked
included how informers could be recruited from within terrorist
cells or how those on the outside could be infiltrated into such cells?
Or, for that matter, what would motivate them to cooperate with the
American state? One source that introduced a note of realism into the
debate actually appeared just prior to 9/11 when Reuel Marc Gerecht,
a former CIA agent, quoted a CIA Near East Division operative on
the difficulties the CIA was having in the Middle East and Central
Asia:

> The CIA probably doesn't have a single truly qualified Arabic-speaking
> officer of Middle Eastern background who can play a believable Muslim
> fundamentalist who would volunteer to spend years of his life with
> shitty food and no women in the mountains of Afghanistan. For Christ's
> sake, most case officers live in the suburbs of Virginia. We don't do that
> kind of thing.[44]

Gerecht provided an even more succinct statement from another CIA
member about the difficulties developing human intelligence about
al-Qaeda: 'Operations that include diarrhea as a way of life don't
happen.'[45]

In the UK, acquiring what has been labelled 'community
intelligence' has proven difficult. The then head of the police's
Counter-Terrorism Command, Peter Clarke, admitted in 2007 that
security agencies needed to generate more domestic human intelligence, preferably through volunteered information:

> We must increase the flow of intelligence coming from communities.
> Almost all of our prosecutions have their origins in intelligence that
> came from overseas, the intelligence agencies or from technical means.
> Few have yet originated from what is sometimes called 'community
> intelligence'. This is something we are working hard to change.[46]

In July 2007, a former director general of MI5, Dame Eliza Manningham-Buller, echoed Clarke's remarks when she called for the recruitment of networks of, in the words of the newspaper *The Times*, 'Muslim spies'. Her intervention strongly indicates that her former organization had failed to do this already. In turn, her comments resembled earlier ones by the minister for counter-terrorism in the government of Prime Minister Gordon Brown, Admiral Sir Alan West. West openly advocated 'snitching or talking about someone . . . because the people we are talking about are trying to destroy our entire way of life'.[47]

One reason for the apparent failure to generate quality domestic informers stems again, as in the case with the US, from the lack of linguistic and cultural expertise in police forces and intelligence services. MI5, for example, fails to reflect the diversity of modern Britain. At the end of 2006 only 6 per cent of its members were drawn from ethnic minorities, although it did manage to recruit 14 per cent of its 400-person intake for the same year from ethnic minorities. London's Metropolitan Police Service, in charge of one of the most ethnically diverse cities in the world, was not much better, with just under 8 per cent of its officers coming from ethnic minorities.[48] These factors not only made it hard for the agencies themselves to infiltrate targeted organizations, but the members' lack of diversity also equalled a lack of knowledge about, and contacts within, the type of communities where informers would need to be recruited.

More vital, however, in the context of the 'war on terror', is the fact that Britain is failing to generate domestic human intelligence because it is losing the war to win 'hearts and minds'. The reasons for this are multi-fold, including weaknesses on the part of those charged with the UK's security. Ultimately, however, the responsibility lies at the feet of the elected politicians. Too often since *9/11*, many of these allowed the domestic war on terror to be driven by short-term political considerations, instead of long-term strategic needs that address the 'root causes' of grievances felt by some in Muslim communities, and which the government itself is well aware of.[49] Repeated emphasis on the law and the targeting of British Muslims through stop and search measures, plus wider repressive measures, like botched police raids and a proposal to allow terrorism suspects to be held for 42 days without charge, coupled with general Islamophobia whipped up by elements within the British media, do not encourage individuals to come forward to assist the state.[50] Former intelligence officer Crispin Black points out specifically the impact of legislation perceived as repressive, on cooperation with the state:

> Everything we do in response to terrorism should have two factors in mind. One is hearts and minds and the other is the flow of intelligence. . . . If you [sic] sitting, say, in a Muslim part of Yorkshire and you are looking at your telephone thinking those three young men that I saw last night outside the garage, maybe I should phone the police? And you've suddenly been presented with the fact that they can be detained for 90 days [as proposed at one point by the government of Tony Blair], does that make you more or less likely to produce that information to the authorities?[51]

Backing up the impact of heavy-handed state measures on informing, a survey of British Muslim students found that among those unwilling to inform the authorities if they knew of a planned terrorist attack, one of the main reasons was a lack of trust of the police.[52]

Despite such obstacles to recruitment, in the tense security world after 9/11, all methods were deployed to sign up informers, as domestic intelligence agencies found themselves at a linguistic and cultural disadvantage. If money did not work to recruit informers then coercive methods might be tried. In dealing with the newly arrived, recently naturalized, or those unnaturalized, intelligence services have resorted to a carrot (citizenship) and stick (deportation) approach, traditional methods used by governments against immigrants.[53] The American immigration system allows for the awarding of special visas to informers and their immediate families. In November 2001, Attorney General John Ashcroft announced the 'Responsible Cooperators Program' in an effort to reiterate to potential informers a path to citizenship if they supplied information pertaining to terrorism.[54]

Informing as a route to citizenship extended to those performing such tasks outside of the US. In Iraq, where for a considerable period the insurgents were better at recruiting informers within the fledgling Iraqi government than the reverse,[55] the Americans embraced individuals who did come forward.[56] The danger for informers was, of course, great. Those suspected of involvement, and even their families could face death.[57] Some informers received sanctuary in the US. In 2004, the American media carried stories of two Iraqi teenage 'heroes' who gained citizenship because of their informing efforts in Iraq. One was 'Johnny', an Iraqi 16-year-old who warned a US military unit of an impending attack and received sanctuary in the US in return because of death threats against him in Iraq.[58] The other, a 13-year-old Iraqi, was given the nickname 'Steve-O' by US soldiers. His assistance involved turning in to the American military his own insurgent father who had apparently brutalized him in the past.[59]

Other countries offer similar inducements. Reda Hassaine, an Algerian by birth, infiltrated the Finsbury Park Mosque in London on behalf of Scotland Yard and MI5 and received British citizenship in January 2008. Since 1994, a special body called the Security Administration for Assistance, run through Shabak, has settled Palestinian informers within Israel. Israel also provides collaborators with more basic rewards, through work permits or the speeding up of family reunifications.[60]

Conversely, those who decline offers from government agencies to assist or who do not assist in the desired way can experience a rather different fate. In 2002, MI5 alerted authorities in Gambia of the arrival of three Arab men, who it claimed were Islamic radicals. They were acquaintances of Abu Qatada, an Islamic radical residing in the UK. MI5 had already approached the men to serve as informers but only one of the three had offered a degree of unpaid cooperation as an informer, which the Security Service still viewed as insufficient. Instead, two of the three men would be picked up in Gambia and turned over to American custody. Next stop was Guantanamo Bay, where they faced sustained pressure to offer their assistance. MI5 members made frequent trips to try to convince them to begin working as informers in exchange for their release.[61] The Security Service allegedly approached several other British citizens and residents held at various times since 2001 in Pakistan, Afghanistan or Guantanamo

Bay. All received offers of their freedom in return for either agreeing to become long-term informers, including undergoing formal training once back in the UK, or for immediately supplying details about a set group of individuals. Another, Binyam Mohamed, a British resident who spent time in Guantanamo Bay before being released without charge, alleges that a Briton from a Moroccan background tried to recruit him as an informer while he was being held prisoner and brutally tortured in Morocco. Freedom was to be the reward for his assistance.[62]

The domestic use of informers raises traditional issues that predate the campaign against terrorism. Charges of entrapment abound. Take the case of Shahed Hussain, a Pakistani immigrant to the US who arrived in the early 1990s. Involved in a variety of ventures and occupations, he was arrested in 2002 for aiding others in illegally obtaining drivers' licenses. He agreed to become an FBI informer to evade a jail sentence and being sent back to Pakistan. That eventually led to his being an *agent provocateur* in 2004 when he, under the FBI's guidance, set up a sting in which he offered to sell a missile to two American Muslims for use in an attack on a Pakistani diplomat. Both men were later convicted and sentenced to 15 years in prison. The same individual then allegedly turned up in 2009 as an informer in a plot involving four men arrested for trying to blow up a New York City synagogue and shoot down a US military jet. He had apparently sold the men a phoney bomb and missile.[63]

Other informers toiled for large amounts of money, generating additional controversy over their believability. In a case involving a British businessmen charged with trying to sell weapons to terrorist groups, an informer received $250,000 to $270,000 from the FBI over a five-year period.[64] Another FBI informer, who had infiltrated a Muslim charity in return for money, which, in turn, led to the largest terrorism trial in the history of the state of Ohio, had declared bankruptcy a few years earlier.[65] Then there was the Bureau's confidential informer CI1, otherwise known as Mohamed Alanssi. A Yemeni by birth, he was recruited by the FBI in the US and his assistance helped lead to terrorism arrests in New York. Alanssi, however, had debt problems and demanded increased payments from the FBI while in their employ. In November 2004, unhappy with the $100,000 he received, and still writing bad cheques and facing bank fraud charges, he set himself on fire in front of the White House to protest his treatment.[66] In an instance near Sacramento, California, an informer who received $250,000 was heard in recordings berating an individual subsequently charged with terrorism offences for not following through on a promise to attend a terrorism training camp while in Pakistan: 'You told me, "I'm going to a camp. I'll do this, I'll do that." You're sitting idle. You're wasting time. Be a man — do something!'[67] Then there were the Miami terrorism arrests in 2006 that the administration of President George W. Bush highlighted as the disruption of a serious plot against the US. Seven men, involved in a bizarre religious group, were charged with various terrorism offences, including plotting to destroy the Sears Tower in Chicago. The Bureau used at least two informers pretending to be al-Qaeda operatives against them; one, who began informing about drug dealers to the New York City Police when he was 16 years of age, received $40,000, while the other collected double that amount. In the end, after two mistrials, a jury convicted five of the accused, although only one on all of the original charges.[68]

In a Canadian example, Mubin Shaikh, an openly radical Muslim, turned informer for the Royal Canadian Mounted Police (RCMP) against a group of young Muslim-Canadian men allegedly seeking to carry out terrorist attacks within Canada, including against Prime Minister Stephen Harper. Shaikh was heavily involved in what became known as the Toronto 18, going so far as to provide weapons training to the accused, but a judge later ruled that he did not entrap those eventually charged. Unusually for informers, he actively courted media attention, seeking to portray his motivation for assisting the state as altruism; it soon emerged that he had also received $300,000 (Can) for his efforts.[69]

Another major danger in relying on informers, particularly in areas where handlers lack linguistic and cultural skills, is the possibility of being fed false information. Israeli army intelligence found that a campaign to generate more tips from Palestinians led to about 10 per cent of the calls being legitimate, while the remainder consisted of deliberately bogus information.[70] A similar problem has existed in the US since *9/11*, with a number of false leads, including a supposed plan to blow up New York City's Verrazano-Narrows Bridge with trucks loaded with petrol, provided by informers seeking asylum or other favours from the government or simply looking for revenge against a foe. In 2004, the US Congress passed a law making it a criminal offence to supply false or deceiving information related to terrorism, but the monetary and citizenship inducements for such practices continue to remain. Within a few weeks of each other, spurious tips came in from different sources about a plot in the Baltimore area to blow up a traffic tunnel and to attack the New York City subway system in the fall of 2005.[71] In the UK, in June 2006, the Metropolitan Police carried out an early morning raid on a home in Forest Gate in London in pursuit of a chemical weapon, based on information supplied from an MI5 informer. Doors were broken down in the process of seizing two brothers and one of them was accidentally shot. The police later released both without charge and eventually apologized to them.[72] Particularly in this case, the damage done to community relations by the police raid raises the possibility of more hoaxes designed to encourage an overreaction by the police and, as a result, set back government efforts at winning 'hearts and minds'.

That point leads directly to the ultimate impact of informers. In liberal-democratic societies, marginalized communities disproportionately experience the uses of such tactics. As mentioned in Chapter 2, sociologist David Lyon has written of the tendency to portray the impact of surveillance in 'individualistic terms as a potential threat to privacy' while missing another important component, specifically 'social sorting', a 'key means of reproducing and reinforcing social, economic, and cultural divisions in informational societies'.[73] In Canada, the US and the UK, it is the turn of Muslims to encounter what groups such as Communists, feminists, African Americans, Native Americans and countless others have previously experienced. As in the past with other groups infiltrated by informers, a sense of being under siege arises. Members of communities magically become responsible for the actions of other community members, while governments and government agencies seek their assistance through informing. Prime Minister John Howard controversially appealed to Australian Muslims to inform on radicals within their midst, as did government officials in the UK. In the latter, an academic case study of British Muslims in London interviewed several who complained about attempts to recruit them as informers and said that, as a result, they were less likely to cooperate with the police.[74] The head of an Islamic organization responsible for 70 mosques across southern California protested that between 2004 and early 2006, the FBI had attempted to recruit four Muslim immigrants to inform on clergy in return for assistance in being allowed to remain in the US.[75] In New York, the revelation that a city police informer named Osama Eldawoody, who received over $100,000 in payment in return for following the orders of his handlers to 'keep your eyes and ears open for any radical thing', had attended 575 prayer services at Staten Island Mosque prompted Wael Mousfar, the president of the Arab Muslim American Federation, to lament the impact of such spying on his community:

> We feel that we've been violated and being spied on is not an easy thing. When you sit and pray, you're not worried about only paying attention to a prayer, concentrating on your prayer, you're worried about whether the person next to you is spying on you, is working for the Government, working for the FBI, whoever, and this is not an easy feeling — not only to take news or listen to what's going on, but also to twist around what is said.[76]

A line exists around the general acceptance of the use of informers. If focused on marginalized communities, informers generally do not ignite controversy, except within those targeted communities, where the use of informers can be divisive and destructive. Nevertheless, the negative associations connected with informing remain, even when it comes to terrorism investigations. Wider efforts at recruiting informers can generate controversy, as an example in the US in 2002 demonstrated. After 9/11, there was an immediate realization that more human intelligence through informers of various stripes was desperately required, both domestically and internationally. The

US government responded to both needs, with a new domestic program, known as the Terrorism Information and Prevention System, or Operation TIPS (or just TIPS) and with the expansion of a foreign program called Rewards for Justice that had been around since the 1980s.

TIPS emerged as part of the domestic component of the administration of President George W. Bush's domestic 'war on terror'. It relied on patriotism as a motivating factor and it paralleled US efforts to recruit thousands of domestic informers during World War II and the Cold War, as profiled in Chapter 3.[77] The first public mention of the program appeared in an oblique reference by President Bush in the 2002 State of the Union speech, famous for his use of the phrase 'Axis of Evil'. The general details of the trial plan soon emerged. It was to be part of a newly created Citizen Corps under the control of Federal Emergency Management Agency (FEMA) and designed to increase public participation in Homeland Security. The original description of TIPS was thus: 'Operation TIPS will enable millions of America transportation workers, postal workers, and public utility employees to identify and report suspicious activities linked to terrorism and crime.' The program escaped attention and criticism despite a public speech by Bush in April 2002, when he mistakenly called it TIP, and another by the Deputy Attorney General of the US in which she hailed TIPS as providing 'millions of American truckers, letter carriers, train conductors, ship captains, utility employees, and others, whose routines allow them to be the "eyes and ears" of police, a formal way to report suspicious or potential terrorist activity'.[78]

TIPS existed outside of any sustained public discussion until July 2002 when a story about it appeared in the *Sydney Morning Herald*. The piece, by a self-described American dissident living in exile in Sweden, claimed that 4 per cent of Americans, or approximately 12 million people, would be recruited as part of the plan, leaving the US with 'a higher percentage of citizen informants than the former East Germany through the infamous Stasi secret police'.[79] Both the numbers and the comparison were dubious, as was the notion that these individuals would be 'recruited' along the lines of the Stasi and its informers. Nevertheless, the story sparked a negative reaction that ran across the American political spectrum from the American Civil Liberties Union and the *Village Voice* on the left to the *New York Times* in the centre to Republican Congressmen Dick Armey and Bob Barr on the right. Barr called TIPS a 'snitch system', that appeared to typify 'the very type of fascist or Communist government we fought so hard to eradicate in other countries in decades past'.[80]

The criticism caused the Bush administration to clarify the aims of the program and who the targets would be:

> This reporting system is being developed by the Department of Justice in coordination with several other federal agencies, including the Office of Homeland Security, the Department of Labor, the Federal Bureau of Investigation, and FEMA, as a part of Citizen Corps. The program was announced in concept in January 2002 for the stated purpose of creating a national information sharing system for specific industry groups to report suspicious, publicly observable activity that could be related to terrorism.[81]

The fact that the workers who would be encouraged to inform under TIPS had access to private property sparked much of the criticism. As a result, the Department of Justice, to address critics, announced that 'the hotline number will not be shared with any workers, including postal and utility workers, whose work puts them in contact with homes and private property'.[82] Instead, only specific private industries would have access to the 'single number for reporting potentially terrorist-related activities occurring in public areas'.[83]

Despite the reforms and additional efforts to clarify the goals of the program,[84] criticism only grew with a slew of negative news stories appearing in July and August 2002.[85] The *New York Times*, for example, ran interviews with workers who potentially might be encouraged to report information. A Federal Express driver remarked on the increased number of satellite dishes he had delivered to 'Arabs' after 9/11, while another driver complained that '[i]mmigrants stare more than anybody else'.[86] In an editorial, the paper decried the new version of the program: 'Even if it is limited to public places, the program is offensive. The idea of citizens spying on citizens, and the government collecting data on everyone who is accused, is a staple of totalitarian regimes.'[87]

More significant was that TIPS had made enemies of powerful politicians, in particular Dick Armey, the Republican Majority leader in the House of Representatives. He took upon it himself to kill Operation TIPS and, more than anyone else, he was responsible for its death. With little fanfare in relation to the controversy the program engendered in the summer, its demise came in the form of Section 880, which Armey shepherded through in the Homeland Security Act under the heading 'Prohibition of the Terrorism Information and Prevention System': 'Any and all activities of the Federal Government to implement the proposed component program of the Citizen Corps known as Operation TIPS (Terrorism Information and Prevention System) are hereby prohibited'. TIPS died on 25 November 2002 when President Bush signed the Homeland Security Act into law.[88] The idea of a program that would recruit large numbers of individuals within a society to be the ears and eyes of the state remains appealing, however. In 2007, a British newspaper reported on a plan to recruit government workers, including doctors, to report not just on crimes that had been committed but even on profiles of individuals who might commit crimes in the future.[89]

While the Bush administration's TIPS program failed to win support domestically, another American effort designed internationally to generate human intelligence about terrorism through informers has largely received acclaim. The effort began not with *9/11* but one of the first major terrorist attacks to target Americans, the 1983 suicide bombing of the Marine barracks in Beirut. Almost exactly a year later, Congress passed 'An Act to Combat International Terrorism'. Quickly signed into law by President Ronald Reagan, one aspect effectively launched an informer-recruiting program, offering a reward of up to $500,000 to 'any individual who furnishes information regarding an act of terrorism directed against a U.S. person or U.S. property'.[90] The model for the campaign seemingly came from criminal enforcement, specifically from a program called Crime Stoppers that began in Albuquerque, New Mexico in July 1976 and offered rewards for information which led to convictions.[91]

Accordingly, recruiting informers as part of a counter-terrorism effort took on ordinary crime fighting dimensions. As sociologists Malin Åkerström and Gary T. Marx have shown, the key motivator for those who become informers is monetary reward.[92] 'Money talks' was how one State Department official justified the emphasis on a monetary reward for helping the US.[93] This approach also inherently reflected the inability on the part of American intelligence, specifically the CIA, to develop human sources of its own in its pursuit of terrorists. In the 1980s, for example, Brent Scowcroft, a senior official in both the Reagan and Bush, Sr administrations, expressed frustration at the lack of human intelligence available relating to Americans kidnapped in Lebanon.[94] There is a certain difficulty, however, with applying such a model to recruiting informers related to terrorism. At its essence, the approach asserts that everyone has his or her price. In some ways it is the opposite of the model frequently connected to espionage in the first few decades of the Cold War where the expectation was, in the aftermath of spies like the Cambridge Five, five committed Communists recruited by Soviet intelligence while students at Cambridge University, that people would betray for ideological reasons. This type of motivation was forgotten later in the Cold War, when spies such as Aldrich Ames and Robert Hanssen burned the CIA and FBI respectively for cold hard cash.[95] The weakness in applying this money-led approach to the current terrorism threat is that it is problematic as a recruiting tool for members of small terrorist cells with ideologically committed members prepared to die for their cause, or as one observer put it, 'individuals who forged their ties over decades in the dust of Palestinian refugee camps, the chaos of Beirut or the killing fields of Afghanistan'.[96] The former head of the CIA's Osama bin Laden team, Michael Scheuer, points to the high level of ideological commitment, particularly among senior al-Qaeda figures, as the primary obstacle to informer recruitment. He argues that the 'odds of our ever having an informant among the senior al-Qaeda decision-makers are remote'.[97]

Perhaps because of the nature of the approach, the program was ineffective throughout the 1980s and by the end of 1988, it had not paid out a cent for information in six terrorist cases for which a reward was on offer.[98] This prompted a reform of the program, including expanding it to cover not only the arrest and conviction of those involved in terrorist attacks that had already occurred, but also to provide for 'payment for information that leads to the prevention, frustration or favorable resolution of terrorist acts against US persons or property overseas'. A new global advertising campaign initiated as part of the agenda emphasized that the 'identities of informants' would be protected.[99] The effort soon became the 'Heroes Program' and an accompanying advertising campaign began.[100] The US government distributed matchbooks and over 7,000 posters advertising the program and television and radio commercials, fronted by Hollywood stars Charlton Heston, Charles Bronson and Charlie Sheen, called upon 'ordinary people' to do 'extraordinary things'.[101]

The combination of the expanded program and high-profile terrorist attacks led to the paying of rewards. By November 1995, the US government had paid out $3 million in a handful of the 20 cases for which rewards were being offered.[102] Two-thirds of that amount came in one payment. The first big contribution to battling terrorism occurred in the mid-1990s in the aftermath of the first attack on the World Trade Center. In emphasizing the successes of the program, US officials turned a single individual, Ramzi Yousef, into the program's poster boy. Yousef organized the 26 February 1993 bomb attack on the World Trade Center that left six people dead and over a thousand injured. He quickly fled the US after the attack and became involved in the planning of other terrorist attacks with his uncle, Khalid Sheikh Mohammed, the apparent planner of the 2001 *9/11* attacks. While operating in Pakistan, he recruited a South African Muslim to assist him. That individual in the end turned Yousef in for the $2 million reward after he heard about the program, not through a $100,000 advertising effort underway at the time, but by reading an article in *Newsweek*.[103] To demonstrate the effectiveness of the program, the US government would repeatedly cite Yousef's arrest over subsequent years, even ten years later in 2006.[104]

Despite the repeated rhetoric about the success of the program, by 2000 only $6 million had been distributed, with approximately one-third of that amount having gone to the informer who turned in

Yousef. With the growing problem of al-Qaeda under the leadership of Osama bin Laden and Ayman al-Zawahiri, evident in the suicide bombing of an American warship, the *USS Cole* in Yemen, the US government further expanded the program. The obvious emphasis was on a monetary motivation for assisting the US government, with the slogan 'We Can Give You 7 Million Reasons to Stop Terrorism' appearing over an image of American dollar bills.[105]

All of this represented a prologue to a different program that would emerge in the aftermath of *9/11* as part of the Bush administration's 'war on terror'. Reflecting the gravity of the attacks, the value of the rewards on offer rose dramatically.[106] The Uniting and Strengthening America by Providing Appropriate Tools Required to Intercept and Obstruct Terrorism Act of 2001 (Patriot Act), passed in October 2001, increased the maximum reward to $25 million. A new campaign began, with one important difference that represented discontinuity from what came before: the advertising campaign was to be directed also at Americans. Part of that appeal was to encourage Americans to donate money to the program that would use 'rewards dollars to turn terrorist supporters and sympathizers into terrorist informants'.[107] Similar to TIPS, the program also encouraged citizens to supply information on suspicious activities within the US. The emphasis was on Muslims and Arab Americans, as the ad for Rewards employed an image of Mohammed Atta, the lead hijacker on *9/11*, as a selling point. 'He was spotted in Hamburg, Prague, Florida and Maine', it said. 'And if someone had called us, his picture wouldn't be spotted in this ad. . . . [He] lived among us, attending classes, shopping at the mall, eating pizza, going out now and then with friends.'[108]

The success of Rewards for Justice in generating informers with particulars about al-Qaeda was another story and, in some ways, the emphasis on the terrorist group in the US detracted from operations abroad. By April 2002, 20 reports of Osama bin Laden being spotted in Utah had arrived on FBI desks.[109] Between September and November 2001, the State Department received over 22,000 separate tips about the whereabouts of bin Laden and other senior al-Qaeda members, most via telephone or email. A State Department official dismissed the validity of much of these by noting that not many telephones or computers were in the areas where the leader of al-Qaeda was likely to be hiding. Indeed, many of the tips involved individuals relaying that Osama bin Laden was somewhere near the Pakistan-Afghanistan border and then requesting their reward.[110] Renewed campaigns abroad began in 2004 and, in a tactic previously used, the US distributed thousands of matchbooks in Pakistan and Afghanistan showing Osama bin Laden's face on them.[111] In March 2004, the House of Representatives unanimously passed legislation allowing Rewards to pay out up to $50 million for information about the location of individuals such as bin Laden and devoting even more money to using radio and television to disseminate details of the program. The Senate followed suit in July 2007 when it passed a similar motion.[112] Additional advertising campaigns started in Pakistan and Afghanistan in the first half of 2005, with the Pakistan leg generating 242 tips between January and June 2005.[113]

As the scale of the program grew, so did the payouts. In 2003, the two largest payments in the history of the program occurred. One of $27 million, which included $2 million in relocation aid to help him move his family, went to an Egyptian al-Qaeda member who supplied information that led to the capture of Khalid Sheikh Mohammed.[114] Surpassing that amount was the new record under Rewards for Justice — $30 million for the information that led the US military to locate and kill Saddam Hussein's sons Uday and Qusay ($15 million for each).[115] Elsewhere, payments went out to Filipinos who aided in the pursuit of an Islamist group Abu Sayyaf.[116] In one case, a US embassy official handed over a suitcase containing $1 million to a masked informer; the exchange received prominent display on US diplomatic websites, apparently in an effort to encourage others to step forward by demonstrating that payments would indeed be made and anonymity assured.[117]

The record of Rewards for Justice as an informer recruitment program against al-Qaeda and the type of terrorism the group represents is mixed to say the least. No payments have occurred in either Pakistan or Afghanistan since the one paid out for Khalid Sheikh Mohammad in 2003.[118] The major problem with Rewards for

Justice is, however, that its premise regarding motivating individuals to become informers against al-Qaeda is misguided. The approach strangely combines a criminal model of informing, as exemplified in Crime Stoppers, with the predominant reason people spied in the later stages of the Cold War when communism had lost its appeal to all but the diehards.[119] How could such logic apply to terrorists, specifically the core members of al-Qaeda, who continue to be motivated by ideology? A question from a reporter to a Bush administration official at a 2002 press conference touched upon this:

> Some of these informants that you hope to get information from as part of this new program are part of whatever terrorist network that you are targeting at the moment. Unfortunately, they are willing — 9/11 showed that they are willing to die for their cause. Can you talk about the challenges in terms of trying to get information from these people who are so loyal, so patriotic to bin Laden or whoever their terrorist leader is, and they'll be not very likely therefore to sell out?[120]

One response is that the program is directed not just at the terrorists but at anyone who might have relevant knowledge, particularly individuals on the fringes who are less motivated by ideology.[121] Still, others concede that money might not be the chief inducement for recruiting informers: House of Representatives' legislation proposed different types of rewards, such as wells, livestock and tractors. One State Department official explained the new philosophy this way: 'We can't come up with 70 virgins, but we can come up with goats.'[122] Although, as terrorism expert Bruce Hoffman points out, anyone using a new tractor or suddenly owning additional goats, for that matter, would raise suspicion and cause themselves to be 'marked' for elimination.[123]

Programs such as TIPS and Rewards for Justice, along with efforts across many countries to recruit informers among Muslim communities, demonstrate the continuing relevance of informers in the twenty-first century. Technological surveillance will continue to play a role. However, the nature of terrorism, in particular the resort to cell-like structures in terms of organizations, coupled with the involvement of members of minority communities with whom the police and security agencies lack familiarity, make the importance of informers that much greater. The problem, and this issue goes back as long as marginalized groups have been targeted through such forms of intelligence collection, is the impact it has on those at the receiving end. Informing is not a neutral activity, as demonstrated by the negative reaction to TIPS when it appeared as if the American government would recruit large numbers of people to spy on their fellow citizens. It is a divisive and destructive force, rendered worse by the resort at times to what amounts to work as *agents provocateurs* on the part of informers. 'It's like a police state here', is how a Muslim-American high school teacher described the impact of police informers in his community. Another, in response to reports of FBI informers attending mosques in California, worried that it 'Makes you think twice about what you say; what if people misunderstand you?'[124] There is a further risk that is unacknowledged in the calls from the prominent for members of communities to spy on each other. At best, such a practice may actively discourage individuals from coming forward with useful information. At worst, the tactic could even radicalize individuals, angry at state tactics against their communities, pushing them down a path toward terrorism. Striking a balance so that needed intelligence about terrorism comes in while the rights of the most vulnerable are protected is essential to ensuring future security. It also remains, as of yet, an unattained goal in the war on terror.

CHAPTER 7

Conclusion: Living in the Informer Age

Men may be without restraints upon their liberty; they may pass to and fro at pleasure: but if their steps are tracked by spies and informers, their words noted down for crimination, their associates watched as conspirators — who shall say that they are free?
— Thomas May, *Constitutional History of England* (1863), p. 275.

Informers have had a long past and will enjoy a lengthy future. Their repeated utilization for centuries, in a variety of forms, plus their systematic, scientific application in the age of the professionalization and bureaucratization of intelligence services and police forces demonstrates not just longevity but, more significantly, adaptability. Despite the unprecedented level of surveillance that is now achievable through technological methods, informing by humans remains a crucial type of intelligence-gathering for modern state security agencies. The reason for this is simple: governmental bodies believe that the practice is valuable. This worth exists on multiple planes. Informing is cost effective. It allows the accessing of the most intimate conversations. It can be proactive instead of simply passively recording what is being said. It can be a powerful force of disruption through *agents provocateurs* or simply because of the knowledge that informers exist or might exist within a group's ranks. Finally, snitching is much easier to deploy than its technological cousins. There is no need, for instance, to obtain a warrant to deploy an informer in the way that such authorization might be required for electronic surveillance. Informers are here to stay.

This is not to say, of course, that informing is not without controversy. The negative response that such practices generated in the past continues into the present. This reaction emanates not from amongst those who employ the informers, but from the midst of the ranks on the receiving end of such unwanted attention. Members of American Muslim communities have criticized the use of police informers against them and there has been a similar response from British and Australian Muslims to state efforts to recruit informers or to encourage informing.[1] In African-American communities across the US anti-informing campaigns have appeared in the shape of slogans on t-shirts and posters such as 'stop snitchin' or 'stop snitching'. A Baltimore rap star, Skinny Suge, went even further, putting out a song 'Stop Fucking Snitching' with an expletive-laden attack on the practice and the practitioners.[2] These campaigns, clearly aimed at individuals who supply information to the police about criminal matters, have generated considerable controversy.[3] Equally contentious has been a website, 'Who's A Rat', which aims to provide a database of the details and names of those who have worked as informers and agents for police forces.[4]

The backlash against informers, even through the violent attacks referenced in earlier chapters, is nothing new. It would not have been out of place in previous centuries. The resistance to informing points not only to the continuing lack of legitimacy of the state in some quarters, but also to an even greater allegiance to human bonds of family, religion, ethnicity, nationality, geographical location, community, gender, sexuality and, most fundamentally, friendship. In the minds of many, any one of these factors or several in combination, trump any special loyalty to the state and thus generate anger toward those who would choose that entity over these fundamentally more important allegiances.

That there is not a greater reaction against the use of informers reflects a theme that runs through this monograph. Groups who are marginalized for a variety of reasons, including that they represent a real or imagined threat to the security of the state or some wider societal status quo, disproportionately experience informing as a practice. Thus, informing is not equal to one form of technological surveillance: the impersonal camera stationed on a pole on a city street. The camera records anyone who walks down the street be they rich or poor, black or white, Christian or Muslim. State informing normally does not function in such an all-encompassing way in liberal-democratic societies. Informers cannot be everywhere, so when they are deployed by intelligence services and police forces they are directed against specific communities, groups and individuals. It is within these same categories that controversy arises over the practices. However, because those targeted are frequently on the margins, their voices receive little attention within dominant discourses. Only when the wider population in liberal democracies feels threatened by informing, and here the parallel exists with certain types of electronic surveillance, does widespread opposition, particularly within societal elites, emerge. This was the case, as described in the previous chapter, with the outcry in the US in 2002 that united those on the left with those on the right against the Terrorism Information and Prevention System (TIPS) that would have recruited letter carriers, cable installers, meter readers, delivery drivers and others engaged in similar occupations as de facto eyes and ears of the state. The hostile response reached a crescendo when Republican members of the House of Representatives led efforts to kill the program.[5] On the other hand, a similar effort at generating more informers, the Rewards for Justice Program, has sparked virtually no disagreement because it focuses on recruiting informers outside of the US. Only in the aftermath of *9/11*, when the Rewards program was brought to the US for the first time, did criticism appear. That came from those who rightly believed they would be the focus of the program, namely members of American Muslim and Arab communities.[6]

Informing, then, remains and will remain a well-used but divisive practice. Both points emerge from the reality that it is not a neutral form of surveillance and information collection. Certainly, it allows the state to gather the material it seeks, but informing and informers equally permit the state to direct, disrupt and even destroy individuals, groups and movements it does not like or finds threatening. In using such tactics, betrayal becomes the sharp edge of a knife of power wielded by those in authority and the institutions under their command. Such power is not always deployed equally. Dependence is greatest when the regime is most vulnerable to popular discontent and has the least legitimacy. Yet even liberal democracies, with relatively strong bases in civil society, rely on the lighter use of informers in political policing. This is a practice that can be managed more unobtrusively in 'open' societies where it is not anticipated, as opposed to closed societies where the hand is expected to be heavier.

In the twenty-first century, informing exists as both an ancient and modern weapon that state agencies around the world employ to different extents. Fundamentally, it is a tool of social control as, ultimately, all forms of surveillance are. That on occasion it benefits the wider society by helping to prevent acts of violence, for instance by the Ku Klux Klan in the 1960s, cannot be denied. Accordingly then, this study is not a plea for informing to end. Rather, the need is for a proper and open debate about the implications of this type of surveillance, especially for those on the receiving end and, ultimately, for greater regulation of and restrictions on the practice in democratic states. Because of the existing lack of limitations and transparency connected to snitching, it is not just a state activity to be concerned about, it is one to be feared.

Notes

Notes to Chapter 1: Introduction

1 'Spy Scandal "Will Remain a Mystery"', *Guardian*, 20 December 2005; Tom Peterkin, 'Sinn Fein Man Was British Agent', *Daily Telegraph*, 17 December 2005; 'Sinn Fein British agent shot dead', *BBC News*, 4 April 2006, http://news.bbc.co.uk/1/hi/northern_ireland/4877516.stm (accessed 10 June 2006); Dan Vergano and Cathy Lynn Grossman, 'Long-Lost Gospel of Judas Recasts "traitor"', *USA Today*, 4 June 2006; Nikos Kazantzakis, *The Last Temptation of Christ* (London: Faber UK, 1996). For more on Judas, see Elaine Pagels and Karen L. King, *Reading Judas: The Gospel of Judas and the Shaping of Christianity* (New York, NY: Viking, 2007).

2 Scott Shane and Andrea Zarate, 'FBI Killed Plot in Talking Stage, a Top Aide Says', *New York Times*, 24 June 2006; Rebecca Cook Dube, 'Leader Turned Informant Rattles Muslims', *Christian Science Monitor*, 31 July 2006; Michael Levi, 'Technology Obsession', *TPM Café*, 10 August 2006, www.tpmcafe.com/blog/americaabroad/2006/aug/10/technology_obsession (accessed 5 September 2007); 'Agent Infiltrated Terror Cell, U.S. Says', *CNN*, 11 August 2006, http://edition.cnn.com/2006/US/08/10/us.security/index.html (accessed 12 February 2009); Richard Norton-Taylor, Sandra Laville, and Vikram Dodd, 'Terror Plot: Pakistan and Al-Qaida Links Revealed', *Guardian*, 12 August 2006; '"Devout Muslim" Informer Aided in Toronto Conspiracy Arrests', *CBC News*, 13 July 2006, www.cbc.ca/canada/story/2006/07/13/terror plot.html (accessed 10 March 2009); Isabel Teotonio, 'No Entrapment, Court Rules in Terror Case', *Toronto Star*, 24 March 2009.

3 Geoff Robertson, *Reluctant Judas: The Life and Death of the Special Branch Informer Kenneth Lennon* (London: Temple Smith, 1976); James Morton, *Supergrasses and Informers: Informal History of Undercover Police Work* (London: Little, Brown, 1995); Oliver Knox, *Rebels & Informers: Stirrings of Irish Independence* (New York, NY: St. Martin's Press, 1997).

4 Larry Grathwohl and Frank Reagan, *Bringing Down America: An FBI Informer with the Weathermen* (New Rochelle, NY: Arlington House Publishers, 1976); William Tulio Divale and James Joseph, *I Lived inside the Campus Revolution* (New York, NY: NY Cowles Book Company, 1970). For an example of the memoirs of an informer in the United Kingdom, see Sean O'Callaghan, *The Informer* (London: Corgi Adult, 1999). For the memoirs of a Canadian informer,

see Carole de Vault, *The Informer: Confessions of an Ex-Terrorist* (Toronto, ON: Fleet Books, 1982).

5   Gary T. Marx, 'Thoughts on a Neglected Category of Social Movement Participant: The Agent Provocateur and the Informant', *American Journal of Sociology*, vol. 80, no. 2 (1974): 402–42; Gary T. Marx, *Undercover: Police Surveillance in America* (Berkeley, CA: University of California Press, 1992); Frank J. Donner, *The Age of Surveillance: The Aims and Methods of America's Political Intelligence System* (New York, NY: Albert A. Knopf, 1980); Malin Åkerström, *Betrayal and Betrayers: The Sociology of Treachery* (New York, NY: Transaction Publishers, 1991); Georg Simmel, 'The Sociology of Secrecy and of Secret Societies', *American Journal of Sociology* vol. 11 (1906): 441–98.

6   Simon Garfinkel, *Database Nation: The Death of Privacy in the 21st Century* (Cambridge, MA: O'Reilly, 2000); Patrick Radden Keefe, *Chatter: Dispatches from the Secret World of Global Eavesdropping* (New York, NY: Random House, 2005); Michael McCahill, *The Surveillance Web: The Rise of Visual Surveillance in an English City* (Cullompton, Devon and Portland, OR: Willan Publishing, 2002); Robert O'Harrow, Jr, *No Place to Hide: Behind the Scenes of Our Emerging Surveillance Society* (New York, NY: Free Press, 2005); Jeffrey Rosen, *The Unwanted Gaze: The Destruction of Privacy in America* (New York, NY: Vintage Books, 2000); William G. Staples, *The Culture of Surveillance: Discipline and Social Control in the United States* (New York, NY: St. Martin's, 1997); Charles J. Sykes, *The End of Privacy: The Attack on Personal Rights — at Home, at Work, On-line, and in Court* (New York, NY: St. Martin's Griffin, 1999); Reg Whitaker, *The End of Privacy: How Total Surveillance Is Becoming a Reality* (New York, NY: The New Press, 1999).

7   Paul Lewis, 'Fears Over Privacy as Police Expand Surveillance Project', *Guardian*, 15 September 2008; Steve Connor, 'Surveillance UK: Why This Revolution Is Only the Start', *Independent*, 22 December 2005; Steve Connor, 'Britain Will Be First Country to Monitor Every Car Journey', *Independent*, 22 December 2005; Steve Hewitt, *The British War on Terror: Terrorism and Counter-Terrorism on the Home Front since 9/11* (London: Continuum, 2008), p. 22.

8   Harrow, *No Place to Hide.*

Notes to Chapter 2: 'Inherent in the Conditions of Human Society': The Nature of Informing

1   Justice William Brennan, as quoted in 'Judicial Control of Secret Agents', *Yale Law Journal*, vol. 76, no. 5 (1967): 1009–10.

2   For more on the importance of informers to counter-terrorist operations, see Mark Urban, *Big Boys' Rules: The Bestselling Story of the SAS and the Secret Struggle against the IRA* (London: Faber and Faber Ltd., 1992), p. 92.

3   Gary T. Marx, *Undercover: Police Surveillance in America* (Berkeley, CA: University of California Press, 1992), pp. 220–1.

4   Thomas Mathiesen, 'The Viewer Society: Michel Foucault's "Panopticon" revisited', *Theoretical Criminology*, vol. 1, no. 2, (1997): 215–34.

5   Saul Hudson, 'Zarqawi Bounty May Go Unpaid but Rewards Aid Fight', *Washington Post*, 9 June 2006.

6   David Lyon, *Surveillance after September 11* (Cambridge, UK: Polity Press, 2003), pp. 34–5; Marx, *Undercover*, p. 219.

7   Admiral Stansfield Turner, as quoted in James Derian, 'Anti-Diplomacy, Intelligence Theory and Surveillance Practice', *Intelligence and National Security*, vol. 8, no. 3 (1993): 42.

8   Gary T. Marx, 'Thoughts on a Neglected Category of Social Movement Participant: The Agent Provocateur and the Informant', *American Journal of Sociology*, vol. 80, no. 2 (1974): 405.

9   As quoted in Urban, *Big Boys' Rules*, p. 101.

10 Walter Pincus, 'An Intelligence Gap Hinders US in Iraq', *Washington Post*, 24 December 2004; Gershom Gorenberg, 'The Collaborator', *New York Times Magazine*, 18 August 2002.

11 Victor S. Navasky, *Naming Names: Historical Perspectives* (London: John Calder, 1982), p. 347.

12 Cyrille Fijnaut and Gary T. Marx, 'Introduction: The Normalization of Undercover Policing in the West: Historical and Contemporary Perspectives', in Cyrille Fijnaut and Gary T. Marx, eds, *Undercover Police Surveillance in Comparative Perspective* (Boston, MA: Kluwer Law International, 1995), p. 11. For a famous example of the use of snitches by a private company, see the 'McLibel' case in which the fast-food chain McDonald's employed as many as seven informers to spy on an anti-McDonald's protest group. Eric Schlosser, *Fast Food Nation: What the All American Meal is Doing to the World* (London: Penguin Books, 2002), pp. 247–8.

13 Marx, 'Thoughts on a Neglected Category . . .', 405.

14 Urban, *Big Boys' Rules*, p. 104.

15 Ward Churchill and Jim Vander Wall, *Agents of Repression: The FBI's Secret Wars against the Black Panther Party and the American Indian Movement* (Cambridge, MA: South End Press, 1988), p. 85. The FBI, for example, considered this tactic against Geronimo Pratt, a Native American activist who turned down FBI entreaties.

16 Churchill and Vander Wall, *Agents of Repression*, p. 49.

17 Ibid.

18 Urban, *Big Boys' Rules*, p. 245.

19 Tom Williamson and Peter Bagshaw, 'The Ethics of Informer Handling', in Roger Billingsley, Teresa Nemitz, and Philip Bean, eds, *Informers: Policing, Policy, Practice* (Uffculme, UK: Willan Publishing, 2001), p. 55; Steve Hewitt, *Spying 101: The RCMP's Secret Activities at Canadian Universities, 1917–1997* (Toronto, ON: University of Toronto Press, 2002), pp. 190–1.

20 E.P. Thompson, *The Making of the English Working Class* (London: Penguin Books, 1986), pp. 493–4. Emphasis is his.

21   Louis Bertrand, as quoted in Luc Keunings, 'The Secret Police in Nineteenth-Century Brussels', *Intelligence and National Security*, vol. 4, no. 1 (1989): 77.

22   J.S. Woodsworth as quoted in Canada, House of Commons' *Debates*, 3 May 1932, pp. 2591–2.

23   Ruth Rosen, *The World Split Open: How the Modern Women's Movement Changed America* (New York, NY: Penguin Books, 2001), p. 260.

24   Marx, 'Thoughts on a Neglected Category . . .', 428.

25   Ibid, 421.

26   James Risen and Eric Lichtblau, 'Bush Lets US Spy on Callers Without Courts', *New York Times*, 16 December 2005. See also, James Risen, *State of War: The Secret History of the CIA and the Bush Administration* (New York, NY: Free Press, 2006).

27   For more on FISA, see 'Foreign Intelligence Surveillance Act', Federation of American Scientists, www.fas.org/irp/agency/doj/fisa/ (accessed 8 April 2009).

28   Civil liberties groups have campaigned for tighter rules. See, for example, a campaign by the American Civil Liberties Union (ACLU): 'Unnecessary Evil: Blind Trust and Unchecked Abuse in America's Informant System', American Civil Liberties Union, www.aclu.org/drugpolicy/search/informantabuse.html (accessed 23 April 2009).

29   Church Committee, 'Final Report of the Select Committee to Study Governmental Operations with Respect to Intelligence Activities', (Washington, DC: Congress, 1976), www.icdc.com/~paulwolf/cointelpro/churchfinalreportIIIj.htm (accessed 13 May 2009).

30   FBI 'Manual of Instructions', as quoted in Church Committee, 'Final Report'.

31   Hewitt, *Spying 101*, pp. 208–11.

32   'Regulation of Investigatory Powers Act 2000', Office of Public Sector Information, www.opsi.gov.uk/acts/acts2000/ukpga_20000023_en_5#pt2 (accessed 21 March 2009); Sandra Laville, 'Analysis: The Rules on Police Informants', *Guardian*, 25 April 2009.

33   'Judicial Control of Secret Agents', p. 996.

34   The three cases were Hoffa vs United States, Osborn vs United States, and Lewis vs United States. 'Judicial Control of Secret Agents', 994–1019. See also Robert L. Misner and John H. Clough, 'Arrestees as Informants: A Thirteenth Amendment Analysis', *Stanford Law Review* vol. 29, no. 4 (1977): 714–15.

35   Ibid.

36   'Judicial Control of Secret Agents', 1009–10.

37   FBI, 'Exhibit 33: Request for Information Concerning This Bureau's Operation of Informants in the Internal Security Field', Church Committee (Washington, DC: Congress, 1975).

38   Church Committee, 'Final Report'.

39   Tony Scott, director, *Enemy of the State*, 1998; Steven Spielberg, director, *Minority Report*, 2002; Francis Ford Coppola, director, *The Conversation*, 1974.

40   www.surveillance-and-society.org/ojs/index.php/journal (23 April 2009).

41 Bob Woodward, *Plan of Attack* (New York, NY: Simon and Shuster, 2004), p. 213; Patrick Radden Keefe, *Chatter: Dispatches from the Secret World of Global Eavesdropping* (New York, NY: Random House, 2005), p. xiv.

42 Jeff Sallot, 'Canada Could Escape Attack, CSIS Says', *Globe and Mail*, 20 June 2006; Hewitt, *Spying 101*, p. 32.

43 Florian Henckel von Donnersmarck, director, *Das Leben der Anderen (The Lives of Others)*, 2006.

44 Church Committee, 'Final Report of the Select Committee to Study Governmental Operations with Respect to Intelligence Activities United States Senate, Book 3', (Washington, DC: Congress, 1976), www.icdc.com/~paulwolf/cointelpro/churchfinalreportIIIj.htm (accessed 13 July 2008).

45 'Miami Tops "Foreign-born" Cities', *BBC News*, 15 July 2004, http://news.bbc.co.uk/1/hi/world/americas/3898795.stm (accessed 23 April 2009).

46 Spike Lee, director, *Inside Job* (2005).

47 Lee Romney, 'The Trouble with Informants', *Houston Chronicle*, 12 August 2006.

48 Phillip Johnston, 'MI5 Seeks "Older, Wiser Women"', *Daily Telegraph*, 10 May 2005; Michael Evans, 'More Britons Are Turning to Terror, Says MI5 Director', *Times*, 10 November 2006; Barney Calman, 'Policing with Passion; Is the Met Police Still Prejudiced against Ethnic Minorities and Women?', *Evening Standard*, 10 July 2006; Martin Bright, 'Revealed: MI6 Plan to Infiltrate Extremists', *Observer*, 4 September 2005. For a discussion of the problems the CIA had in infiltrating Al Qaeda pre-9/11 see Reuel Marc Gerecht, 'The Counterterrorist Myth', *Atlantic Monthly*, July/August 2001.

49 Hewitt, *Spying 101*, pp. 188–9; Ruth Rosen, *The World Split Open: How the Modern Women's Movement Changed America* (New York, NY: Penguin Books, 2001), pp. 240–60.

50 Larry Grathwohl and Frank Reagan, *Bringing Down America: An FBI Informer with the Weathermen* (New Rochelle, NY: Arlington House Publishers, 1976), p. 122.

51 Jeff Sallot, 'Canada Could Escape Attack, CSIS Says', *Globe and Mail*, 20 June 2006; 'Biggest US Spy Agency Choking on Too Much Information', *CNN*, 25 November 1999, www.cnn.com/US/9911/25/nsa.woes/ (accessed 1 November 2005).

52 Steven Greer, *Supergrasses: Study in Anti-Terrorist Law Enforcement in Northern Ireland* (Oxford, UK: Clarendon Press, 1995); Paddy Hillyard and Janie Percy-Smith, 'Converting Terrorists: The Use of Supergrasses in Northern Ireland', *Journal of Law and Society*, vol. 11, no. 3 (1984): 335–55.

53 McDonald Commission, *Second Report: Freedom and Security, Vol. 1*, 296–7.

54 Ibid, 300.

55 Peter Klerks, 'Covert Policing in the Netherlands', in Cyrille Fijnaut and Gary T. Marx, eds, *Undercover Police Surveillance in Comparative Perspective* (Boston: Kluwer Law International, 1995), p. 130.

56   Boston Police, 'Boston Police Guidelines Regarding Use of Informants', in Robert M. Bloom, *Ratting: The Use and Abuse of Informants in the American Justice System* (London: Praeger, 2002), pp. 50–61.

57   Colin Dunninghan, and Clive Norris, 'A Risky Business: The Recruitment and Running of Informers by English Police Officers', *Police Studies*, vol. 19, no. 2 (1996): 3.

58   Greer, *Supergrasses*, p. 4.

59   Navasky, as quoted in Steven Greer, 'Towards a Sociological Model of the Police Informant', *British Journal of Sociology*, vol. 46, no. 3 (1995): 516.

60   For a longer list see Greer, 'Towards a Sociological Model . . .', 513.

61   Malachi L. Harney and John C. Cross, *The Informer in Law Enforcement* (Springfield, IL: Charles C. Thomas, 1968), p. 4.

62   Elia Kazan, director, *On the Waterfront*, 1954; 'Colleagues Labelled Oscar Winner as "Informer"', *Age*, 8 August 2009. For more on the film, see Kenneth Hey, 'Ambivalence as a Theme in "On the Waterfront" (1954: An Interdisciplinary Approach to Film Study)', *American Quarterly*, vol. 31, no. 5 (1979): 666–96.

63   Dalton Trumbo, screenwriter, *Spartacus*, 1960; 'Dalton Trumbo, Film Writer, Dies', *New York Times*, 11 September 1976.

64   Martin Ritt, director, *The Molly Maguires*, 1970; John Sayles, director, *Matewan*, 1987; Martin Scorsese, director, *The Departed*, 2006; von Donnersmarck, director, *Das Leben der Anderen (The Lives of Others)*.

65   'Seven Beer Snitch', *The Simpsons*, broadcast 3 April 2005; 'The Trouble with Trillions', *The Simpsons*, broadcast 5 April 1998; 'The Debarted', *The Simpsons*, broadcast 2 March 2008; *Sleeper Cell*, Showtime, first broadcast on 4 December 2005; Nellie Andreeva, 'Australian "Informant" Talks to Fox', *Hollywood Reporter*, 7 August 2008.

66   Jeremy Kahn, 'The Story of a Snitch', *Atlantic Monthly*, April 2007. For an example of the British effort, see 'Rat on a Rat', Sussex Police Online, www.sussex.police.uk/campaigns/ratonrat.asp (accessed 15 April 2009).

67   Malin Åkerström, *Betrayal and Betrayers: The Sociology of Treachery* (New York: Transaction Publishers, 1991), pp. 27–8.

68   J. Edgar Hoover, as quoted in Åkerström, *Betrayal and Betrayers*, p. 39.

69   Navasky, as quoted in Ibid, 122.

70   Ibid, 39.

71   Harney and Cross, *The Informer in Law Enforcement*, p. 65.

72   Laville, 'Analysis: The Rules on Police Informants'; Urban, *Big Boys' Rules*, 97; Frank J. Donner, *Protectors of Privilege: Red Squads and Police Repression in Urban America* (Los Angeles, CA: University of California Press, 1990), p. 464.

73   Borzou Daragahi, 'A Tragic End to an Unlikely Friendship', *Houston Chronicle*, 18 September 2005; 'Real IRA Claim Donaldson Killing', *Donegal Democrat*, 14 April 2009.

74   Urban, *Big Boys' Rules*, pp. 102, 244; Greer, *Supergrasses*, pp. 41–2; Louise

Richardson, *What Terrorists Want: Understanding the Terrorist Threat* (London: John Murray, 2006), p. 54.

75 India News, 'Naxals Killed a TDP Worker', *New Kerala*, 2 February 2005; Press Trust of India, 'Terrorists Chop Off Man's Tongue in J&K', *Hindustan Times*, 14 August 2005; 'Woman Killed for Being Informer, Claims KCP', *Sangai Express*, 5 September 2005; 'Jharkhand Lures Informers with Huge Compensation', *WebIndia*, 11 November 2005 http://news.webindia123.com/news/showdetails. asp?id=159789&cat=India (accessed 11 November 2005); 'Maoists Kill One under Suspicion of Being an Informer', *India News*, 17 November 2005; 'Maoists Kill Civilian Branding Him Informer', *WebIndia*, 8 December 2005.

76 Gorenberg, 'The Collaborator'.

77 'US Soldiers Die in Baghdad Blast', *BBC News*, 6 June 2004, http://news.bbc. co.uk/1/hi/world/middle_east/3778897.stm (accessed 15 September 2006); Marx, *Undercover*, pp. 146–7. An archivist once told me that the names of informers involved in the 1919 Winnipeg General Strike would never be released because even though those involved may be long dead, the descendants of the strikers might seek vengeance against the descendants of the informers.

78 Richard A. Kaba, 'Threshold Requirements for the FBI under Exemption 7 of the Freedom of Information Act', *Michigan Law Review* vol. 86, no. 3 (1987): 629.

79 Dunninghan and Norris, 'A Risky Business . . .', 5.

80 'Swedish Secret Service Seeks Informers: Chief', *Agence France Presse*, 7 March 2001.

81 Paul Lewis, 'Police Caught on Tape Trying to Recruit Plane Stupid Protester as Spy', *Guardian*, 24 April 2009. The recordings can be listened to at: www.guardian.co.uk/uk/audio/2009/apr/24/police-surveillance-intelligence-3 (accessed 25 April 2009).

82 Steve Hewitt, 'The Professoriate and the Police during the Cold War', in Paul Stortz and E. Lisa Panayotidis, eds, *Historical Identities: The Professoriate in Canada* (Toronto, ON: University of Toronto Press, 2006), pp. 84–105.

83 Stanislav Levchenko, *On the Wrong Side: My Life in the KGB* (Washington, DC: Pergamon-Brassey's, 1988); see also Åkerström, *Betrayal and Betrayers*, p. 22.

84 Alexander Stephan, *Communazis:* FBI Surveillance of German Émigré Writers (New Haven, CT: Yale University Press, 2000), p. 22.

85 FBI, 'Exhibit 33'.

86 'Crime Pays — If You're a Snitch', *Otago Daily Times*, 20 April 2004.

87 Brian McGrory, 'Drug War's Odd Couple: Informants and Police', *Boston Globe*, 15 April 1994.

88 Stephanie Barry, 'FBI Paid Informant $135,000', *Republican*, 8 January 2005; Benjamin Weiser, 'Videotapes of a Qaeda Informer Offer Glimpse into a Secret Life', *New York Times*, 1 May 2004; Rebecca Cook Dube, 'Leader Turned Informant Rattles Muslims', *Christian Science Monitor*, 31 July 2006.

89 Church Committee, 'Final Report'.

90 Dunninghan and Norris, 'A Risky Business . . .', 5.

91 Klerks, 'Covert Policing in the Netherlands', 131.

92 Yaakov Peri, former head of Shin Bet, as quoted in Gorenberg, 'The Collaborator'.

93 Paul Lewis and Marc Vallée, '"UK Plc Can Afford More than 20 Quid," the Officer Said', *Guardian*, 25 April 2009.

94 Harney and Cross, *The Informer in Law Enforcement*, pp. 41–8.

95 Levchenko, *On the Wrong Side*, 106. For a variation on the MICE concept, see Stan A. Taylor and Daniel Snow, 'Cold War Spies: Why They Spied and How They Got Caught', *Intelligence and National Security*, vol. 12, no. 2 (Spring 1997), 101–25; Klerks, 'Covert Policing in the Netherlands', 130; Åkerström, *Betrayal and Betrayals*, p. 3; Mark Leier, *Rebel Life: The Life and Times of Robert Gosden, Revolutionary, Mystic, Labour Spy* (Vancouver, BC: New Star Books, 1999), p. 103.

96 Greer, 'Towards a Sociological Model . . .', 515–17.

97 Taylor and Snow, 'Cold War Spies', 102.

98 Jamal Ahmed al-Fadl, as quoted in Benjamin Weiser, 'Videotapes of a Qaeda Informer Offer Glimpse into a Secret Life', *New York Times*, 1 May 2004; Åkerström, *Betrayal and Betrayals*, p. 3; Taylor and Snow, 'Cold War Spies', 108.

99 Hewitt, *Spying 101*, pp. 32–4.

100 For instance, an alleged Islamist apparently approached British intelligence offering to be an informer, to ensure that London would not 'become a centre for settling Islamic scores'. Richard Norton-Taylor, 'Detained Leader Offered to Inform on Extremists', *Guardian*, 24 March 2004.

101 Roger Billingsley, 'Informers' Careers: Motivations and Change', in Roger Billingsley, Teresa Nemitz, and Philip Bean, eds, *Informers: Policing, Policy, Practice* (Uffculme, UK: Willan Publishing, 2001), p. 86; Nemitz, 'Gender Issues in Informer Handling', 101; Martin Ingram and Greg Harkin, *Stakeknife: Britain's Secret Agents in Ireland* (Dublin: The O'Brien Press Ltd., 2004), p. 38; Williamson and Bagshaw, 'The Ethics of Informer Handling', 59–60; Marx, 'Thoughts on a Neglected Category . . .', 414; Richard Ericson, *Making Crime: A Study of Detective Work* (Toronto, ON: University of Toronto Press, 1993), p. 123.

102 FBI, 'Exhibit 33'.

103 Hoover, as quoted in Harney and Cross, *The Informer in Law Enforcement*, p. 15.

104 Liam Clarke, 'Focus: The Spy at the Heart of the IRA', *Sunday Times*, 18 December 2005.

105 Marx, *Undercover*, p. 155; Gorenberg, 'The Collaborator'. In a recent case a police recruiter advised a potential informer that money paid to her would not be done through her bank account, to avoid leaving a paper trail. Lewis, 'Police Caught on Tape Trying to Recruit Plane Stupid Protester as Spy'.

106 Williamson and Bagshaw, 'The Ethics of Informer Handling', 59.

107 Marx, 'Thoughts on a Neglected Category . . .', 415.

108 Severin Carrell, 'MI5 "Left Al-Qaeda Informant to Rot in Guantanamo Bay"',

Independent, 5 June 2005; Vikram Dodd, 'Guantanamo Inmate Says Us Told Him to Spy on Al-Jazeera', *Guardian*, 26 September 2005; Craig Whitlock, 'Courted as Spies; Held as Combatants: British Residents Enlisted by MI5 after Sept 11 Languish at Guantanamo', *Washington Post*, 2 April 2006; 'Abductee El-Masri Offered Job as Informer: Report', *Expatica*, 19 December 2005.

109 Brendan Lyons, 'Mosque Welcomed in Informant', *Albany Times-Union*, 8 August 2004.

110 Lawrence Wright, *The Looming Tower* (New York, NY: Albert A. Knopf, 2006), p. 215.

111 Barbara Miller, *Narratives of Guilt and Compliance in Unified Germany* (London and New York: Routledge, 1999), pp. 47–9.

112 Ibid, 107–8.

113 For an example from the Central Intelligence Agency, see Anthony F. Czajkowski, 'Techniques of Domestic Intelligence Collection', in H. Bradford Westerfield, ed, *Inside CIA's Private World: Declassified Articles from the Agency's Internal Journal, 1955–1992* (New Haven and London: Yale University Press, 1995), pp. 51–62.

114 Church Committee, 'Final Report'; Gorenberg, 'The Collaborator'.

115 Anonymous Israeli soldier, as quoted in Bruce Hoffman, 'The Logic of Suicide Terrorism', *Atlantic Monthly*, June 2003.

116 Marx, 'Thoughts on a Neglected Category . . .', 409–11.

117 Gordon Thomas, *Gideon's Spies: The Secret History of the Mossad* (New York, NY: Thomas Dunne Books, 1999), p. 5; Hewitt, *Spying 101*, pp. 32–5; James T. Stark, *Cold War Blues: The Operation Dismantle Story* (Hull, PQ 1991), pp. 320–62.

118 Marx, *Undercover*, p. 165.

119 'RCMP Defend Methods', *Edmonton Journal*, 5 February 1999.

120 Marx, 'Thoughts on a Neglected Category . . .', 421–2.

121 Tim Weiner, 'Records Tie CIA Informer to Two Guatemala Killings', *New York Times*, 7 May 1996.

122 Paul Pillar, *Terrorism and US Foreign Policy* (Washington, DC: Brookings Institute Press, 2001), p. 112.

123 Vernon Loeb, 'CIA Giving Fired Agent Top Award', *Washington Post*, 10 March 2000; James Risen, 'Report Faults CIA's Recruitment Rules', *New York Times*, 18 July 2002.

124 Harney and Cross, *The Informer in Law Enforcement*, p. 40.

125 William Tulio Divale and James Joseph, *I Lived inside the Campus Revolution* (New York, NY: NY Cowles Book Company, 1970), p. 19.

126 Richard Bernstein, 'Poland Exhumes the Skeletons in Its Communist Closet', *New York Times*, 14 January 2005.

127 Church Committee, 'Final Report'; M. Wesley Swearingen, *FBI Secrets: An Agent's Exposé* (Boston, MA: South End Press, 1995), p. 68.

128 Annie Machon, *Spies, Lies and Whistleblowers: MI5, MI6 and the Shayler Affair* (Sussex, UK: The Book Guild Ltd, 2005), p. 229.

129 Frank J. Donner, *The Age of Surveillance: The Aims and Methods of America's Political Intelligence System* (New York, NY: Albert A. Knopf, 1980), p. 183.

130 Marx, *Undercover*, pp. 146–9.

131 Nigel South, 'Informers, Agents and Accountability', in Roger Billingsley, Teresa Nemitz, and Philip Bean, eds, *Informers: Policing, Policy, Practice* (Uffculme, UK: Willan Publishing, 2001), p. 72; Marx, *Undercover*, pp. 155, 174; Machon, *Spies, Lies and Whistleblowers*, p. 311; 'Spy Agency Hid Fact that Source Lied in Harkat Case', *Globe and Mail*, 6 June 2009.

132 William C. Sullivan, with Bill Brown, *The Bureau: My Thirty Years in Hoover's FBI* (New York, NY: W.W. Norton and Company, 1979), p. 128.

133 Harney and Cross, *The Informer in Law Enforcement*, p. 79.

134 Miller, *Narratives of Guilt . . .*', p. 14.

135 Hewitt, *Spying 101*, p. 35.

136 Carole de Vault, *The Informer: Confessions of an Ex-Terrorist* (Toronto, ON: Fleet Books, 1982), p. 240.

137 'Sheriff's Deputy Fired for Allegedly Impregnating Informant', *Newsnet 5*, 22 February 2005, www.newsnet5.com/news/4219821/detail.html (accessed 22 February 2005); Margaret F. Bonafide, 'Woman Says Cops Ignored Detective's Sex with Her', *Ashbury Park Press*, 19 November 2005.

138 'FBI Agent in Affair with Informant Makes Deal', *Pasadena Star-News*, 18 July 2005; 'Ex-FBI Official Guilty of Lying About Affair with Informant', *Washington Post*, 5 May 2004; Eric Lichtblau, 'FBI Missed Many "Red Flags" on Key Informer, Review Finds', *New York Times*, 25 May 2006.

139 Ironically, the FBI agent in question, John Connolly Jr, became a jailhouse informer once he was imprisoned over his illegal activities surrounding Bulger. 'Ex-FBI Agent Who Helped Bulger Escape Turns Jailhouse Informant', *Associated Press*, 20 December 2004.

140 Machon, *Spies, Lies and Whistleblowers*, p. 52; Gorenberg, 'The Collaborator'.

141 Peter Klerks, 'Covert Policing in the Netherlands', in Cyrille Fijnaut and Gary T. Marx, eds, *Undercover Police Surveillance in Comparative Perspective* (Boston, MA: Kluwer Law International, 1995), p. 132.

142 'Mueller Tightens FBI Rules on Informants', *Yahoo News*, 2 May 2006, http://news.yahoo.com/s/ap/fbi_informants;_ylt=AsKjCnmtdkjoi5Lm4BdQf.Os0NUE;_ylu=X3oDMTA2Z2szazkxBHNlYwN0bQ–, (accessed 3 January 2007). For a copy of the new rules see Janet Reno, 'Department of Justice Guidelines Regarding the Use of Confidential Informants', (Washington, DC: US Department of Justice, 2001).

143 Boston Police, 'Boston Police Guidelines Regarding Use of Informants', in Bloom, *Ratting*, pp. 50–61.

144 Dunninghan and Norris, 'A Risky Business', 22.

145 Dan Eggen, 'FBI Agents Often Break Informant Rules', *Washington Post*, 13 September 2005; Daniel Engber, 'How Do You Handle an FBI Informant? If You Pay Him, Get a Receipt', *Slate*, 13 September 2005, www.slate.com/id/2126246/ (accessed 4 May 2006).

146   Mike Maguire, *Intelligence, Surveillance and Informants: Integrated Approaches,* (London: Home Office Police Research Group, 1995), pp. 11–13.

Notes to Chapter 3: Informing History

1   Gary T. Marx, *Undercover: Police Surveillance in America* (Berkeley, CA: University of California Press, 1992), p. 17.

2   Mark 14.10 *The Bible* (King James Version).

3   Steven Greer, *Supergrasses: Study in Anti-Terrorist Law Enforcement in Northern Ireland* (Oxford, UK: Clarendon Press, 1995), p. 10. For more on this see D. Kaufman, 'Jewish Informers in the Middle Ages', *Jewish Quarterly Review*, vol. 8, no. 2 (1896): 217–38.

4   Malin Åkerström, *Betrayal and Betrayers: The Sociology of Treachery* (New York, NY: Transaction Publishers, 1991), p. 2.

5   Robert M. Bloom, *Ratting: The Use and Abuse of Informants in the American Justice System* (London: Praeger, 2002), p. 2.

6   Rose Mary Sheldon, *Intelligence Activities in Ancient Rome: Trust in the Gods, but Verify* (London: Routledge, 2005), p. 152; Bloom, *Ratting*, p. 5; Steven H. Rutledge, *Imperial Inquisitions: Prosecutors and Informants from Tiberius to Domitian* (London: Routledge, 2001), p. 4.

7   Rutledge, *Imperial Inquisitions*, pp. 12–15.

8   *Epigrams of Martial*, as quoted in Ibid, p. 13.

9   Bloom, *Ratting*, p. 5.

10   Edward Coke, *The Third Part of the Institutes of the Laws of England* (E. and R. Brooke, 1797), p. 194.

11   For more on popular perceptions of informers, see Albert H. Tricomi, *Reading Tudor-Stuart Texts through Cultural Historicism* (Gainesville, FL: University Press of Florida, 1996), p. 82.

12   Ben Jonson, 'On Spies', as quoted in *Intelligence and National Security*, vol. 8, no. 4 (October 1993).

13   William Shakespeare, as quoted in Bernard Porter, *Plots and Paranoia: A History of Political Espionage in Britain, 1790–1988* (London: Routledge, 1989), p. 21.

14   David Dean, *Law-Making and Society in Late Elizabethan England* (Cambridge: Cambridge University Press, 2002), pp. 204–7.

15   Anthony Tyrrell, as quoted in Lowell Gallagher, *Medusa's Gaze: Casuistry and Conscience in the Renaissance* (Palo Alto, CA: Stanford University Press, 1991), p. 99.

16   Peter Holmes, 'Tyrrell, Anthony (1552–1615)', in H. C. G. Matthew and Brian Harrison, eds, *Oxford Dictionary of National Biography* (Oxford: Oxford University Press, 2004), www.oxforddnb.com/view/article/27950 (accessed 9 May 2009); Gallagher, *Medusa's Gaze*, pp. 98–103.

17   Robert J. Stove, *The Unsleeping Eye: Secret Police and Their Victims* (San

Francisco, CA: Encounter Books, 2003), pp. 28–32. See also Stephen Budiansky, *Her Majesty's Spymaster: Elizabeth 1, Sir Francis Walsingham, and the Birth of Modern Espionage* (London: Plume, 2005), and Alan Haynes, *The Elizabethan Secret Services* (London: Sutton Publishing, 2002).

18 Richard L. Greaves, *Secrets of the Kingdom: British Radicals from the Popish Plot to the Revolution of 1688–1689* (Palo Alto, CA: Stanford University Press, 1992), pp. 337–8; Richard L. Greaves, *Deliver Us from Evil: The Radical Underground in Britain, 1660–1663* (Oxford: Oxford University Press, 1986), p. 14.

19 Edward Potter, as quoted in Greaves, *Deliver Us from Evil*, p. 14.

20 Alan Marshall, *Intelligence and Espionage in the Reign of Charles II, 1660–1685* (Cambridge: Cambridge University Press, 1994), p. 4; Greaves, *Deliver Us from Evil*, p. 14.

21 Samuel Bold, 'A Sermon against Persecutions Preached March 26 1682', (1682), 7–9, as quoted in Marshall, *Intelligence and Espionage in the Reign of Charles II*, p. 207.

22 Greaves, *Deliver Us from Evil*, p. 14.

23 James Beckman, *Comparative Legal Approaches to Homeland Security and Anti-Terrorism* (London: Ashgate Publishing Ltd., 2007), p. 56. For more on the evolution of British policing, see T. A. Critchley, *A History of Police in England and Wales, 900–1966* (London: Constable, 1967), and Clive Emsley, *The English Police: A Political and Social History* (London: Longman, 1996).

24 Richard C. Donnelly, 'Judicial Control of Informants, Spies, Stool Pigeons, and Agent Provocateurs', *Yale Law Journal*, vol. 60, no. 7 (1951): 1091; G.R. Elton, 'Informing for Profit: A Sidelight on Tudor Methods of Law-Enforcement', *Cambridge Historical Journal*, vol. 11, no. 2 (1954): 150; Marx, *Undercover*, pp. 19–20.

25 See, for example, Robert M. Fogelson, *Big City Police* (Cambridge, MA: Harvard University Press, 1979); DeLloyd J. Guth, 'The Traditional Common Law Constable, 1235–1829: From Bracton to the Fieldings of Canada', in R.C. Macleod and David Schneiderman, eds, *Police Powers in Canada: The Evolution and Practice of Authority* (Toronto, ON: University of Toronto Press, 1994), p. 18.

26 Clive Emsley, 'The Home Office and Its Sources of Information and Investigation, 1791–1801', *English Historical Review*, vol. 94, no. 372 (1979): 544.

27 Emsley, 'The Home Office . . .', 547–9.

28 Robert Holden, as quoted in Ibid, 541.

29 Brother of Lyman, as quoted in Ibid, 547.

30 Ibid, 560–1; Elaine A. Reynolds, *Before the Bobbies: The Night Watch and Police Reform in Metropolitan London, 1720–1830* (London: Macmillan Press Ltd., 1998), pp. 107–8.

31 Jean-Paul Brodeur, 'High Policing and Low Policing: Remarks About the Policing of Political Activities', *Social Problems*, vol. 30, no. 5 (1983): 514.

32 Chief of Police Sartine, as quoted in James Morton, *The First Detective: The Life and Revolutionary Times of Vidocq* (London: Ebury Press, 2005), p. 130.

33 Cyrille Fijnaut and Gary T. Marx, 'Introduction: The Normalization of Undercover Policing in the West: Historical and Contemporary Perspectives', in Cyrille Fijnaut and Gary T. Marx, eds, *Undercover: Police Surveillance in Comparative Perspective* (Boston, MA: Kluwer Law International, 1995), pp. 2–3.

34 Morton, *The First Detective*, p. 130.

35 Fijnaut and Marx, 'Introduction', 2–3; Paul Metzner, *Crescendo of the Virtuoso: Spectacle, Skill, and Self-promotion in Paris during the Age of Revolution* (Berkeley, CA: University of California Press, 1998), p. 95; Martin L. Van Creveld, *The Rise and Decline of the State* (Cambridge: Cambridge University Press, 1999), p. 167.

36 Marx, *Undercover*, pp. 17–19; Morton, *The First Detective*, p. 131; Bloom, *Ratting*, p. 6; Howard G. Brown, 'Tips, Traps and Tropes: Catching Thieves in Post-Revolutionary Paris', in Clive Emsley and Haia Shpayer-Makov, eds, *Police Detectives in History, 1750–1950* (London: Ashgate Publishing, Ltd., 2006), p. 38. For more on Vidocq, see Eugène Francois Vidocq, *Memoirs of Vidocq: Master of Crime (Nabat)* (London: AK Press, 2003).

37 Fijnaut and Marx, 'Introduction . . .', 6–7; Walter Laqueur, *A History of Terrorism* (London: Transaction Publishers, 2002), p. 98.

38 Count Otto von Bismarck, as quoted in Laqueur, *A History of Terrorism*, p. 98.

39 Luc Keunings, 'The Secret Police in Nineteenth-Century Brussels', *Intelligence and National Security*, vol. 4, no. 1 (January 1989): 60–1, 77.

40 Reynolds, *Before the Bobbies*, p. 151.

41 Marx, *Undercover*, pp. 22–7.

42 Bloom, *Ratting*, p. 6.

43 Marx, *Undercover*, pp. 22–3; Fijnaut and Marx, 'Introduction . . .', 7–8.

44 Rhodri Jeffreys-Jones, *Cloak and Dollar: A History of American Secret Intelligence* (New Haven, CT: Yale University Press, 2002), pp. 24–43.

45 Marx, *Undercover*, p. 29; Pamala L. Griset and Sue Mahan, *Terrorism in Perspective* (London: SAGE, 2007), pp. 41–2, 326; Robert Niemi, *History in the Media: Film and Television* (Santa Barbara, CA: ABC-CLIO, 2006), p. 326; Martin Ritt, director, *The Molly Maguires*, 1970.

46 Steve Hewitt, *Riding to the Rescue: The Transformation of the RCMP in Alberta and Saskatchewan, 1914–1939* (Toronto, ON: University of Toronto Press, 2006), p. 88.

47 Steve Hewitt, 'Royal Canadian Mounted Spy: The Secret Life of John Leopold/ Jack Esselwein', *Intelligence and National Security*, vol. 15, no. 1 (Spring 2000): 144–68.

48 Richard Gid Powers, *Secrecy and Power: The Life of J. Edgar Hoover* (London: Collier Macmillan Publishers, 1992), pp. 67–9.

49 David Garrow, 'FBI Historiography: Analyzing Informants and Measuring the Effects', *The Public Historian*, vol. 10, no. 4 (fall 1988): 7.

50 Winston A. Grady-Willis, 'The Black Panther Party: State Repression and Political

Prisoners', in Charles E. Jones, ed, *The Black Panther Party (Reconsidered)* (Baltimore, MD: Black Classic Press, 2005), p. 364; Bureau Report, 4 January 1923, www.marcusgarvey.com/wmview.php?ArtID=425 (accessed 5 May 2007); Bureau Report, 6 September 1922, www.marcusgarvey.com/wmview. php?ArtID=430 (accessed 12 May 2009).

51   Richard C. Thurlow, '"a Very Clever Capitalist Class": British Communism and State Surveillance, 1939–45', *Intelligence and National Security*, vol. 12, no. 2 (1997): 1–21.

52   Gary T. Marx, 'Thoughts on a Neglected Category of Social Movement Participant: The Agent Provocateur and the Informant', *American Journal of Sociology*, vol. 80, no. 2 (1974): 429.

53   Joan M. Jensen, *Army Surveillance in America, 1775–1980* (New Haven, CT: Yale University Press, 1991), p. 211.

54   Marx, *Undercover*, p. 31.

55   Robert Cohen, *When the Old Left Was Young: Student Radicals and America's First Mass Student Movement, 1929–1941* (New York, NY: Oxford University Press, 1993), pp. xvi, 44–53, 325–6.

56   Roosevelt, as quoted in Theoharis, Athan G. *The FBI & American Democracy: A Brief Critical History* (Lawrence, KS: University Press of Kansas, 2004), p. 52.

57   Jensen, *Army Surveillance in America*, pp. 219–20.

58   Ibid, pp. 214–15; Athan G. Theoharis, 'The FBI and the American Legion Contact Program, 1940–1966', *Political Science Quarterly*, vol. 100, no. 2 (1985): 272–3, 277; Theoharis, *The FBI & American Democracy*, p. 53.

59   Theoharis, 'The FBI and the American Legion Contact Program', 280.

60   Frank J. Donner, *The Age of Surveillance: The Aims and Methods of America's Political Intelligence System* (New York, NY: Albert A. Knopf, 1980), p. 137.

61   FBI Files related to Joseph P. Kennedy, SAC Boston Director to A.H. Belmont, 16 October 1953. For more on the life of Joseph P. Kennedy, see Thomas Maier, *The Kennedys: America's Emerald Kings* (New York, NY: Basic Books, 2003).

62   Ellen Schrecker, *Many Are the Crimes: McCarthyism in America* (New York, NY: Little, Brown and Company, 1998), p. 227.

63   Jeffrey T. Richelson and Desmond Ball, *The Ties That Bind: Intelligence Cooperation between the UKUSA Countries–the United Kingdom, the United States of America, Canada, Australia and New Zealand* (Boston and London: Unwin Hyman, 1990), p. 289.

64   Garrow, 'FBI Political Harassment and FBI Historiography', 8; Marx, 'Thoughts on a Neglected Category of Social Movement Participant', 429.

65   Church Committee, 'Final Report of the Select Committee to Study Governmental Operations with Respect to Intelligence Activities', (Washington, DC: Congress, 1976), www.aarclibrary.org/publib/church/reports/vol6/contents.htm (accessed 10 May 2007); Brodeur, 'High Policing and Low Policing', 515.

66   Athan Theoharis, *Chasing Spies: How the FBI Failed in Counter-Intelligence But Promoted the Politics of McCarthyism in the Cold War Years* (Chicago, IL: Ivan R. Dee, 2002), pp. 100, 103. The FBI was not the only part of the American

government that relied on informers in the early Cold War. The Internal Revenue Service (IRS) also employed informers as a tool to catch tax cheats. W. H. Lawrence, 'Host of Informers Tips Agencies on Spies, Reds and Tax Evaders', *New York Times*, 7 July 1954.

67 Reg Whitaker, 'Cold War Alchemy: How America, Britain and Canada Transformed Espionage into Subversion', *Intelligence and National Security* vol. 15, no. 2 (Summer 2000): 177–210.

68 Lawrence, 'Host of Informers Tips Agencies on Spies, Reds and Tax Evaders'.

69 Robert M. Lichtman and Ronald D. Cohen, *Deadly Farce: Harvey Matusow and the Informer System in the McCarthy Era* (Urbana and Chicago, IL: University of Illinois Press, 2004), pp. 2–3.

70 Schrecker, *Many Are the Crimes*, p. 227.

71 Church Committee, 'Final Report . . .'.

72 Hoover, as quoted in Malachi L. Harney and John C. Cross, *The Informer in Law Enforcement* (Springfield, IL: Charles C. Thomas, 1968), pp. 17–20.

73 M. Wesley Swearingen, *FBI Secrets: An Agent's Exposé* (Boston: South End Press, 1995), pp. 23–4; Ward Churchill, and Jim Vander Wall, *The COINTELPRO Papers: Documents from the FBI's Secret Wars Against Dissent in the United States* (Boston, MA: South End Press, 1990), pp. 33–9. The father of COINTELPRO-CP, USA was William Sullivan, a senior member of the FBI, who later broke with Hoover and had an autobiography published posthumously. See William C. Sullivan, with Bill Brown, *The Bureau: My Thirty Years in Hoover's FBI* (New York, NY: Norton, 1979). For more on those who infiltrated the CPC on behalf of the FBI, see Schrecker, *Many Are the Crimes*, pp. 196–8.

74 McDonald Commission, *Freedom and Security Under the Law: Vol. 1*, 267–8. The text of the letter is available at Library and Archives Canada (LAC), Records of the McDonald Commission, Record Group (RG) 33/128, access to information request AH-1998-00059, accession 1992–93/251, box 130, file 'Covert Measures-Check Mate-'D' Operations, 21 March 1956. For the problems Khrushchev's speech and the Soviet invasion of Hungary caused the Labour Progressive Party see Merrily Weisbord, *The Strangest Dream: Canadian Communists, the Spy Trials, and the Cold War* (Toronto, ON: Véhicule Press, 1983), pp. 214–13; Norman Penner, *Canadian Communism: The Stalin Years and Beyond* (Toronto, ON: Methuen, 1998), pp. 237–49.

75 Peter Hennessy, 'From Secret State to Protective State', in Peter Hennessy, ed, *The New Protective State: Government, Intelligence and Terrorism* (London: Continuum, 2007), p. 22.

76 Frank J. Donner, *Protectors of Privilege: Red Squads and Police Repression in Urban America* (Los Angeles, CA: University of California Press, 1990). For efforts of state police and militias in policing strikes, see Gerda Ray, '"We Can Stay Until Hell Freezes Over": Strike Control and the State Police in New York, 1919–1923', *Labor History*, vol. 36, no. 3 (Summer 1995): 403–25.

77 Church Committee, 'Final Report . . .'.

78 David Cunningham, *There's Something Happening Here: The New Left, the Klan, and FBI Counterintelligence* (London: University of California Press, 2004), pp. 56–9.

79 William Tulio Divale and James Joseph, *I Lived Inside the Campus Revolution* (New York, NY: Cowles Book Company, Inc., 1970), p. ix. For another first-hand account by an FBI informer active in the same period, see Larry Grathwohl and Frank Reagan, *Bringing Down America: An FBI Informer with the Weathermen* (New Rochelle, NY: Arlington House Publishers, 1976).

80 Ibid, pp. 186–7; David C. Rapoport, *Terrorism: The Third or New Left Wave* (London: Taylor & Francis, 2006), p. 198.

81 Cunningham, *There's Something Happening Here*, pp. 238–42.

82 Donner, *The Age of Surveillance*, p. 157.

83 Steve Hewitt, *Spying 101: The RCMP's Secret Activities at Canadian Universities, 1917–1997* (Toronto, ON: University of Toronto Press, 2002), pp. 109–11.

84 Memo of Assistant Commissioner Leonard Higgitt, 29 November 1967, as quoted in McDonald Commission, *Second Report*, Vol. 1, 343–6. The FBI employed similar tactics at American universities. Church Committee, 'Final Report . . .'.

85 David Gallen and Michael Friedly, eds, *Martin Luther King, Jr.: The FBI File* (New York, NY: Carroll & Graf Publishing, 1993).

86 Donner, *Protectors of Privilege*, p. 187.

87 Churchill and Vander Wall, *Agents of Repression*, pp. 67–70.

88 Church Committee, 'Final Report'; Swearingen, *FBI Secrets*, p. 68.

89 Ibid.

90 Ibid.

91 FBI report, as quoted in Marx, 'Thoughts on a Neglected Category of Social Movement Participant', 412.

92 Church Committee, 'Final Report . . .'.

93 Ruth Rosen, *The World Split Open: How the Modern Women's Movement Changed America* (New York, NY: Penguin Books, 2001), p. 255.

94 Rosen, *The World Split Open*, pp. 244, 247–8, 251.

95 FBI report as quoted in Ibid, 244. For the quote, see Church Committee, 'Final Report . . .'.

96 LAC, RG 146, files related to Women's Liberation Movement, access request A2005-00441, Royal Canadian Mounted Police report, 17 April 1972. See another example in Rosen, *The World Split Open*, p. 247.

97 Rosen, *The World Split Open*, p. 253.

98 Ibid, p. 260.

99 Robert Kennedy, as quoted in Church Committee, 'Final Report . . .'; Jerrold K. Footlick and Anthony Marro, 'What Price Informants?' *Newsweek*, 8 March 1976. For more on a specific informer in the Klan, see Gary May, *The Informant: The FBI, the Ku Klux Klan, and the Murder of Viola Liuzzo* (New Haven and London: Yale University Press, 2005).

100 Marx, *Undercover*, p. 149; Church Committee, 'Final Report . . .'.

101 Cunningham, *There's Something Happening Here*, pp. 76, 130–2, 144.

102 Ibid, p. 3.

103 Church Committee, 'Final Report . . .'.

104 Marx, *Undercover*, p. 147.

105 Church Committee, 'Final Report . . .'.

106 Ibid.

107 Anthony Marro, 'Rising Concern over Informers Being Voiced by Legal Officials', *New York Times*, 23 July 1978.

108 Marx. *Undercover*, p. 181.

109 Church Committee, 'Final Report . . .'.

110 Marro, 'Rising Concern over Informers . . .'; Theoharis, *The FBI & American Democracy*, p. 147.

111 James Risen, 'Report Faults C.I.A.'s Recruitment Rules', *New York Times*, 18 July 2002; Bill Gertz, *Breakdown: How America's Intelligence Failure Led to September 11* (New York, NY: Plume, 2003), p. 68.

112 British military commander, as quoted in Mark Urban, *Big Boys' Rules: The Bestselling Story of the SAS and the Secret Struggle against the IRA* (London: Faber and Faber Ltd., 1992), p. 101.

113 Thomas R. Mockaitis, *British Counterinsurgency in the Post-Imperial Era* (Manchester and New York: Manchester University Press, 1995), p. 108.

114 Peter Taylor, *Brits: The War against the IRA* (London: Bloomsbury, 2002), p. 150.

115 Urban, *Big Boys' Rules*, pp. 102, 244; Greer, *Supergrasses*, pp. 41–2; Louise Richardson, *What Terrorists Want: Understanding the Terrorist Threat* (London: John Murray, 2006), p. 54; Angelique Chrisafis, 'Mystery of Sinn Féin Man Who Spied for British', *Guardian*, 17 December 2005; Martin Ingram and Greg Harkin, *Stakeknife: Britain's Secret Agents in Ireland* (Dublin: The O'Brien Press Ltd., 2004), pp. 16, 39, 83–93, 120–1; Urban, *Big Boys' Rules*, pp. 103–4; Annie Machon, *Spies, Lies and Whistleblowers: MI5, MI6 and the Shayler Affair* (Sussex, UK: The Book Guild Ltd, 2005), p. 1.

116 Liam Clarke, 'New MI5 Chief Named in Probe over Murder of Policewoman', *Sunday Times*, 18 March 2007; Ingram and Harkin, *Stakeknife*, pp. 39–40.

117 Taylor, *Brits*, pp. 150–1.

118 Urban, *Big Boys' Rules*, pp. 104–5; Ingram and Harkin, *Stakeknife*, p. 37.

119 Liam Clarke, 'Focus: The Spy at the Heart of the IRA', *Sunday Times*, 18 December 2005.

120 For a specific example of the impact of such an informer see the story of Sean O'Callaghan, an informer within the IRA. Sean O'Callaghan, *The Informer* (London: Bantam Books, 1998).

121 Matthew Teague, 'Double Blind', *Atlantic Monthly*, April 2006.

Notes to Chapter 4: Famous Informers

1 For more on the implications of such records see Greg Kealey, 'Filing and Defiling: The Organization of the Canadian State's Security Archives in the Interwar Years', in Franca Iacovetta and Wendy Mitchinson, eds, *On the Case: Explorations in Social History* (Toronto, ON: University of Toronto Press, 1998), pp. 88–105.

2 Peter Finn, 'Walesa Cleared as Informer; Court Finds Plot to Sabotage His Nobel Nomination', *Washington Post*, 12 April 2000; Richard Bernstein, 'Poland Exhumes the Skeletons in Its Communist Closet', *New York Times*, 14 January 2005; Tina Rosenberg, 'A Polish Election Vexed by Communist Spies', *New York Times*, 11 August 2000.

3 Liam Clarke, 'McGuinness in New Spy Claims', *Sunday Times*, 4 June 2006; 'New Informer Claims Denied', *Irish Abroad*, 6 January 2006.

4 Antoniu de Gabriela, 'Băsescu: To Be or Not to Be Informer', *Jurnalul*, 11 April 2006.

5 Matt Kelley, 'New Iraqi Prime Minister CIA Source', *Seattle Post-Intelligencer*, 6 September 2004.

6 'PM Denies Being a British Informant', *SIFY*, 5 April 2004.

7 Richard Bernstein, 'Poland Exhumes the Skeletons in Its Communist Closet', *New York Times*, 14 January 2005.

8 'Daily Prints Hungarian Bishop's Note to Secret Police', BBC Summary of World Broadcasts, 5 January 1995; Jeffrey Fleishman, 'Romania Torn over Whether to Expose Communist Informers', *Philadelphia Inquirer*, 20 December 1998.

9 'Ethnic Hungarian bishop admits to writing contract with Securitate', BBC Summary of World Broadcasts, 12 August 2000.

10 Roger Billingsley, 'Informers' Careers: Motivations and Change', in Roger Billingsley, and Teresa Nemitz, and Philip Bean, eds, *Informers: Policing, Policy, Practice* (Uffculme, UK: Willan Publishing, 2001), p. 86.

11 Georg Simmel, as quoted in Åkerström, *Betrayal and Betrayers: The Sociology of Treachery* (New York, NY: Transaction Publishers, 1991), p. 22; Georg Simmel, 'The Sociology of Secrecy and of Secret Societies', *American Journal of Sociology*, vol. 11 (1906): 441–98.

12 Anna Geifman, *Entangled in Terror: The Azef Affair and the Russian Revolution* (Wilmington, DE: SR Books, 2000), p. 143.

13 Geifman, *Entangled in Terror*, p. 108.

14 Ibid, pp. 55, 62, 65.

15 'Reagan Was FBI Informant in Hunt for Communists', *United Press International*, 26 August 1985.

16 Stephen Vaughn, *Ronald Reagan in Hollywood: Movies and Politics* (Cambridge: Cambridge University Press, 1994), p. 130; Gary Wills, *Reagan's America: Innocents at Home* (New York, NY: Penguin Books, 1985), p. 292. See also Alexander Stephan, *Communazis: FBI Surveillance of German Émigré Writers* (New Haven, CT: Yale University Press, 2000), pp. 20–2.

17   Reagan, as quoted in Wills, *Reagan's America*, p. 293.

18   Ibid, pp. 291–2.

19   Federal Bureau of Investigation (FBI), 'Communist Infiltration — Motion Picture Industry (Compic)', file 100-138754, serial 251x1, pt. 7 of 15, 6–7.

20   FBI, Communist Infiltration — Motion Picture Industry (Compic)', file 100-138754, serial 1106, pt. 12 of 15, 4.

21   Vaughn, *Ronald Reagan in Hollywood*, p. 130.

22   FBI, Communist Infiltration — Motion Picture Industry (Compic)', file 100-138754, serial 1106, pt. 12 of 15, FBI Report, 15 May 1958, 6.

23   Wills, *Reagan's America*, pp. 295–7.

24   FBI, 'Communist Infiltration — Motion Picture Industry (Compic)', file 100-138754, serial 157x1, pt. 3 of 15, 15.

25   FBI, 'Communist Infiltration — Motion Picture Industry (Compic)', file 100-138754, serial 157x1, pt. 2 of 15, 1.

26   FBI, 'Communist Infiltration — Motion Picture Industry (COMPIC)', file 100-138754, serial 1003, pt. 8 of 15, 30.

27   FBI, 'Communist Infiltration — Motion Picture Industry (Compic)', file 100-138754, serial 1106, pt. 12 of 15, 7.

28   FBI, 'Communist Infiltration — Motion Picture Industry (COMPIC)', file 100-138754, serial 1003, pt. 8 of 15, 3.

29   'Reagan Was FBI Informant in Hunt for Communists', *United Press International*, 26 August 1985.

30   Marc Eliot, *Walt Disney: Hollywood's Dark Prince* (London: Andre Deutsch, 1993), p. 123.

31   Ibid, p. 124.

32   FBI, 'Communist Infiltration — Motion Picture Industry (COMPIC)', file 100-138754, serial 1003, pt. 8 of 15, 14.

33   Eliot, *Dark Prince*, pp. 169–70.

34   FBI, Walt Disney File, HQ 94-4-4667.

35   Eliot, *Dark Prince*, pp. 223–4.

36   FBI, Walt Disney File, HQ 94-4-4667, SAC, Los Angeles, to Hoover, 16 March 1961.

37   FBI, Walt Disney File, HQ 94-4-4667, SAC, Los Angeles, 10 May 1961.

38   Eliot, *Dark Prince*, p. 243.

39   FBI, file Joseph P. Kennedy, Boston Office to FBI Headquarters, 7 September 1943.

40   Ibid, FBI Report, 27 December 1943.

41   Ibid, Hoover to Boston FBI office, 24 August 1945.

42   Ibid, E.A. Tamm to Director, 16 October 1945.

43   Ibid, SAC Boston to FBI Director, 4 August 1950; Ibid, SAC Boston to FBI Director, 26 September 1950; Ibid, SAC Boston to FBI Director, 31 July 1950; Ibid, D.M. Ladd to A.H. Belmont, 16 October 1953.

44   Ibid, SAC Miami to Director, FBI, 7 January 1953.

45   Ibid, Hoover to Kennedy, 14 January 1953.

46 Ibid, 'Edgar' to 'Joe' 5 May 1953.

47 Ibid, SAC Boston to Director, FBI, 28 August 1953.

48 Stephan, *Communazis*, pp. 97–102.

49 Alexander Charns, *Cloak and Gavel: FBI Wiretaps, Bugs, Informers, and the Supreme Court* (Chicago, IL: University of Illinois Press, 1992), pp. 56–62, 65–6.

50 Sigmund Diamond, *Compromised Campus: The Collaboration of Universities with the Intelligence Community, 1945–1955* (New York, NY: Oxford University Press, 1992) pp. 139–40, 147–9.

51 Ibid, pp. 151–66.

52 Timothy Garton Ash, 'Orwell's List', *New York Review of Books*, vol. 50, no. 14, 25 September 2003; Hugh Wilford, *The CIA, the British Left, and the Cold War: Calling the Tune* (London: Routledge, 2003), pp. 60–2; Scott Lucas, *Orwell* (London: Haus Publishing, 2003), pp. 105–10. Malin Åkerström's description of such rationales as the 'denial of injury' argument would fit the defence made by Orwell supporters. Malin Åkerström, *Betrayal and Betrayers: The Sociology of Treachery* (London: Transaction Publishers, 1991), p. 123.

53 Herbert A. Philbrick, *I Led 3 Lives: Citizen, 'Communist', Counterspy* (London: Hamish Hamilton, 1952), pp. 63–5.

54 Ibid, pp. 65, 157, 285.

55 Kathryn S. Olmsted, *Red Spy Queen: Elizabeth Bentley and the Cold War at Home* (Chapel Hill, NC: University of North Carolina Press, 2002), pp. x, 70, 75, 124; Kathryn S. Olmsted, 'Blond Queens, Red Spiders and Neurotic Old Maids: Gender and Espionage in the Early Cold War', *Intelligence and National Security*, vol. 19, no. 1 (Spring 2004): 78–94.

56 Olmsted, *Red Spy Queen*, p. 134.

57 Robert M. Lichtman and Ronald D. Cohen, *Deadly Farce: Harvey Matusow and the Informer System in the McCarthy Era* (Urbana and Chicago: University of Illinois Press, 2004), pp. 28–34.

58 Matusow, as quoted in Lichtman and Cohen, *Deadly Farce*, p. 29.

59 Ellen Schrecker, *Many Are the Crimes: McCarthyism in America* (New York, NY: Little, Brown and Company, 1998), p. 312.

60 'The Professional Informer', *New York Times*, 5 February 1955.

61 Gordon Douglas, director, *I Was a Communist for the FBI*, 1951.

62 Daniel J. Leab, 'I Was a Communist for the FBI', *History Today*, vol. 46, no. 12 (1996): 42–7; R.E. 'Gus' Payne, *I Was a Communist for the FBI: Matt Cvetic* (Bloomington, IN: AuthorHouse, 2004), pp. 5, 10, 34–40. For more on the popular culture versions of these stories see Michael Kackman, 'Citizen, Communist, Counterspy: "I Led 3 Lives" and Television's Masculine Agent of History', *Cinema Journal*, vol. 38, no. 1 (1998): 98–114.

63 William Tulio Divale and James Joseph, *I Lived Inside the Campus Revolution* (New York, NY: Cowles Book Company, Inc., 1970), pp. vii–ix, 1–7,18–20, 48, 50, 82.

64 Ibid, p. 143.

65 Larry Grathwohl and Frank Reagan, *Bringing Down America: An FBI Informer with the Weathermen* (New Rochelle, NY: Arlington House Publishers, 1976), pp. 26–7, 43–5. For more on the history of the Weather Underground, see Ron Jacobs *The Way the Wind Blew: A History of the Weather Underground* (London: Verso, 1997).

66 Ibid, pp. 75–6, 110–11, 123–4, 154. For a critical view of Grathwohl, see Ward Churchill and Jim Vander Wall, *The COINTEPRO Papers* (Boston, MA: South End Press, 2002), pp. 223–4.

67 Grathwohl and Reagan, *Bringing Down America*, pp. 164, 179; David Cunningham, *There's Something Happening Here: The New Left, the Klan, and FBI Counterintelligence* (London: University of California Press, 2004), pp. 176–7.

68 'Former FBI Informant Details Spying on Radical William Ayers', *The O'Reilly Factor*, 28 October 2008, www.foxnews.com/story/0,2933,445684,00.html (accessed 18 May 2009); 'Eyewitness to the Ayers' Revolution', *Pajamas Media*, 28 October 2008, http://pajamasmedia.com/blog/eyewitness-to-the-ayers-revolution/ (accessed 18 May 2009).

69 Church Committee, 'Final Report of the Select Committee to Study Governmental Operations with Respect to Intelligence Activities United States Senate', (Washington: Congress, 1976), www.aarclibrary.org/publib/church/reports/vol6/contents.htm (accessed 15 November 2007).

70 Ibid.

71 Cunningham, *There's Something Happening Here*, p. 75.

72 Gary May, *The Informant: The FBI, the Ku Klux Klan, and the Murder of Viola Liuzzo* (New Haven and London: Yale University Press, 2005), pp. 368–9.

73 Luke Fisher, with Warren Caragata, 'Spies under Fire', *Maclean's*, 31 October 1994; Jim Bronskill, 'CSIS Informant Defends Heritage Front Role', *Canadian Press*, 10 August 2004; Andrew Mitrovica, 'Front Man', *The Walrus*, September 2004; Andrew Mitrovica, 'Droege Is Gone, but the Hate Lives On', *The Walrus Online*, 25 April 2005.

74 Rhéal Séguin, 'In Book, Morin Defends His Role as Informant', *Globe and Mail*, 3 April 2006; Jean-Paul Brodeur, 'Undercover Policing in Canada: A Study of Its Consequences', in Cyrille Fijnaut and Gary T. Marx, eds, *Undercover Policing in Comparative Perspective* (London: Kluwer, 1995), p. 84; Robert McKenzie, 'Morin Shakes the Soul of Quebec Independence', *Toronto Star*, 10 May 1992; 'Witness Believes News of Morin Gave Lévesque a Mild Heart Attack', *Toronto Star*, 13 May 1992; For more on Morin's activities, see Normand Lester, *Enquêtes sur les services secrets* (Montreal, QC: Les Éditions de l'Homme, 1998); Claude Morin, *L'affaire Morin: légendes, sottises et calomnies* (Montreal, QC: Boréal, 2006).

75 Montreal Police report, 14 November 1970, as quoted in Carole de Vault and William Johnson, *The Informer: Confessions of an Ex-Terrorist* (Toronto, ON: Fleet Books, 1982), pp. 143–4.

76 de Vault and Johnson, *The Informer*, pp. 113–21, 196, 240; 'The Saga of Carole de Vault', www.mcgill.ca/files/maritimelaw/Q.doc (accessed 18 May 2009).

77   David Leppard, 'Diana Driver Was Secret Informer', *Times*, 26 February 2006; Giles Tremlett, 'Spanish Novelist Spied for Franco's Regime', *Guardian*, 25 September 2004; 'Spanish Laureate "Was Informer"', *BBC News*, 28 September 2004, http://news.bbc.co.uk/2/hi/europe/3689746.stm (accessed 29 September 2004); Donald Macintyre, 'Jerusalem Mayor Spied on Terrorists for MI5', *Independent*, 30 March 2007; 'Timothy Leary Was FBI Informer', *BBC News*, 29 June 1999, http://news.bbc.co.uk/2/hi/americas/380815.stm (accessed 15 June 2005); 'Turn On, Tune In, Rat Out', *The Smoking Gun*, www.thesmokinggun.com/leary/leary.html (accessed 10 December 2008).

Notes to Chapter 5: The Informer State

1   Malin Åkerström, *Betrayal and Betrayers: The Sociology of Treachery* (London: Transaction Publishers, 1991), p. 21.
2   David Childs and Richard Popplewell, *The Stasi: The East German Intelligence and Security Service* (London: Macmillan Press Ltd, 1996), p. 111.
3   On the phenomenon of 'lustration' see, for example, later in this chapter and Tina Rosenberg, *The Haunted Land: Facing Europe's Ghosts after Communism* (New York, NY: Vintage Books, 1995).
4   Michel Foucault, *Discipline and Punish: The Birth of the Prison* Trans. by Alan Sheridan (London: Penguin, 1977), pp. 200–9; William G. Staples, *The Culture of Surveillance: Discipline and Social Control in the United States* (New York, NY: St. Martin's, 1997), p. 4.
5   Robert Gellately, 'Denunciations in Twentieth-Century Germany: Aspects of Self-Policing in the Third Reich and the German Democratic Republic', *Journal of Modern History*, vol. 68, no. 4 (1996): 931.
6   Cyrille Fijnaut, and Gary T. Marx, 'Introduction: The Normalization of Undercover Policing in the West: Historical and Contemporary Perspectives', in Cyrille Fijnaut, and Gary T. Marx, eds, *Undercover Police Surveillance in Comparative Perspective* (Boston, MA: Kluwer Law International, 1995), p. 22.
7   Fijnaut and Marx, 'Introduction', 22.
8   Nurit Schleifman, *Undercover Agents in the Russian Revolutionary Movement: The SR Party, 1902–1914* (New York, NY: St. Martin's Press, 1988), p. ix.
9   Schleifman, *Undercover Agents . . .*', p. 19.
10 Ibid, 12; Walter Laqueur, *A History of Terrorism* (London: Transaction Publishers, 2002), p. 98.
11 Anna Geifman, *Entangled in Terror: The Azef Affair and the Russian Revolution* (Wilmington, DE: SR Books, 2000), p. 167. The higher figures were supplied by Maurice LaPorte in his 1935 history of the Okhrana that he based on the organization's actual records. See Schleifman, *Undercover Agents . . .*', p. 47.
12 Schleifman, *Undercover Agents . . .*', p. 35.
13 Ibid, p. 48.

14   Frederic S. Zuckerman, *The Tsarist Secret Police in Russian Society, 1880–1917* (London: Macmillan Press Ltd, 1996), pp. 39–42.

15   Zuckerman, *The Tsarist Secret Police . . .*', p. 41.

16   Schleifman, *Undercover Agents . . .*', p. 38.

17   Steven Greer, 'Towards a Sociological Model of the Police Informant', *British Journal of Sociology*, vol. 46, no. 3 (1995): 509–27, 516.

18   Ibid.

19   Zuckerman, *The Tsarist Secret Police . . .*', pp. 47–8, 51.

20   Ibid, pp. 55–7.

21   Schleifman, *Undercover Agents . . .*', pp. 27, 70. Some years later, an informer in Northern Ireland would allegedly perform a similar function on behalf of British intelligence, which tampered with bullets intended for Sinn Féin president Gerry Adams, who was shot but survived. Martin Ingram, and Greg Harkin, *Stakeknife: Britain's Secret Agents in Ireland* (Dublin: The O'Brien Press Ltd, 2004), pp. 174–8.

22   Zuckerman, *The Tsarist Secret Police . . .*', p. 47.

23   Ibid, p. 43.

24   Schleifman, *Undercover Agents . . .*', p. 57.

25   Ibid, pp. 75, 81, 194–6.

26   E. P. Thompson, *The Making of the English Working Class* (London: Penguin Books, 1986), p. 493.

27   Foucault, *Discipline and Punish*, p. 201.

28   Not surprisingly, the actual story was far more complicated. See Catriona Kelly, *Comrade Pavlik: The Rise and Fall of a Soviet Boy Hero* (London: Granta Books, 2005). See also Barrington Moore, *Terror and Progress USSR: Some Sources of Change and Stability in the Soviet Dictatorship* (Cambridge, MA: Harvard University Press, 1954).

29   Fijnaut and Marx, 'Introduction', 22.

30   Louise Shelley, 'Soviet Undercover Work', in Cyrille Fijnaut and Gary T. Marx, eds, *Undercover Police Surveillance in Comparative Perspective* (London: Kluwer, 1995), p. 156.

31   A fear of *stukach*, meaning someone who knocks at the door but which was a term for a 'stool-pigeon', existed. Vladimir A. Kozlov, 'Denunciation and Its Functions in Soviet Governance', in Sheila Fitzpatrick and Robert Gellately, eds, *Accusatory Practices: Denunciations in Modern European History, 1789–1989* (Chicago and London: University of Chicago Press, 1997), p. 129; Ilya Zemtsov, *Encyclopedia of Soviet Life* (Edison, NJ: Transaction Publishers, 1991), p. 96; Shelley, 'Soviet Undercover Work', pp. 162–3.

32   Shelley, 'Soviet Undercover Work', pp. 162–3.

33   Ibid, p. 168.

34   Ibid, p. 168.

35   Robert Gellately, 'Denunciations in Twentieth-Century Germany: Aspects of Self-Policing in the Third Reich and the German Democratic Republic', *Journal of Modern History*, vol. 68, no. 4 (1996): 931.

36 Sheila Fitzpatrick, 'Signals from Below: Soviet Letters of Denunciation of the 1930s', in Sheila Fitzpatrick and Robert Gellately, eds, *Accusatory Practices: Denunciations in Modern European History, 1789–1989* (Chicago and London: University of Chicago Press, 1997), pp. 110, 112.

37 Fitzpatrick, 'Signals from Below', p. 117.

38 Ibid, p. 117; Vladimir A. Kozlov, 'Denunciation and Its Functions in Soviet Governance', in Sheila Fitzpatrick and Robert Gellately, eds, *Accusatory Practices: Denunciations in Modern European History, 1789–1989* (Chicago and London: University of Chicago Press, 1997), pp. 130–1, 137.

39 Ilona Vinogradova, 'The Return of the Snitch: a Despised Soviet-Era Custom Enjoys a New Vogue after Beslan, *Russia Profile*, October 2004, www.russiaprofile. org (accessed 3 November 2004); 'KGB Veteran Calls for Restoration of Soviet Informer System to Fight Terror', *Moscow News*, 7 September 2004, www. mosnews.com/news/2004/09/07/kgbterror.shtml (accessed 7 September 2004).

40 Shelley, 'Soviet Undercover Work', p. 157.

41 Anthony Glees, *The Stasi Files: East Germany's Secret Operations against Britain* (London: Free Press, 2003), p. 3; Anna Funder, *Stasiland: Stories from Behind the Berlin Wall* (London: Granta Books, 2003), p. 57. Funder has the numbers as Gestapo 1 to 2,000, the KGB 1 to 5,830 and the GDR 1 to 63, although she inexplicably includes IMs in the GDR figure.

42 Robert Gellately, 'The Gestapo and German Society: Political Denunciation in the Gestapo Case Files', *Journal of Modern History*, vol. 60, no. 4 (1988): 654–94, 657, 660–1; Robert Gellately, *The Gestapo and German Society: Enforcing Racial Policy, 1933–1945* (Oxford: Clarendon, 1991), p. 5.

43 George C. Browder, *Hitler's Enforcers: The Gestapo and the SS Security Service in the Nazi Revolution* (New York, NY: Oxford University Press, 1996), p. 73.

44 Gellately, *The Gestapo and German Society*, pp. 61, 64.

45 Gellately, 'The Gestapo and German Society', 688; Gellately, *The Gestapo and German Society*, pp. 61–5.

46 Gellately, 'The Gestapo and German Society', 687–8.

47 Ibid, 688.

48 Ibid, 689–90; Gellately, *The Gestapo and German Society*, pp. 63–4.

49 Gellately, 'Denunciations in Twentieth-Century Germany', 949; Gellately, 'The Gestapo and German Society', 687.

50 Gellately, 'Denunciations in Twentieth-Century Germany', 949.

51 Ibid, 944.

52 Gellately, 'The Gestapo and German Society', 686; Gellately, 'Denunciations in Twentieth-Century Germany', 961, 943, 940.

53 Gellately, 'Denunciations in Twentieth-Century Germany', 945.

54 Gellately, 'The Gestapo and German Society', 670.

55 Ibid, 663.

56 Mary Fulbrook, *Anatomy of a Dictatorship: Inside the GDR, 1949–1989* (Oxford: Oxford University Press, 1995), p. 52.

57 Funder, *Stasiland*, p. 57; Glees, *The Stasi Files*, p. 3.

58 Gellately, 'Denunciations in Twentieth-Century Germany', 956, 958.

59 For the various categories see Mike Dennis, *The Stasi: Myth and Reality* (London: Pearson, 2003), p. 93.

60 John O. Koehler, *Stasi: The Untold Story of the East German Secret Police*. Boulder, CO: Westview Press, 1999), p. 8; Fulbrook, *Anatomy of a Dictatorship*, p. 50; Funder, *Stasiland*, p. 57; Dennis, *The Stasi*, p. 92; Childs and Popplewell, *The Stasi*, p. 84.

61 Fulbrook, *Anatomy of a Dictatorship*, p. 50; Gellately, 'Denunciations in Twentieth-Century Germany', 954–5.

62 Koehler, *Stasi*, p. 8; Childs and Popplewell, *The Stasi*, p. 86.

63 Barbara Miller, *Narratives of Guilt and Compliance in Unified Germany* (London and New York: Routledge, 1999), pp. 73, 94; Dennis, *The Stasi*, p. 91.

64 Gellately, 'Denunciations in Twentieth-Century Germany', 963.

65 Alison Lewis, 'Ex-Gendering Remembrance: Memory, Gender, and Informers for the Stasi', *New German Critique*, vol. 86 (2002): 113–15; Childs and Popplewell, *The Stasi*, p. 85.

66 Miller, *Narratives of Guilt . . .*', pp. 19–20, 46.

67 Ibid, pp. 14, 21.

68 Fulbrook, *Anatomy of a Dictatorship*, p. 51.

69 As quoted and translated from the Stasi original in Miller, *Narratives of Guilt . . .*', p. 23.

70 Funder, *Stasiland*, p. 200.

71 Miller, *Narratives of Guilt . . .*', pp. 14–16.

72 Gellately, 'Denunciations in Twentieth-Century Germany', 958.

73 Miller, *Narratives of Guilt . . .*', p. 36.

74 Dennis, *The Stasi*, p. 97.

75 Miller, *Narratives of Guilt . . .*', pp. 39–40; Dennis, *The Stasi*, pp. 96–7.

76 Miller, *Narratives of Guilt . . .*', pp. 35, 46; Gellately, 'Denunciations in Twentieth-Century Germany', 957.

77 Miller, *Narratives of Guilt . . .*', p. 47; Dennis, *The Stasi*, pp. 97, 99.

78 Funder, *Stasiland*, p. 267; Miller, *Narratives of Guilt . . .*', p. 49; Lewis, 'Ex-Gendering Remembrance', 121; Dennis, *The Stasi*, pp. 104–6.

79 Dennis, *The Stasi*, p. 97.

80 Åkerström, *Betrayal and Betrayers*, p. 123. This was the argument made by a defender of George Orwell against charges that he was an informer. Timothy Garton Ash, 'Orwell's List', *New York Review of Books*, vol. 50, no. 14, 25 September 2003.

81 Funder, *Stasiland*, p. 55; Miller, *Narratives of Guilt . . .*', p. 77.

82 Fulbrook, *Anatomy of a Dictatorship*, p. 50.

83 Gellately, 'Denunciations in Twentieth-Century Germany', 956. Miller, *Narratives of Guilt . . .*', p. 41.

84 Dennis, *The Stasi*, p. 101.

85 Ibid, p. 100.

86 Gellately, 'Denunciations in Twentieth-Century Germany', 957.

87 Dennis, *The Stasi*, p. 92.

88 Miller, *Narratives of Guilt . . .*', pp. 21–2.

89 Ibid, p. 41.

90 Koehler, *Stasi*, p. 143.

91 Miller, *Narratives of Guilt . . .*', p. 22; Gellately, 'Denunciations in Twentieth-Century Germany', 958.

92 Lewis, 'Ex-Gendering Remembrance', 127, 131–2.

93 Dennis, *The Stasi*, p. 99.

94 Miller, *Narratives of Guilt . . .*', p. 45; Dennis, *The Stasi*, p. 100.

95 Miller, *Narratives of Guilt . . .*', p. 68.

96 Rosenberg, *The Haunted Land*, pp. 379–92.

97 Dennis, *The Stasi*, p. 95; Rosenberg, *The Haunted Land*, pp. 299–300.

98 Miller, *Narratives of Guilt . . .*', pp. 53, 61–5; Dennis, *The Stasi*, p. 100.

99 Edward Peterson, *The Limits of Secret Police Power: The Magdeburger Stasi, 1953–1989* (New York, NY: Peter Lang Publishing Inc., 2004), p. 96.

100 Dennis, *The Stasi*, pp. 102–3.

101 Ibid, pp. 135, 164, 166.

102 Miller, *Narratives of Guilt . . .*', p. 136.

103 Ibid, pp. 107, 141; Dennis, *The Stasi*, pp. 116–18. For Sacha Anderson's reaction to his exposure as an informer, see Feiwel Kupferberg, *The Rise and Fall of the German Democratic Republic* (Transaction Publishers, Edison, NJ: 2002), pp. 179–80.

104 Ibid, p. 133.

105 'Germany Won't Ban Sledder Who Informed', *New York Times*, 11 February 1992.

106 'How Should We Judge Katarina Witt Today?' *Ottawa Citizen*, 13 May 2002; 'Sports Notebook', *Houston Chronicle*, 24 June 1992.

107 Toby Helm, 'Witt Wanted to Join Stasi', *Daily Telegraph*, 13 May 2002; Tony Paterson, 'Witt Had Alliance with Stasi: Police Files Show Star Got Special Treatment', *Calgary Herald*, 5 May 2002; Tony Paterson, 'Stasi Files Reveal Katarina Witt Was Willing Accomplice', *Guardian*, 2 February 2002.

108 Dennis, *The Stasi*, pp. 146–8.

109 Popplewell and Childs, *The Stasi*, p. 92.

110 Miller, *Narratives of Guilt . . .*', p. 75; Childs and Popplewell, *The Stasi*, p. 84; Dennis, *The Stasi*, pp. 158–9.

111 Tony Paterson, 'My Mother Spied on Me for the Stasi Secret Police', *Daily Telegraph*, 7 April 2002; Dennis, *The Stasi*, p. 159; Miller, *Narratives of Guilt . . .*', p. 94; Childs and Popplewell, *The Stasi*, p. 110.

112 Rosenberg, *The Haunted Land*, pp. 72, 53–4, 87–8, 58.

113 Former StB member, as quoted in Rosenberg, *The Haunted Land*, p. 58.

114 Dennis Deletant, *Ceauşescu and the Securitate: Coercion and Dissent in Romania, 1965–1989* (London: Hurst & Company, 1995), p. 394; Marian Chiriac, 'Rights-Romania: Few Apply for Access to Secret Police Files', Inter

Press Service, 2 August 2001; Phelim McAleer, 'Few Interested in Tales of Ceauşescu's Informers', *Financial Times*, 25 April 2001.

115 'Romania: Author of Law on Securitate Files Reveals Names of Members', BBC Monitoring, 9 January 2002.

116 Deletant, *Ceauşescu and the Securitate*, p. 395; Chiriac, 'Rights-Romania'.

117 Ben Aris, 'Fresh Stasi Files Could Name German MPs', *Guardian*, 8 July 2003.

118 '"Lustration" Loses in Poland', *New York Times*, 7 June 1992.

119 Corey Ross, *The East German Dictatorship: Problems and Perspectives in the Interpretation of the GDR* (London: Oxford University Press, 2002), p. 183; Rosenberg, *The Haunted Land*, p. 297.

120 Miller, *Narratives of Guilt . . .*', p. 129.

121 Dennis, *The Stasi*, p. 241; Miller, *Narratives of Guilt . . .*', p. 89; Rosenberg, *The Haunted Land*, pp. 320–7.

122 Julius Strauss, 'Communist Files Open to Public: Names of Informers Are Withheld from "Enemies"', *Daily Telegraph*, 14 October 1997.

123 Gabriel Ronay, 'Hungary's Secret Police Informers Unmasked', *Japan Today*, 1 October 2002; Pablo Gorondi, 'Hungary Agent, Informant Names Leaked', *Kansas City Star*, 11 February 2005. For a list of stories about informing revelations in Hungary see www.eurotopics.net/en/magazin/stasi-2008-01/ int-link-stasi-2008-01/ (accessed 15 March 2008).

124 Alison Mutler, 'Old Secret Police Files Cast Shadow Over Romanians', *Associated Press*, 19 June 1998; Jeffrey Fleischman, 'Romania Torn Over Whether To Expose Communist Informers', *Philadelphia Inquirer*, 20 December 1998.

125 Marian Chiriac, 'Romania: Author of Law on Securitate Files Reveals Names of Members', BBC Monitoring, 9 January 2002; McAleer, 'Few Interested in Tales of Ceauşescu's Informers'.

126 Alison Mutler, 'Thousands Form Human Chain, Calling for the Opening of Romania's Communist-Era Secret Police Files', *Associated Press*, 11 March 2003; 'Names of Former Informers to be Published in Romania', Hungarian News Agency Corporation, 11 September 2003.

127 'AP Wins Cleric Libel Case', *Associated Press*, 6 November 2001; 'Toekes Did Not Collaborate with the Securitate, Says Publisher of Files', *Associated Press*, 9 February 2001.

128 'Daily Prints Hungarian Bishop's Note to Secret Police', BBC Summary of World Broadcasts, 5 January 1995. For the printed pledge, see Chapter 4.

129 Rosenberg, *The Haunted Land*, p. 89.

130 Peter Finn, 'Walesa Cleared as Informer; Court Finds Plot to Sabotage His Nobel Nomination', *Washington Post*, 12 April 2000; Stephen Erlanger, 'Polish Watchdog Nips at Walesa's Heels', *New York Times*, 21 August 2000.

131 Finn, 'Walesa Cleared as Informer'.

132 'Poland in Uproar over Leak of Spy Files', *Guardian*, 5 February 2005. A similar issue arose in Hungary, where a handful of names of alleged Hungarian informers were posted on a website in February 2005 with the threat that more would follow. Pablo Gorondi, 'Researchers Threaten to Publish Names

of Hungarian Communist Agents, Informants', *Associated Press*, 11 February 2005.

133   Richard Bernstein, 'Poland Exhumes the Skeletons in Its Communist Closet', *New York Times*, 14 January 2005; Kamil Tchorek, 'Poland's Communist Informers Caught Red-Handed on the Net', *Independent*, 15 February 2005; Jan Cienski, 'Poles Nervous as their Secret Past Becomes Public', *Financial Times*, 22 February 2005; Monika Scislowska, 'Publication of List of Communist-Era Agents and Informers Is Painful Experience for Many Poles', *New York Times*, 13 February 2005; Vanessa Gera, 'Polish Parliament Approves New Law to Help People on List of Communist-Era Secret Police, Victims', *Associated Press*, 4 March 2005.

134   Tina Rosenberg, '15 Years after the Fall, Poland Asks: Who Was Nowak?' *New York Times*, 24 January 2005.

135   'Former Government Spokeswoman Challenges Accusations of Communist Collaboration', *Associated Press*, 20 May 2005.

136   Richard Bernstein, 'Poland Exhumes the Skeletons in Its Communist Closet', *New York Times*, 14 January 2005; Rosenberg, '15 Years after the Fall . . .'.

137   Rosenberg, *The Haunted Land*, pp. 100–5.

138   Rosenberg, '15 Years after the Fall . . .'.

139   Martina Jurinová, 'Banáš Listed as StB Informer', *Slovak Spectator*, 12 January 2005.

140   RSI, 'Former President Schuster Was an StB Informant', *Novy Cas*, 18 November 2004.

141   In Iran, for example, networks of informers have been established at the country's universities, hotbeds of opposition to the regime. Genevieve Abdo, 'The Next Generation in the Gulf', *Washington Quarterly*, vol. 24, no. 4 (2001): 163.

Notes to Chapter 6: Informers in the 'War on Terror'

1   John Hiscock, 'LA's Spy-in-the-Sky Drone Sparks Privacy Concerns', *Independent*, 20 June 2006.

2   'Spooked Spooks at the CIA', *Time*, 28 November 1977.

3   Bob Woodward, *Plan of Attack: The Road to War* (New York, NY: Simon and Schuster, 2004), p. 213. Patrick Radden Keefe, *Chatter: Dispatches from the Secret World of Global Eavesdropping* (New York, NY: Random House, 2005), p. xiv.

4   Jason Burke, 'Omar Was a Normal British Teenager Who Loved His Little Brother and Man Utd. So Why at 24 Did He Plan to Blow up a Nightclub in Central London?', *Observer*, 20 January 2008.

5   Craig Whitlock, 'Al Qaeda Detainee's Mysterious Release', *Washington Post*, 30 January 2006; Paul Pillar, *Terrorism and US Foreign Policy* (Washington, DC: Brookings Institution Press, 2004), p. 112.

6   James Bamford, 'Big Brother Is Listening', *Atlantic Monthly*, April 2006.

7 Assistant Commissioner Peter Clarke of the Metropolitan Police, as quoted in Transcript of 'Real Spooks', *BBC Panorama*, 30 April 2007; Jeff Sallot, 'Canada Could Escape Attack, CSIS Says', *Globe and Mail*, 20 June 2006.

8 Intelligence and Security Committee, 'Could 7/7 Have Been Prevented', as quoted in Richard Norton-Taylor, 'MI5 and Police Had Limited Relationship', *Guardian*, 19 May 2009.

9 Robert Mueller, as quoted in Office of the Inspector General, 'The Federal Bureau of Investigation's Compliance with the Attorney General's Investigative Guidelines', (Washington, DC: Office of the Inspector General, Department of Justice, 2005), 65.

10 'Preparing for the 21st century', www.gpoaccess.gov/int/report.html, as quoted in Mark D. Villaverde, 'Structuring the Prosecutor's Duty to Search the Intelligence Community for Brady Material', *Cornell Law Review*, vol. 88, no. 5 (2003): 1521.

11 Suzanne Breen, 'Nobody Knows Who to Trust', *Sunday Tribune*, 9 January 2005.

12 Amy Waldman, 'Prophetic Justice', *Atlantic Monthly*, October 2006; Andrea Elliott, 'Undercover Work Deepens Police-Muslim Tensions', *New York Times*, 27 May 2006.

13 Jeff Barnard, 'Undercover Informant Used in Ecoterrorism Investigation', *San Diego Union-Tribune*, 12 December 2005; Hal Bernton, 'An Activist-Turned-Informant', *Seattle Times*, 7 May 2006; Jack Grimston, 'Animal Terrorist Group Foiled by Informant Dressed as a Beagle', *Sunday Times*, 1 March 2009.

14 Andrew Roberts, 'Bring Back 007', *Spectator*, 6 October 2001; Troy Sookdeo, 'The Importance of Intelligence', *The Diamondback*, 8 October 2001; Laurence Chollet, 'Billions for Security, but Feeling Insecure', *Record*, 15 September 2001; Jonathan Freedland, 'Use Brains, Not Brawn', *Guardian*, 4 December 2002; Rob de Wijk, 'Tools to Combat Terrorism', *Washington Quarterly*, vol. 25, no. 1 (Winter 2002); Max Hastings, 'In the Fight against Al-Qaida We Need People, Not Tanks', *Guardian*, 17 October 2005.

15 Douglas Pasternak, 'Squeezing Them, Leaving Them', *US News and World Report*, 8 July 2002.

16 Amy Zegart, *Spying Blind: The CIA, The FBI, and the Origins of 9/11* (Princeton, NJ: Princeton University Press, 2007), p. 87.

17 Edward Jenkinson, as quoted in Bernard Porter, *The Origins of the Vigilant State: The London Metropolitan Police Special Branch before the First World War* (London: Weidenfeld and Nicolson, 1987), p. 66; Bernard Porter, *Plots and Paranoia: A History of Political Espionage in Britain, 1790–1988* (London: Routledge, 1989), p. 97. Henri Le Caron made a career out of infiltrating Fenian groups and later wrote about his experiences. Henri Le Caron, *Twenty-Five Years in the Secret Service: The Recollections of a Spy* (London: EP Publishing, 1974).

18 Bruce Hoffman, 'A Nasty Business', *Atlantic Monthly*, January 2002; Alistair Horne, *A Savage War of Peace: Algeria, 1954–1962* (New York, NY: New York Review of Books, 2006), pp. 259–61.

19   Caroline Elkins, *Imperial Reckoning: The Untold Story of Britain's Gulag in Kenya* (New York, NY: Henry Holt and Company, 2005), pp. 182–4.

20   Matthew Teague, 'Double Blind', *Atlantic Monthly*, April 2006; Caroline Elkins, 'The Wrong Lesson', *Atlantic Monthly*, July/August 2005.

21   Frank Kitson, *Low Intensity Operations: Subversion, Insurgency, and Peacekeeping* (St. Petersburg, FL: Hailer Publisher, 1992).

22   Steven Greer, *Supergrasses: Study in Anti-Terrorist Law Enforcement in Northern Ireland* (Oxford, UK: Clarendon Press, 1995), pp. 32, 34–42; Peter Taylor, *Brits: The War against the IRA* (London: Bloomsbury, 2002), pp. 3, 55; Teague, 'Double Blind'.

23   Greer, *Supergrasses*, p. 3; Sean O'Callaghan, *The Informer* (London: Corgi Books, 1999); Teague, 'Double Blind'.

24   Thomas Mockaitis, *British Counterinsurgency in the Post-Imperial Era*, p. 121; Coogan, *The I.R.A.*, p. 519.

25   British military commander as quoted in Mark Urban, *Big Boy' Rules: The Bestselling Story of the SAS and the Secret Struggle against the IRA* (London: Faber and Faber Ltd., 1992), p. 101.

26   Teague, 'Double Blind'.

27   Bruce Hoffman, 'The Logic of Suicide Terrorism', *Atlantic Monthly*, June 2003.

28   Vernon Loeb, 'CIA Giving Fired Agent Top Award', *Washington Post*, 10 March 2000; Tim Weiner, 'What the Widows Weren't Told', *New York Times*, 12 May 1996.

29   Amy Zegart, *Spying Blind: The CIA, the FBI, and the Origins of 9/11* (Princeton, NJ: Princeton University Press, 2007), p. 37.

30   Bill Gertz, *Breakdown: How America's Intelligence Failures Led to September 11* (Washington: Regnery, 2002), p. 68.

31   James Risen, 'Report Faults CIA's Recruitment Rules', *New York Times*, 18 July 2002.

32   Pillar, *Terrorism and US Foreign Policy*, p. 112.

33   Risen, 'Report Faults C.I.A.'s Recruitment Rules'.

34   Richard K. Betts, 'Fixing Intelligence', in Russell D. Howard and Reid L. Sawyer, eds, *Terrorism and Counterterrorism: Understanding the New Security Environment* (New York, NY: McGraw-Hill, 2003), p. 461.

35   Pillar, *Terrorism and US Foreign Policy*, pp. 110–11; Michael Scheuer, 'Why It's So Hard to Infiltrate Al-Qaeda', *Atlantic Monthly*, April 2005.

36   Robert Baer, *See No Evil: The True Story of a Ground Soldier in the CIA's War on Terrorism* (New York, NY: Three Rivers Press, 2003), pp. xv–xvi.

37   Permanent Select Committee on Intelligence, House of Representatives, 'IC21: The Intelligence Community in the 21st century', 12 June 1996, www.access. gpo.gov/congress/house/intel/ic21/ic21009.html (accessed 15 January 2007).

38   Villaverde, 'Structuring The Prosecutor's Duty . . .', 1527–28.

39   9/11 Commission Final Report, 415, 433.

40   Craig Whitlock, 'After a Decade at War with West, Al-Qaeda Still Impervious to Spies', *Washington Post*, 20 March 2008.

41 Melinda Liu, with Robin Sparkman, 'The Mysterious Informant', *Newsweek*, 16 August 1993, 28; Timothy Naftali, *Blind Spot: The Secret History of American Counterterrorism* (New York, NY: Basic Books, 2005), pp. 230–4.

42 Seth Ackerman, 'Who Knew? The Unanswered Questions of 9/11', *In These Times*, 29 September 2003. For the profile of another valuable FBI informer named Jamal Ahmed al-Fadl, see Jane Mayer, *The Dark Side: The Inside Story of How the War on Terror Turned into a War on American Ideals* (New York, NY: Anchor Books, 2009), pp. 116–17.

43 Dan Eggen, 'FBI Agents Still Lacking Arabic Skills', *Washington Post*, 11 October 2006. See also 'Intel Agencies Seek Help Recruiting Immigrants', *Associated Press*, 17 May 2008.

44 Reuel Marc Gerecht, 'The Counterterrorist Myth', *Atlantic Monthly*, July/August 2001.

45 Ibid.

46 Peter Clarke, 'Learning from Experience — Counter Terrorism in the UK since 9/11', Colin Cramphorn Memorial Lecture, 24 April 2007.

47 Michael Evans, 'Recruit Muslim Spies in War on Terror, Urges New Security Chief', *Times*, 9 July 2007; Patrick Hennessy, 'Fight Against Terror Could Take 15 Years', *Sunday Telegraph*, 8 July 2007. See also 'Britain Needs More Terror Informers: Call', *Washington Times*, 27 May 2005.

48 Phillip Johnston, 'MI5 Seeks "Older, Wiser Women"', *Daily Telegraph*, 10 May 2005; Michael Evans, 'More Britons Are Turning to Terror, Says MI5 Director', *Times*, 10 November 2006; Barney Calman, 'Policing with Passion; Is the Met Police Still Prejudiced against Ethnic Minorities and Women?', *Evening Standard*, 10 July 2006; Martin Bright, 'Revealed: MI6 Plan to Infiltrate Extremists', *Observer*, 4 September 2005. For a discussion of the problems the CIA had in infiltrating Al Qaeda pre-9/11 see Gerecht, 'The Counterterrorist Myth'.

49 For example, see Home Office and Foreign Office, 'Young Muslims and Extremism', 2004, www.globalsecurity.org/security/library/report/2004/muslimext-uk.htm#gfc (accessed 20 December 2006).

50 Robert Verkaik, 'Muslims Hit by Trebling in Stop and Search', *Independent*, 1 May 2009.

51 Crispin Black as quoted in Peter Oborne, *The Use and Abuse of Terror: The Construction of a False Narrative on the Domestic Terror Threat* (London: Centre for Policy Studies, 2006), p. 35.

52 'One-in-Ten Muslim Students Would Not Turn Police Informer, Survey', *Kuwait News Agency*, 21 September 2005.

53 Reg Whitaker, 'Refugees: The Security Dimension', *Citizenship Studies*, vol. 2, no. 3 (November 1998): 413–33; Peter Cheney, 'CSIS Agents Forced Him to Spy, Man Says', *Globe and Mail*, 15 January 2003.

54 Douglas A. Kash, 'Hunting Terrorists Using Confidential Informant Reward Programs', *Federal Bureau of Investigation's Law Enforcement Bulletin*, vol. 71, no. 4 (2002).

55 Walter Pincus, 'An Intelligence Gap Hinders US in Iraq', *Washington Post*, 24 December 2004.

56 Jonathan Finer, 'Informants Decide Fate of Iraqi Detainees', *Washington Post*, 13 September 2005.

57 'Revenge for Betraying Saddam's Sons', *Reuters*, www.iol.co.za/index.php?click_id=123&art_id=qw1086431402502B262&set_id=1 (accessed 12 February 2008).

58 Cindy Gonzalez, 'Baghdad Orphan Finds a New Home — Girls and Boys Town Takes in an Iraqi Teen Who Came to the Aid of US Forces', *Omaha World-Herald*, 20 October 2004.

59 'How a Boy Named Steve-O Became a Secret Weapon', *Age*, 5 October 2004.

60 Sean O'Neill, 'Proud Day for Spy Who Infiltrated Mosque', *Times*, 28 January 2008; Gershom Gorenberg, 'The Collaborator', *New York Times Magazine*, 18 August 2002.

61 Severin Carrell, 'MI5 "Left Al-Qa'ida Informant to Rot in Guantanamo Bay"', *Independent*, 5 June 2005; Craig Whitlock, 'Courted as Spies; Held as Combatants: British Residents Enlisted by MI5 after Sept. 11 Languish at Guantanamo', *Washington Post*, 2 April 2006. For an account of a prisoner at Guantanamo and MI5 efforts to recruit informers among British Muslims, see Moazzam Begg and Victoria Brittain, *Enemy Combatant: The Terrifying True Story of a Briton in Guantanamo* (London: Pocket Books, 2007), p. 90.

62 Robert Verkaik, 'How MI5 Attempted to Recruit Prison Camp Inmates', *Independent*, 6 May 2009; David Rose, 'MI5 "used Muslim 007" to Turn British Torture Victim in Moroccan Prison', *Daily Mail*, 16 May 2009.

63 Brendan Lyons, 'Mosque Welcomed in Informant', *Albany Times Union*, 8 August 2004; William K. Rashbaum and Kareem Fahim, 'Informer's Role in Bombing Plot', *New York Times*, Deborah Hastings, 'Terrorism Arrests: Snitch, Sting, then Controversy', *Associated Press*, 24 May 2009.

64 'FBI Informant Got Thousands of Dollars from FBI', *Newsday*, 10 February 2005.

65 Christopher Evans, Mark Rollenhagen and Mike Tobin, 'Terror Case Informant Has Had Money Woes', *Cleveland Plain Dealer*, 28 April 2006; Mike Tobin, Mark Rollenhagen and Christopher Evans, 'FBI's Informant Worked at Muslim Charity 3 Years', *Cleveland Plain Dealer*, 2 March 2006.

66 Carlyle Murphy and Wilbur Del Quenton, 'Terror Informant Ignites Himself near White House', *Washington Post*, 16 November 2004; William Glaberson, 'Terror Case Hinges on a Wobbly Key Player', *New York Times*, 27 November 2004; Anthony M. Destefano, 'Informant Says He Set Self on Fire as a Ploy', *Newsday*, 23 February 2005.

67 Don Thompson, 'Tapes: FBI Informer Pushed Suspect into Al-Qaida Camp', *Los Angeles Daily News*, 1 March 2006; Lee Romney, Eric Bailey and Josh Meyer, 'Sighting of Terrorist in Lodi Questioned', *Los Angeles Times*, 15 March 2006. For more on the case see Waldman, 'Prophetic Justice'.

68 Mark Hosenball, 'Terror Plot Takedown', *Newsweek*, 3–10 July 2006; Bob

Norman, 'Have Terror, Will Travel', *Broward-Palm Beach*, 22 November 2007; Kirk Semple, 'US Falters in Terror Case Against 7 in Miami', *New York Times*, 14 December 2007; Damien Cave and Carmen Gentile, 'Five Convicted in Plot to Blow Up Sears Tower', *New York Times*, 12 May 2009.

69   Tom Regan, 'Is Using Informants in Terror Cases Entrapment?', *Christian Science Monitor*, 13 July 2006; Colin Freeze, 'RCMP Agent Concedes Key Role in Set-Up, Running of Terrorist Training Camp', *Globe and Mail*, 31 January 2009; Isabel Teotonio, 'No Entrapment, Court Rules in Terror Case', *Toronto Star*, 24 March 2009.

70   'Army Intelligence Opposes Informant Campaign', 30 October 2005, www.israelnn.com/news.php3?id=91991 (accessed 30 November 2005).

71   Tom Hays, 'Fake Threats Frustrate Officials', *Buffalo News*, 15 October 2005; 'FBI Believes Tip about Tunnel Plot Was Not Accurate', *WTOP News*, 23 October 2005, www.wtopnews.com/index.php?nid=25&sid=601499 (accessed 28 October 2005); 'Subway Threat May Have Been Informant's Hoax', *Washington Post*, 12 October 2005.

72   Phillip Knightley, 'MI5, the Police and the Inside Story of a Raid that Went Wrong', *Daily Mail*, 6 June 2006; Sophie Goodchild and Francis Elliott, 'Tip-Off by Police Informer Led to Forest Gate Raid', *Independent*, 11 June 2006; Audrey Gillan, Richard Norton-Taylor and Vikram Dodd, 'Raided, Arrested, Released: The Price of Wrong Intelligence', *Guardian*, 12 June 2006; Terri Judd, 'Informant Who Triggered Forest Gate Raid Was an "Utter Incompetent"', *Independent*, 19 June 2006.

73   David Lyon, *Surveillance after September 11* (Cambridge, UK: Polity Press, 2003), pp. 34–5.

74   'Australian Islamic Leader Rejects Call to "Spy" on Muslims', *Agence France Presse*, 13 November 2005; Michael Evans, 'Recruit Muslim Spies in War on Terror, Urges New Security Chief', *Times*, 9 July 2007; Basia Spalek, Salwa El Awa, Laura Zahra McDonald, 'Police-Muslim Engagement and Partnerships for the Purposes of Counter-Terrorism: An Examination', University of Birmingham Report, May 2009, 12, 33, 36–7.

75   Rone Tempest, 'FBI Informer Begins His Testimony in Terror Trial', *Los Angeles Times*, 23 February 2006.

76   Wael Mousfar, as quoted in *File on 4*: 'US Muslims', BBC Radio Transcript, 4 July 2006; William K. Rashbaum, 'Police Informer in Terror Trial Takes Stand', *New York Times*, 25 April 2006; Elliott, 'Undercover Work Deepens Police-Muslim Tensions'.

77   Athan G. Theoharis, 'The FBI and the American Legion Contact Program, 1940–1966', *Political Science Quarterly*, vol. 100, no. 2 (1985): 272–82.

78   'Remarks of President Bush', 8 April 2002, www.whitehouse.gov/news/releases/2002/04/20020408-4.html (accessed 15 June 2006); Deborah J. Daniels, 'Remarks of the Honorable Deborah J. Daniels, Assistant Attorney General', Department of Justice, 18 June 2002, www.ojp.usdoj.gov/archives/speeches/2002/EOWSNO.htm (accessed 18 August 2008).

79   Ritt Goldstein, 'US Planning to Recruit One in 24 Americans as Citizen Spies', *Sydney Morning Herald*, 15 July 2002.

80   Adam Clymer, 'Traces of Terror: Security and Liberty; Worker Corps to Be Formed to Report Odd Activity', *New York Times*, 26 July 2002.

81   Department of Homeland Security, 'Operation Tips Fact Sheet', 2002, www.thetip.org/tips.html (accessed 1 February 2006).

82   Ibid.

83   citizencorps@fema.gov, 13 August 2002, http://cryptome.org/tips081302.htm (accessed 10 August 2007).

84   Barbara Comstock, 'Statement of Barbara Comstock, Director of Public Affairs, Regarding the Tips Program', 2002, www.usdoj.gov (accessed 25 January 2006).

85   Clymer, 'Traces of Terror'; Dave Lindorff, 'When Neighbors Attack!' *Salon*, 6 August 2006, www.salon.com/news/feature/2002/08/06/tips/index.html (accessed 20 April 2007); Dave Lindorff, 'New Life for Operation TIPS', *Salon*, 30 August 2002, www.salon.com/news/feature/2002/08/30/tips/index.html (accessed 12 February 2005).

86   Andy Newman, 'Ideas & Trends: Look out; Citizen Snoops Wanted (Call Toll-Free)', *New York Times*, 21 July 2002.

87   'Informant Fever', *New York Times*, 22 July 2002; 'The War on Civil Liberties', *New York Times*, 10 September 2002.

88   Nat Hentoff, 'The Death of Operation TIPS', *Village Voice*, 13 December 2002.

89   Francis Elliott, 'Secret Plans to Turn Staff into Police Informers', *Times*, 21 May 2007.

90   US Congress, 'A Bill to Combat International Terrorism', H.R. 6311, 1984.

91   'History of Crime Stoppers', http://crimestoppers.ns.ca/index.php/about/history-of-crime-stoppers/ (accessed 10 February 2008).

92   Tom Williamson and Peter Bagshaw, 'The Ethics of Informer Handling', in Roger Billingsley, and Teresa Nemitz, and Philip Bean, eds, *Informers: Policing, Policy, Practice* (Uffculme, UK: Willan Publishing, 2001), pp. 59–60; Roger Billingsley, 'Informers' Careers: Motivations and Change', in Roger Billingsley, and Teresa Nemitz, and Philip Bean, eds, *Informers: Policing, Policy, Practice* (Uffculme, UK: Willan Publishing, 2001), p. 86; Gary T. Marx, 'Thoughts on a Neglected Category of Social Movement Participant: The Agent Provocateur and the Informant', *American Journal of Sociology*, vol. 80, no. 2 (1974): 414–17; Malin Åkerström, *Betrayal and Betrayers: The Sociology of Treachery* (New York, NY: Transaction Publishers, 1991), p. 22; Colin Dunninghan and Clive Norris, 'A Risky Business: The Recruitment and Running of Informers by English Police Officers', *Police Studies*, vol. 19, no. 2 (1996): 4.

93   Susan Ellis, 'US Offers up to $7 Million for Tips on Terrorists', US Department of State, 2000.

94   Naftali, *Blind Spot*, p. 208.

95   Stan A. Taylor and Daniel Snow, 'Cold War Spies: Why They Spied and How

They Got Caught', *Intelligence and National Security*, vol. 12, no. 2 (1997): 101–25; David Wise, *Spy: The Inside Story of How the FBI's Robert Hanssen Betrayed America* (New York, NY: Random House Books, 2003).

96 Randy Scheunemann, as quoted in Andrew Roberts, 'Bring Back 007', *Spectator*, 6 October 2001.

97 Michael Scheuer, 'Why It's So Hard to Infiltrate Al-Qaeda', *Atlantic Monthly*, April 2005.

98 The six were: the 28 June 1988 murder of the US Defense Attaché in Athens ($500,000); the terrorist bombing of TWA Flight 840 on 2 April 1986 ($250,000); the assassination of four US Marines and two US civilians in San Salvador on 19 June 1985 ($100,000); the hijacking of TWA Flight 847 on 13 June 1985 ($250,000); the hijacking of Kuwaiti Airlines Flight 221 on 4 December 1984 ($250,000); and the hijacking of the cruise ship *Achille Lauro* on 7 October 1985 ($250,000). Phyllis Oakley, 'From the State Department (Expansion of Rewards Program)', State Department Briefing, 21 December 1988.

99 Ibid.

100 Kyodo News Service, 'US Offers Reward for Information on Terrorism', 8 June 1990.

101 James Baker, 'Rewards for Terrorism Information Program', Washington: State Department, 22 October 1990.

102 'State Dept. Offers $2 Million Reward', *United Press International*, 24 November 1995.

103 Sid Balman, Jr, 'US Offers $2 Million for New York Bombing Suspect', *United Press International*, 23 July 1993; Naftali, 242; Andy Laine, Interview by Daniel Zwerdling, 'State Department Rewards', *Weekend All Things Considered*, National Public Radio Transcripts, 9 November 1998.

104 US Federal News, 'Rewards for Justice Program Pays Three Filipinos $1 Million for Information on Abu Sayyaf Leaders', *US Fed News (HT Media)*, 26 October 2004.

105 Richard Boucher, 'Rewards for Justice Program — Prevention of Terrorism Advertising Campaign', Washington, 2000; Susan Ellis, 'US Offers up to $7 Million for Tips on Terrorists', US Department of State, 2000.

106 'Bush Pledges to Get bin Laden, Dead or Alive', *USA Today*, 14 December 2001.

107 'Transcript of Interview with Scott Case and Joe Rutledge', *Hannity and Colmes*, Fox News, 15 October 2001.

108 'US to Expand Terrorist Bounty to Palestinians, New Ad Campaign', *Agence France Presse*, 13 December 2001.

109 '*Harper's* Index for April 2002', www.harpers.org/HarpersIndex2002-04. html#230553581536753 (accessed 17 March 2006).

110 Eli J. Lake, 'How the Bounty on Bin Laden Works', *United Press International*, 21 November 2001; Kevin Whitelaw, 'Just a Phone Call Away', *US News and World Report*, 31 January 2005, 32.

111 Bill Gertz and Rowan Scarborough, 'Inside the Ring', *Washington Times*, 23 January 2004.

112 Kari Haskell, 'Turning in Terrorists: Take the Money and Run', *New York Times*, 28 March 2004; 'Senate Doubles bin Laden Bounty to 50 Million Dollars', *Japan Today*, 14 July 2007.

113 Amani Whaidullah, 'First War, Now PR to Get Bin Laden', *Times Union*, 3 September 2005.

114 Brendan Koerner, 'Do Terrorist Informants Have to Pay Taxes?', *Slate*, 13 March 2003.

115 'Powell Signs Off on 30 Million Reward to Saddam Sons Informant', *Agence France Presse*, 31 July 2003.

116 State News Service, 'Rewards for Justice Program Pays Three Filipinos $1 Million for Information on Abu Sayyaf Leaders', *States News Service*, 26 October 2004.

117 See, for example, 'Rewards for Justice', www.rewardsforjustice.net/index. cfm?page=p_payout&language=english (accessed 10 May 2008).

118 Whitlock, 'After a Decade at War with West . . .'.

119 Ibid; Taylor and Snow, 'Cold War Spies'.

120 'News Conference with Jimmy Gurule, Treasury Undersecretary for Enforcement and Frank Taylor, State Department Coordinator for Counterterrorism', *Federal News Service*, 13 November 2002.

121 Ibid.

122 Kevin Whitelaw, 'Just a Phone Call Away', *US News and World Report*, 31 January 2005.

123 Koerner, 'Do Terrorist Informants Have to Pay Taxes?'

124 Elliott, 'Undercover Work Deepens Police-Muslim Tensions'; Teresa Watanabe and Paloma Esquivel, 'L.A. Area Muslims Say FBI Surveillance Has a Chilling Effect', *Los Angeles Times*, 1 March 2009.

Notes to Chapter 7: Conclusion: Living in the Informer Age

1 Amy Waldman, 'Prophetic Justice', *Atlantic Monthly*, (October 2006); Andrea Elliott, 'Undercover Work Deepens Police-Muslim Tensions', *New York Times*, 27 May 2006; BBC Radio, *File on 4*: 'US Muslims', 4 July 2006; 'Recruiting Muslim Spies', BBC Radio 4, 18 December 2007; 'Australian Islamic Leader Rejects Call to "Spy" on Muslims', *Agence France Presse*, 13 November 2005.

2 The video can be viewed at www.youtube.com/watch?v=vWSsQ-CzSEM (accessed 20 March 2008).

3 '"Stop Snitching" Shirts Don't Wear Well with Cops', *Fox News*, 20 August 2005, www.foxnews.com/story/0,2933,166310,00.html (accessed 13 March 2006); Rick Hampson, 'Anti-snitch Campaign Riles Police, Prosecutors', *USA*

Today, 29 March 2006; Jeremy Kahn, 'The Story of a Snitch', *Atlantic Monthly*, April 2007.

4 'Who's A Rat', www.whosarat.com/aboutus.php (accessed 12 February 2008).

5 See Chapter 6 for more information on the program and the reaction against it.

6 'Rewards for Justice Program Expands to Encourage Reporting of Information About Possible Terrorists Domestically', in National Public Radio Weekend *All Things Considered*, 15 December 2001.

Selected Bibliography

Primary Sources

Coke, Edward. *The Third Part of the Institutes of the Laws of England*. London: E. and R. Brooke, 1797.
Comstock, Barbara. Statement of Barbara Comstock, Director of Public Affairs, Regarding the TIPS Program, 16 July 2002, www.usdoj.gov/opa/pr/2002/July/02_ag_405.htm (accessed 25 January 2006).
'Department of Justice Regulations Regarding the Use of Confidential Informants'. Washington, DC: Department of Justice, 2001.
Federal Bureau of Investigation. 'Communist Infiltration — Motion Picture Industry (Compic) (Excerpts)'. File 100-138754.
Federal Bureau of Investigation. Files Related to Joseph P. Kennedy. File 9-41998.
'Final Report of the Select Committee to Study Governmental Operations with Respect to Intelligence Activities'. Washington, DC: Congress, 1976.
McDonald Commission. *Third Report: Certain R.C.M.P. Activities and the Question of Governmental Knowledge*. Ottawa, ON: Minister of Supply and Services, 1981.
Office of the Inspector General. 'The Federal Bureau of Investigation's Compliance with the Attorney General's Investigative Guidelines'. Washington, DC: Office of the Inspector General, Department of Justice, 2005.
'Operation TIPS Fact Sheet'. Washington, DC: Department of Homeland Security, 1 February 2002.
'Rewards for Justice Program — Prevention of Terrorism Advertising Campaign'. Washington, DC, 18 December 2000.
'Rewards for Justice Program'. US State Department, 2 February 2006, www.state.gov/m/ds/terrorism/c8651.htm (accessed 27 February 2006).
'Rewards for Justice Targets Al-Qaida in Iraq's New Leader'. US State Department USINFO Washington File, 28 April 2006, http://usinfo.state.gov/is/Archive/2006/Apr/28-283728.html (accessed 5 July 2006).
'Rewards Program: Release of Public Service Announcement'. US State Department, 6 August 1999.
'State Department Regular Briefing'. Washington, DC: State Department, 30 January 1997.
'US Offers Rewards for Terrorism'. Washington, DC: US State Department, 17 October 1985.

Books

Åkerström, Malin. *Betrayal and Betrayers: The Sociology of Treachery*. New York, NY: Transaction Publishers, 1991.

Baer, Robert. *See No Evil: The True Story of a Ground Soldier in the CIA's War on Terrorism*. New York, NY: Three Rivers Press, 2003.

Beckman, James. *Comparative Legal Approaches to Homeland Security and Anti-Terrorism*. London: Ashgate Publishing Ltd, 2007.

Begg, Moazzam, and Victoria Brittain. *Enemy Combatant: The Terrifying True Story of a Briton in Guantanamo*. London: Pocket Books, 2007.

Bergen, Peter L. *The Osama Bin Laden I Know: An Oral History of Al Qaeda's Leader*. New York, NY: Free Press, 2006.

Blackstock, Nelson. *Cointelpro: The FBI's Secret War on Political Freedom*. New York, NY: Vintage Books, 1976.

Bloom, Robert M. *Ratting: The Use and Abuse of Informants in the American Justice System*. London: Praeger, 2002.

Browder, George C. *Hitler's Enforcers: The Gestapo and the SS Security Service in the Nazi Revolution*. New York, NY: Oxford University Press, 1996.

Budiansky, Stephen. *Her Majesty's Spymaster: Elizabeth 1, Sir Francis Walsingham, and the Birth of Modern Espionage*. London: Plume, 2005.

Carr, Caleb. *The Lessons of Terror*. New York, NY: Random House, 2003.

Charns, Alexander. *Cloak and Gavel: FBI Wiretaps, Bugs, Informers, and the Supreme Court*. Chicago, IL: University of Illinois Press, 1992.

Childs, David, and Richard Popplewell. *The Stasi: The East German Intelligence and Security Service*. London: Macmillan Press Ltd, 1996.

Churchill, Ward, and Jim Vander Wall, eds, *Agents of Repression: The FBI's Secret Wars against the Black Panther Party and the American Indian Movement*. Cambridge, MA: South End Press, 1988.

Churchill, Ward, and Jim Vander Wall, eds, *The Cointelpro Papers: Documents from the FBI's Secret Wars against Dissent in the United States*. Boston, MA: South End Press, 1990.

Critchley, T. A. *A History of Police in England and Wales, 900–1966*. London: Constable, 1967.

Cunningham, David. *There's Something Happening Here: The New Left, the Klan, and FBI Counterintelligence*. London: University of California Press, 2004.

Davis, John Kirkpatrick. *Assault on the Left: The FBI and the Sixties Antiwar Movement*. Westport, CT and London: Praeger, 1997.

de Vault, Carole, and William Johnson. *The Informer: Confessions of an Ex-Terrorist*. Toronto, ON: Fleet Books, 1982.

Dean, David. *Law-Making and Society in Late Elizabethan England*. Cambridge: Cambridge University Press, 2002.

Deletant, Dennis. *Ceauşescu and the Securitate: Coercion and Dissent in Romania, 1965–1989*. London: Hurst & Company, 1995.

Dennis, Mike. *The Stasi: Myth and Reality*. London: Pearson, 2003.

Diamond, Sigmund. *Compromised Campus: The Collaboration of Universities with the Intelligence Community, 1945–1955*. New York, NY: Oxford University Press, 1992.

Dillon, Martin. *The Dirty War*. London: Arrow, 1990.

Divale, William Tulio and James Joseph. *I Lived Inside the Campus Revolution.* New York, NY: NY Cowles Book Company, 1970.

Donner, Frank J. *The Age of Surveillance: The Aims and Methods of America's Political Intelligence System.* New York, NY: Albert A. Knopf, 1980.

Donner, Frank J. *Protectors of Privilege: Red Squads and Police Repression in Urban America.* Los Angeles, CA: University of California Press, 1990.

Eliot, Marc. *Walt Disney: Hollywood's Dark Prince.* London: Andre Deutsch, 1993.

Elkins, Caroline. *Imperial Reckoning: The Untold Story of Britain's Gulag in Kenya.* New York, NY: Henry Holt and Company, 2005.

Emsley, Clive. *The English Police: A Political and Social History.* London: Longman, 1996.

Ericson, Richard. *Making Crime: A Study of Detective Work.* Toronto, ON: University of Toronto Press, 1993.

Farebrother, Ron and Martin Short. *Informer: Life in the Shadows as an Undercover Agent.* London: Smith Gryphon Ltd, 1997.

Fogelson, Robert M. *Big City Police.* Cambridge, MA: Harvard University Press, 1979.

Foucault, Michel. *Discipline and Punish: The Birth of the Prison.* Translated by Alan Sheridan. London: Penguin, 1977.

Friedman, Robert I. *The False Prophet: Rabbi Meir Kahane — from FBI Informant to Knesset Member.* London: Faber and Faber, 1990.

Fulbrook, Mary. *Anatomy of a Dictatorship: Inside the GDR, 1949–1989.* Oxford: Oxford University Press, 1995.

Funder, Anna. *Stasiland: Stories from Behind the Berlin Wall.* London: Granta Books, 2003.

Gallagher, Lowell. *Medusa's Gaze: Casuistry and Conscience in the Renaissance.* Palo Alto, CA: Stanford University Press, 1991.

Gallen, David, and Michael Friedly, eds, *Martin Luther King, Jr.: The FBI File.* New York, NY: Carroll & Graf Publishing, 1993.

Garfinkel, Simson. *Database Nation: The Death of Privacy in the 21st Century.* Cambridge, MA: O'Reilly, 2000.

Geifman, Anna. *Entangled in Terror: The Azef Affair and the Russian Revolution.* Wilmington, DE: SR Books, 2000.

Gellately, Robert. *The Gestapo and German Society: Enforcing Racial Policy, 1933–1945.* Oxford: Clarendon, 1991.

Geraghty, Tony. *The Irish War: The Hidden Conflict between the IRA and British Intelligence.* New York, NY: Johns Hopkins University Press, 2000.

Gertz, Bill. *Breakdown: How America's Intelligence Failure Led to September 11.* New York, NY: Plume, 2003.

Glees, Anthony. *The Stasi Files: East Germany's Secret Operations against Britain.* London: Free Press, 2003.

Grathwohl, Larry, and Frank Reagan. *Bringing Down America: An FBI Informer with the Weathermen.* New Rochelle, NY: Arlington House Publishers, 1976.

Greaves, Richard L. *Deliver Us from Evil: The Radical Underground in Britain, 1660–1663.* Oxford: Oxford University Press, 1986.

Greaves, Richard L. *Secrets of the Kingdom: British Radicals from the Popish Plot to the Revolution of 1688–1689.* Palo Alto, CA: Stanford University Press, 1992.

Greer, Steven. *Supergrasses: Study in Anti-Terrorist Law Enforcement in Northern Ireland*. Oxford, UK: Clarendon Press, 1995.

Griset, Pamala, and Sue Mahan. *Terrorism in Perspective*. London: SAGE, 2007.

Haynes, Alan. *The Elizabethan Secret Services*. London: Sutton Publishing, 2002.

Hewitt, Steve. *Riding to the Rescue: The Transformation of the RCMP in Alberta and Saskatchewan, 1914–1939*. Toronto, ON: University of Toronto Press, 2006.

Hewitt, Steve. *Spying 101: The RCMP's Secret Activities at Canadian Universities, 1917–1997*. Toronto, ON: University of Toronto Press, 2002.

Hewitt, Steve. *The British War on Terror: Terrorism and Counter-Terrorism on the Home Front since 9/11*. London: Continuum, 2008.

Horne, Alistair. *A Savage War of Peace: Algeria, 1954–1962*. New York, NY: New York Review of Books, 2006.

Ingram, Martin, and Greg Harkin. *Stakeknife: Britain's Secret Agents in Ireland*. Dublin: The O'Brien Press Ltd, 2004.

Jacobs, Ron. *The Way the Wind Blew: A History of the Weather Underground*. London: Verso, 1997.

James, Robert. *The Informant Files: The FBI's Most Valuable Snitch*. Las Vegas, NV: Electronic Media Publishing Co., Inc., 1994.

Jeffreys-Jones, Rhodri. *Cloak and Dollar: A History of American Secret Intelligence*. New Haven, CT: Yale University Press, 2002.

Jensen, Joan M. *Army Surveillance in America, 1775–1980*. New Haven, CT: Yale University Press, 1991.

Kazantzakis, Nikos. *The Last Temptation of Christ*. London: Faber UK, 1996.

Keefe, Patrick Radden. *Chatter: Dispatches from the Secret World of Global Eavesdropping*. New York, NY: Random House, 2005.

Kelly, Catriona. *Comrade Pavlik: The Rise and Fall of a Soviet Boy Hero*. London: Granta Books, 2005.

Kitson, Frank. *Low Intensity Operations: Subversion, Insurgency, and Peacekeeping*. St. Petersburg, FL: Hailer Publisher, 1992.

Knox, Oliver. *Rebels & Informers: Stirrings of Irish Independence*. New York, NY: St. Martin's Press, 1997.

Koehler, John O. *Stasi: The Untold Story of the East German Secret Police*. Boulder, CO: Westview Press, 1999.

Kupferberg, Feiwel. *The Rise and Fall of the German Democratic Republic*. Transaction Publishers, Edison, NJ: 2002.

Laqueur, Walter. *A History of Terrorism*. London: Transaction Publishers, 2002.

Laqueur, Walter. *No End to War: Terrorism in the Twenty-First Century*. New York and London: Continuum, 2003.

Le Caron, Henri. *Twenty-Five Years in the Secret Service: The Recollections of a Spy*. London: EP Publishing, 1974.

Leier, Mark. *Rebel Life: The Life and Times of Robert Gosden: Revolutionary, Mystic, Labour Spy*. Vancouver, BC: New Star Books, 1999.

Lester, Normand. *Enquêtes sur les services secrets*. Montreal, QC: Les Éditions de l'Homme, 1998.

Levchenko, Stanislav. *On the Wrong Side: My Life in the KGB*. Washington, DC: Pergamon-Brassey's, 1988.

Lichtman, Robert M., and Ronald D. Cohen. *Deadly Farce: Harvey Matusow and the Informer System in the McCarthy Era*. Urbana and Chicago: University of Illinois Press, 2004.

Lucas, Scott *Orwell*. London: Haus Publishing, 2003.

Luger, Jack. *Snitch: A Handbook for Informants*. Port Townsend, WA: Loompanics Unlimited, 1991.

Lyon, David. *Surveillance After September 11*. Cambridge, UK: Polity Press, 2003.

Machon, Annie. *Spies, Lies and Whistleblowers: MI5, MI6 and the Shayler Affair*. Sussex, UK: The Book Guild Ltd, 2005.

Maguire, Mike. *Intelligence, Surveillance and Informants: Integrated Approaches*. London: Home Office Police Research Group, 1995.

Maier, Thomas. *The Kennedys: America's Emerald Kings*. New York, NY: Basic Books, 2003.

Marshall, Alan. *Intelligence and Espionage in the Reign of Charles II, 1660–1685*. Cambridge: Cambridge University Press, 1994.

Martin, David C. and John Walcott. *Best Laid Plans: The Inside Story of America's War against Terrorism*. New York, NY: Harper & Row, 1988.

Marx, Gary T. *Undercover: Police Surveillance in America*. Berkeley, CA: University of California Press, 1992.

May, Gary. *The Informant: The FBI, the Ku Klux Klan, and the Murder of Viola Liuzzo*. New Haven, CT: Yale University Press, 2005.

Mayer, Jane. *The Dark Side: The Inside Story of How the War on Terror Turned into a War on American Ideals*. New York, NY: Anchor Books, 2009.

Metzner, Paul. *Crescendo of the Virtuoso: Spectacle, Skill, and Self-promotion in Paris during the Age of Revolution*. Berkeley, CA: University of California Press, 1998.

Miller, Barbara. *Narratives of Guilt and Compliance in Unified Germany*. London and New York, NY: Routledge, 1999.

Milne, Seamus. *The Enemy Within: The Secret War against the Miners*. London: Verso, 2004.

Mockaitis, Thomas R. *British Counterinsurgency in the Post-Imperial Era*. Manchester and New York, NY: Manchester University Press, 1995.

Moore, Barrington. *Terror and Progress USSR: Some Sources of Change and Stability in the Soviet Dictatorship*. Cambridge, MA: Harvard University Press, 1954.

Morin, Claude. *L'affaire Morin: légendes, sottises et calumnies*. Montreal, QC: Boréal, 2006.

Morton, James. *Supergrasses and Informers: Informal History of Undercover Police Work*. London: Little, Brown, 1995.

Morton, James. *The First Detective: The Life and Revolutionary Times of Vidocq*. London: Ebury Press, 2005.

Mueller, John. *Overblown: How Politicians and the Terrorism Industry Inflate National Security Threats, and Why We Believe Them*. New York, NY: Free Press, 2006.

Naftali, Timothy. *Blind Spot: The Secret History of American Counterterrorism*. New York, NY: Basic Books, 2005.

Navasky, Victor S. *Naming Names: Historical Perspectives*. London: John Calder, 1982.

Niemi, Robert. *History in the Media: Film and Television*. Santa Barbara, CA: ABC-CLIO, 2006.

Oborne, Peter. *The Use and Abuse of Terror: The Construction of a False Narrative on the Domestic Terror Threat*. London: Centre for Policy Studies, 2006.

O'Callaghan, Sean. *The Informer*. London: Corgi, 1999.

O'Harrow, Jr. Robert. *No Place to Hide: Behind the Scenes of Our Emerging Surveillance Society*. New York, NY: Free Press, 2005.

Olmsted, Kathryn S. *Red Spy Queen: Elizabeth Bentley and the Cold War at Home*. Chapel Hill, NC: University of North Carolina Press, 2002.

Pagels, Elaine, and Karen L. King, *Reading Judas: The Gospel of Judas and the Shaping of Christianity*. New York, NY: Viking, 2007.

Payne, R.E. 'Gus'. *I Was a Communist for the FBI: Matt Cvetic*. Bloomington: AuthorHouse, 2004.

Penner, Norman. *Canadian Communism: The Stalin Years and Beyond*. Toronto, ON: Methuen, 1998.

Peterson, Edward N. *The Limits of Secret Police Power: The Magdeburger Stasi, 1953–1989*. New York, NY: Peter Lang Publishing Inc., 2004.

Philbrick, Herbert A. *I Led 3 Lives: Citizen, 'Communist', Counterspy*. London: Hamish Hamilton, 1952.

Pillar, Paul. *Terrorism and US Foreign Policy*. Washington, DC: Brookings Institute Press, 2001.

Porter, Bernard. *Plots and Paranoia: A History of Political Espionage in Britain, 1790–1988*. London: Routledge, 1989.

Porter, Bernard. *The Origins of the Vigilant State: The London Metropolitan Police Special Branch before the First World War*. London: Weidenfeld and Nicolson, 1987.

Powers, Richard Gid. *Secrecy and Power: The Life of J. Edgar Hoover*. London: Collier Macmillan Publishers, 1992.

Rapoport, David C. *Terrorism: The Third or New Left Wave*. London: Taylor & Francis, 2006.

Reynolds, Elaine A. *Before the Bobbies: The Night Watch and Police Reform in Metropolitan London, 1720–1830*. London: Macmillan Press Ltd, 1998.

Richardson, Louise. *What Terrorists Want: Understanding the Terrorist Threat*. London: John Murray, 2006.

Richelson, Jeffrey T., and Desmond Ball. *The Ties That Bind: Intelligence Cooperation between the UKUSA Countries — the United Kingdom, the United States of America, Canada, Australia and New Zealand*. Boston and London: Unwin Hyman, 1990.

Risen, James. *State of War: The Secret History of the CIA and the Bush Administration*. New York, NY: Free Press, 2006.

Robertson, Geoff. *Reluctant Judas: The Life and Death of the Special Branch Informer Kenneth Lennon*. London: Temple Smith, 1976.

Rosen, Jeffrey. *The Unwanted Gaze: The Destruction of Privacy in America*. New York, NY: Vintage Books, 2000.

Rosen, Ruth. *The World Split Open: How the Modern Women's Movement Changed America*. New York, NY: Penguin Books, 2001.

Rosenberg, Tina. *The Haunted Land: Facing Europe's Ghosts after Communism*. New York, NY: Vintage Books, 1995.

Ross, Corey. *The East German Dictatorship: Problems and Perspectives in the Interpretation of the GDR*. London: Oxford University Press, 2002.

Rutledge, Steven H. *Imperial Inquisitions: Prosecutors and Informants from Tiberius to Domitian*. London: Routledge, 2001.

Ruud, Charles A., and Sergei A. Stepanov. *Fontanka 16: The Tsars' Secret Police*. Phoenix Mill, Stroud: Sutton Publishing, 1999.

Schleifman, Nurit. *Undercover Agents in the Russian Revolutionary Movement: The SR Party, 1902–1914*. New York, NY: St. Martin's Press, 1988.

Schlosser, Eric. *Fast Food Nation: What the All American Meal is Doing to the World*. London: Penguin Books, 2002.

Schrecker, Ellen. *Many Are the Crimes: McCarthyism in America*. New York, NY: Little, Brown and Company, 1998.

Sheldon, Rose Mary. *Intelligence Activities in Ancient Rome: Trust in the Gods, but Verify*. London: Routledge, 2005.

Staples, William G. *The Culture of Surveillance: Discipline and Social Control in the United States*. New York, NY: St. Martin's, 1997.

Stark, James T. *Cold War Blues: The Operation Dismantle Story*. Hull, PQ, 1991.

Stephan, Alexander. *Communazis*. New Haven, CT: Yale University Press, 2000.

Stove, Robert J. *The Unsleeping Eye: Secret Police and Their Victims*. San Francisco, CA: Encounter Books, 2003.

Sullivan, William C., with Bill Brown. *The Bureau: My Thirty Years in Hoover's FBI*. New York, NY: W.W. Norton and Company, 1979.

Swearingen, M. Wesley. *FBI Secrets: An Agent's Exposé*. Boston, MA: South End Press, 1995.

Sykes, Charles J. *The End of Privacy: The Attack on Personal Rights — at Home, at Work, on-Line, and in Court*. New York, NY: St. Martin's Griffin, 1999.

Taylor, Peter. *Brits: The War against the IRA*. London: Bloomsbury, 2002.

Theoharis, Athan G. *Chasing Spies: How the FBI Failed in Counter-Intelligence But Promoted the Politics of McCarthyism in the Cold War Years*. Chicago, IL: Ivan R. Dee, 2002.

Theoharis, Athan G. *From the Secret Files of J. Edgar Hoover*. Chicago, IL: Ivan R. Dee, 1991.

Theoharis, Athan G. *Spying on Americans: Political Surveillance from Hoover to the Huston Plan*. Philadelphia, PA: Temple University, 1978.

Theoharis, Athan G. *The FBI & American Democracy: A Brief Critical History*. Lawrence, KS: University Press of Kansas, 2004.

Theoharis, Athan G., and John Stuart Cox. *The Boss: J. Edgar Hoover and the Great American Inquisition*. Philadelphia, PA: Temple University Press, 1988.

Thomas, Gordon. *Gideon's Spies: The Secret History of the Mossad*. New York, NY: Thomas Dunne Books, 1999.

Thompson, E.P. *The Making of the English Working Class*. London: Penguin Books, 1986.

Tricomi, Albert H. *Reading Tudor-Stuart Texts through Cultural Historicism*. Gainesville, FL: University Press of Florida, 1996.

Urban, Mark. *Big Boys' Rules: The Bestselling Story of the SAS and the Secret Struggle against the IRA*. London: Faber and Faber Ltd, 1992.

Van Creveld, Martin L. *The Rise and Decline of the State*. Cambridge: Cambridge University Press, 1999.

Vaughn, Stephen. *Ronald Reagan in Hollywood: Movies and Politics*. Cambridge: Cambridge University Press, 1994.
Vidocq, Eugène Francois. *Memoirs of Vidocq: Master of Crime (Nabat)*. London: AK Press, 2003.
Weisbord, Merrily. *The Strangest Dream: Canadian Communists, the Spy Trials, and the Cold War*. Toronto, ON: Véhicule Press, 1983.
Whitaker, Reg. *The End of Privacy: How Total Surveillance Is Becoming a Reality*. New York, NY: The New Press, 1999.
Wilford, Hugh. *The CIA, the British Left, and the Cold War: Calling the Tune*. London: Routledge, 2003.
Wills, Gary. *Reagan's America: Innocents at Home*. New York, NY: Penguin Books, 1985.
Wise, David. *Spy: The Inside Story of How the FBI's Robert Hanssen Betrayed America*. New York, NY: Random House Books, 2003.
Woodward, Bob. *Plan of Attack*. New York, NY: Simon and Shuster, 2004.
Wright, Lawrence. *The Looming Tower*. New York, NY: Albert A. Knopf, 2006.
Zegart, Amy. *Spying Blind: The CIA, The FBI, and the Origins of 9/11*. Princeton, NJ: Princeton University Press, 2007.
Zuckerman, Frederic S. *The Tsarist Secret Police in Russian Society, 1880–1917*. London: Macmillan Press Ltd, 1996.

Journal Articles

Abdo, Geneive. 'Iran's Generation of Outsiders'. *Washington Quarterly*, 24, no. 4 (Autumn 2001): 163–71.
Aid, Matthew M. 'All Glory Is Fleeting: Sigint and the Fight against International Terrorism'. *Intelligence and National Security*, 18, no. 4 (2003): 72–120.
Andrew, Christopher. 'Intelligence, International Relations and "Under-Theorisation."', *Intelligence and National Security*, 19, no. 2 (2004): 170–84.
Biddle, Francis. 'Internal Security and Civil Rights'. *Annals of the American Academy of Political and Social Science*, 300 (1955): 51–61.
Bonner, David. 'Combating Terrorism: Supergrass Trials'. *Modern Law Review*, 51, no. 1 (1988): 23–53.
Brodeur, Jean-Paul. 'High Policing and Low Policing: Remarks About the Policing of Political Activities'. *Social Problems*, 30, no. 5 (1983): 507–20.
Charters, David. 'Eyes of the Underground: Jewish Insurgent Intelligence in Palestine, 1945–47'. *Intelligence and National Security*, 13, no. 4 (1998): 163–77.
Cuordileone, Kyle A. '"Politics in an Age of Anxiety": Cold War Political Culture and the Crisis in American Masculinity, 1949–1960'. *Journal of American History*, 87, no. 2 (2000): 515–45.
Deletant, Dennis. 'The *Securitate* and the Police State in Romania, 1948–64'. *Intelligence and National Security*, 8, no. 4 (1993): 1–25.
Deletant, Dennis. 'The *Securitate* and the Police State in Romania, 1964–89'. *Intelligence and National Security*, 9, no. 1 (1994): 22–49.

Derian, James. 'Anti-Diplomacy, Intelligence Theory and Surveillance Practice'. *Intelligence and National Security*, 8, no. 3 (1993): 29–51.

Donnelly, Richard C. 'Judicial Control of Informants, Spies, Stool Pigeons, and Agent Provocateurs'. *The Yale Law Journal*, 60, no. 7 (1951): 1091–131.

Donnelly, Richard C. 'Police Authority and Practices'. *Annals of the American Academy of Political and Social Science*, 339 (1962): 90–110.

Dunninghan, Colin and Clive Norris. 'A Risky Business: The Recruitment and Running of Informers by English Police Officers'. *Police Studies*, 19, no. 2 (1996): 1–25.

Dupont, Alan. 'Intelligence for the Twenty-First Century'. *Intelligence and National Security*, 18, no. 4 (2003): 15–39.

Elton, Geoffrey R. 'Informing for Profit: A Sidelight on Tudor Methods of Law-Enforcement'. *Cambridge Historical Journal*, 11, no. 2 (1954): 149–67.

Emsley, Clive. 'The Home Office and Its Sources of Information and Investigation, 1791–1801'. *English Historical Review*, 94, no. 372 (1979): 532–61.

Escobar, Edward J. 'The Dialectics of Repression: The Los Angeles Police Department and the Chicano M'. *Journal of American History*, 79, no. 4 (1993): 1483–1514.

Garrow, David J. 'FBI Political Harassment and FBI Historiography: Analyzing Informants and Measuring the Effect'. *The Public Historian*, 10, no. 4 (1988): 5–18.

Gellately, Robert. 'Denunciations in Twentieth-Century Germany: Aspects of Self-Policing in the Third Reich and the German Democratic Republic'. *Journal of Modern History*, 68, no. 4 (1996): 931–67.

Gellately, Robert. 'The Gestapo and German Society: Political Denunciation in the Gestapo Case Files'. *Journal of Modern History*, 60, no. 4 (1988): 654–94.

Gill, Peter. 'Securing the Globe: Intelligence and the Post-9/11 Shift from "Liddism" to Drainism'. *Intelligence and National Security*, 19, no. 3 (2004): 467–89.

Goodman, Melvin. '9/11: The Failure of Strategic Intelligence'. *Intelligence and National Security*, 18, no. 4 (2003): 59–71.

Greer, Steven. 'Towards a Sociological Model of the Police Informant'. *The British Journal of Sociology*, 46, no. 3 (1995): 509–27.

Gutterman, Melvin. 'The Informer Privilege'. *Journal of Criminal Law, Criminology and Police Science*, 58, no. 1 (1967): 32–64.

Hewitt, Steve. 'Royal Canadian Mounted Spy: The Secret Life of John Leopold/Jack Esselwein'. *Intelligence and National Security*, 15, no. 1 (Spring 2000): 144–68.

Hey, Kenneth. 'Ambivalence as a Theme in "On the Waterfront"'. *American Quarterly*, 31, no. 5 (1979): 666–96.

Hight, James E. 'Avoiding the Informant Trap'. *FBI Law Enforcement Bulletin*, 67, no. 11 (1998): 1–6.

Hillyard, Paddy and Janie Percy-Smith. 'Converting Terrorists: The Use of Supergrasses in Northern Ireland'. *Journal of Law and Society*, 11, no. 3 (1984): 335–55.

Hoffman, Bruce. 'Intelligence and Terrorism: Emerging Threats and New Security Challenges in the Post-Cold War Era'. *Intelligence and National Security*, 11, no. 2 (1996): 207–23.

J.W.G. 'The Detective Branch of the Police Service'. *Journal of the American Institute of Criminal Law and Criminology*, 1, no. 3 (1910).

'Judicial Control of Secret Agents'. *Yale Law Journal*, 76, no. 5 (1967): 994–1019.

Kaba, Richard A. 'Threshold Requirements for the FBI under Exemption 7 of the Freedom of Information Act'. *Michigan Law Review*, 86, no. 3 (1987): 620–45.

Kackman, Michael. 'Citizen, Communist, Counterspy: "I Led 3 Lives" and Television's Masculine Agent of History'. *Cinema Journal*, 38, no. 1 (1998): 98–114.

Kash, Douglas A. 'Hunting Terrorists Using Confidential Informant Reward Programs'. *Federal Bureau of Investigation's Law Enforcement Bulletin*, 71, no. 4 (2002).

Kaufman, D. 'Jewish Informers in the Middle Ages'. *Jewish Quarterly Review*, 8, no. 2 (1896): 217–38.

Keunings, Luc. 'The Secret Police in Nineteenth-Century Brussels'. *Intelligence and National Security*, 4, no. 1 (1989): 59–85.

Leab, Daniel J. 'How Red Was My Valley: Hollywood, the Cold War Film, and I Married a Communist'. *Journal of Contemporary History*, 19, no. 1 (1984): 59–88.

Leab, Daniel J. 'I Was a Communist for the FBI'. *History Today*, 46, no. 12 (1996): 42–7.

Lewis, Alison. 'Ex-Gendering Remembrance: Memory, Gender, and Informers for the Stasi'. *New German Critique*, 86 (2002): 103–34.

Lukes, Igor. 'The Birth of a Police State: The Czechoslovak Ministry of the Interior, 1945–48'. *Intelligence and National Security*, 11, no. 1 (1996): 78–88.

Marx, Gary T. 'Some Concepts That May Be Useful in Understanding the Myriad Forms and Contexts of Surveillance'. *Intelligence and National Security*, 19, no. 2 (2004): 226–48.

Marx, Gary T. 'Thoughts on a Neglected Category of Social Movement Participant: The Agent Provocateur and the Informant'. *American Journal of Sociology*, 80, no. 2 (1974): 80–2.

Mathiesen, Thomas. 'The Viewer Society: Michel Foucault's "Panopticon" Revisited'. *Theoretical Criminology*, 1, no. 2, (1997): 215–34.

Misner, Robert L. and John H. Clough. 'Arrestees as Informants: A Thirteenth Amendment Analysis'. *Stanford Law Review*, 29, no. 4 (1977): 713–46.

O'Brien, Kevin A. 'Counter-Intelligence for Counter-Revolutionary Warfare: The South African Police Security Branch 1979–1990'. *Intelligence and National Security*, 16, no. 3 (2001): 27–59.

Olmsted, Kathryn S. 'Blond Queens, Red Spiders and Neurotic Old Maids: Gender and Espionage in the Early Cold War'. *Intelligence and National Security*, 19, no. 1 (Spring 2004): 78–94.

Rathmell, Andrew. 'Towards Postmodern Intelligence'. *Intelligence and National Security*, 17, no. 3 (2002): 87–104.

Ray, Gerda. '"We Can Stay Until Hell Freezes Over": Strike Control and the State Police in New York, 1919–1923'. *Labor History*, 36, no. 3 (Summer 1995): 403–25.

Reed, Merl E. 'The FBI, MOWM, and Core, 1941–1946'. *Journal of Black Studies*, 21, no. 4 (1991): 465–79.

Scott, Len and Peter Jackson. 'The Study of Intelligence in Theory and Practice'. *Intelligence and National Security*, 19, no. 2 (2004): 139–69.

Simmel, Georg. 'The Sociology of Secrecy and of Secret Societies'. *American Journal of Sociology*, 11 (1906): 441–98.

Spalek, Basia, Salwa El Awa and Laura Zahra McDonald. 'Police-Muslim Engagement and Partnerships for the Purposes of Counter-Terrorism: An Examination'. University of Birmingham Report, (May 2009).

Taylor, Stan A. and Daniel Snow. 'Cold War Spies: Why They Spied and How They Got Caught'. *Intelligence and National Security*, 12, no. 2 (1997): 101–25.

Theoharis, Athan G. 'The FBI and the American Legion Contact Program, 1940–1966'. *Political Science Quarterly*, 100, no. 2 (1985): 271–86.

Thurlow, Richard C. '"A Very Clever Capitalist Class": British Communism and State Surveillance, 1939–45'. *Intelligence and National Security*, 12, no. 2 (1997): 1–21.

Treverton, Gregory F. 'Terrorism, Intelligence and Law Enforcement: Learning the Right Lessons'. *Intelligence and National Security*, 18, no. 4 (2003): 121–40.

Villaverde, Mark D. 'Structuring the Prosecutor's Duty to Search the Intelligence Community for Brady Material'. *Cornell Law Review*, 88, no. 5 (2003): 1471–548.

Weitzer, Ronald. 'Contested Order: The Struggle over British Security Policy in Northern Ireland'. *Comparative Politics*, 19, no. 3 (1987): 281–98.

Weyrauch, Walter Otto. 'Gestapo Informants: Facts and Theory of Undercover Operations'. *Columbia Journal of Transnational Law*, 24 (1986): 554–96.

Whitaker, Reg. 'Cold War Alchemy: How America, Britain and Canada Transformed Espionage into Subversion'. *Intelligence and National Security*, 15, no. 2 (Summer 2000): 177–210.

Whitaker, Reg. 'Refugees: The Security Dimension'. *Citizenship Studies*, 2, no. 3 (November 1998): 413–33.

Wilson, Veronica A. 'Elizabeth Bentley and Cold War Representation: Some Masks Not Dropped'. *Intelligence and National Security*, 14, no. 2 (1999): 49–69.

Yoder, Jennifer. 'Truth without Reconciliation in Post-Communist Germany: An Appraisal of the Enquete Commission on the SED Dictatorship in Germany'. *German Politics*, 8, no. 3 (1999): 59–80.

Chapters in Books

Armstrong, Gary and Dick Hobbs. 'High Tackles and Professional Fouls: The Policing of Soccer Hooliganism', in Cyrille Fijnaut and Gary T. Marx, eds, *Undercover Policing in Comparative Perspective*. London: Kluwer, 1995, pp. 175–93.

Ballardie, Carole and Paul Iganski. 'Juvenile Informers', in Roger Billingsley, Teresa Nemitz and Philip Bean, eds, *Informers: Policing, Policy, Practice*. Uffculme, UK: Willan Publishing, 2001, pp. 110–22.

Bean, Philip. 'Informers and Witness Protection Schemes', in Roger Billingsley, Teresa Nemitz, and Philip Bean, eds, *Informers: Policing, Policy, Practice*. Uffculme, UK: Willan Publishing, 2001, pp. 153–63.

Betts, Richard K. 'Fixing Intelligence', in Russell D. Howard and Reid L. Sawyer, eds, *Terrorism and Counterterrorism: Understanding the New Security Environment*. New York, NY: McGraw-Hill, 2003, pp. 338–53.

Billingsley, Roger. 'Informers' Careers: Motivations and Change', in Roger Billingsley, Teresa Nemitz, and Philip Bean, eds, *Informers: Policing, Policy, Practice*. Uffculme, UK: Willan Publishing, 2001, pp. 81–97.

Billingsley, Roger and Philip Bean. 'Drugs, Crime and Informers', in Roger Billingsley, Teresa Nemitz, and Philip Bean, eds, *Informers: Policing, Policy, Practice*. Uffculme, UK: Willan Publishing, 2001, pp. 25–37.

Billingsley, Roger, Teresa Nemitz and Philip Bean. 'Introduction', in Roger Billingsley, Teresa Nemitz and Philip Bean, eds, *Informers: Policing, Policy, Practice*. Uffculme, UK: Willan Publishing, 2001, pp. 5–24.

Black, Jason and Jennifer Black. 'The Rhetorical 'Terrorist': Implications of the USA Patriot Act on Animal Liberation', in Steven Best and Anthony J. Nocella II, eds, *Terrorists or Freedom Fighters? Reflections on the Liberation of Animals*. New York, NY: Lantern Books, 2004, pp. 288-99.

Brodeur, Jean-Paul. 'Undercover Policing in Canada: A Study of Its Consequences', in Cyrille Fijnaut and Gary T. Marx, eds, *Undercover Policing in Comparative Perspective*. London: Kluwer, 1995, pp. 71–102.

Brown, Howard G. 'Tips, Traps and Tropes: Catching Thieves in Post-Revolutionary Paris', in Clive Emsley and Haia Shpayer-Makov, eds, *Police Detectives in History, 1750–1950*. London: Ashgate Publishing, Ltd, 2006, pp. 33–60.

Busch, Heiner and Albrecht Funk. 'Undercover Tactics as an Element of Preventive Crime Fighting in the Federal Republic of Germany', in Cyrille Fijnaut and Gary T. Marx, eds, *Undercover Policing in Comparative Perspective*. London: Kluwer, 1995, pp. 55–69.

Clark, Roy. 'Informers and Corruption', in Roger Billingsley, Teresa Nemitz and Philip Bean, eds, *Informers: Policing, Policy, Practice*. Uffculme, UK: Willan Publishing, 2001, pp. 38–49.

Czajkowski, Anthony F. 'Techniques of Domestic Intelligence Collection', in H. Bradford Westerfield, ed, *Inside CIA's Private World: Declassified Articles from the Agency's Internal Journal, 1955–1992*. New Haven and London: Yale University Press, 1995, pp. 51–62.

Fijnaut, Cyrille, and Gary T. Marx. 'Introduction: The Normalization of Undercover Policing in the West: Historical and Contemporary Perspectives', in Cyrille Fijnaut and Gary T. Marx, eds, *Undercover Policing in Comparative Perspective*. London: Kluwer, 1995, pp. 1–27.

Fitzpatrick, Sheila. 'Signals from Below: Soviet Letters of Denunciation of the 1930s', in Sheila and Robert Gellately Fitzpatrick, eds, *Accusatory Practices: Denunciations in Modern European History, 1789–1989*. Chicago and London: University of Chicago Press, 1997, pp. 85-120.

Gellately, Robert, and Sheila Fitzpatrick. 'Introduction to the Practices of Denunciation in Modern European History', in Sheila and Robert Gellately Fitzpatrick, eds, *Accusatory Practices: Denunciation in Modern European History, 1789–1989*. Chicago and London: University of Chicago Press, 1997, pp. 1–21.

Grady-Willis, Winston A. 'The Black Panther Party: State Repression and Political

Prisoners', in Charles E. Jones, ed, *The Black Panther Party (Reconsidered)*. Baltimore, MD: Black Classic Press, 2005, pp. 363–90.

Greer, Steven. 'Where the Grass Is Greener? Supergrasses in Comparative Perspective', in Roger Billingsley, Teresa Nemitz and Philip Bean, eds, *Informers: Policing, Policy, Practice*. Uffculme, UK: Willan Publishing, 2001, pp. 123–40.

Griffiths, Bill and Alan Murphy. 'Managing Anonymous Informants through Crimestoppers', in Roger Billingsley, Teresa Nemitz and Philip Bean, eds, *Informers: Policing, Policy, Practice*. Uffculme, UK: Willan Publishing, 2001, pp. 141–52.

Gunnlaugsson, Helgi and John F. Galliher. 'The Secret Drug Police of Ireland', in Cyrille Fijnaut and Gary T. Marx, eds, *Undercover Policing in Comparative Perspective*. London: Kluwer, 1995, pp. 235–47.

Guth, DeLloyd J. 'The Traditional Common Law Constable, 1235–1829: From Bracton to the Fieldings of Canada', in R. C. Macleod and David Schneiderman, eds, *Police Powers in Canada: The Evolution and Practice of Authority*. Toronto, ON: University of Toronto Press, 1994, pp. 3–23.

Hennessy, Peter. 'From Secret State to Protective State', in Peter Hennessy, ed, *The New Protective State: Government, Intelligence and Terrorism*. London: Continuum, 2007, pp. 1–43.

Kealey, Greg. 'Filing and Defiling: The Organization of the Canadian State's Security Archives in the Interwar Years', in Franca Iacovetta and Wendy Mitchinson, eds, *On the Case: Explorations in Social History*. Toronto, ON: University of Toronto Press, 1998, pp. 88–105.

Klerks, Peter. 'Covert Policing in the Netherlands', in Cyrille Fijnaut and Gary T. Marx, eds, *Undercover Policing in Comparative Perspective*. London: Kluwer, 1995, pp. 103–40.

Kozlov, Vladimir A. 'Denunciation and Its Functions in Soviet Governance', in Sheila and Robert Gellately Fitzpatrick, eds, *Accusatory Practices: Denunciation in Modern European History, 1789–1989*. Chicago and London: University of Chicago Press, 1997, pp. 121–52.

Levi, Michael. 'Covert Policing and the Investigation of "Organized Fraud": The English Experience in International Context', in Cyrille Fijnaut and Gary T. Marx, eds, *Undercover Policing in Comparative Perspective*. London: Kluwer, 1995, pp. 195–212.

Marx, Gary T. 'Undercover in Comparative Perspective: Some Implications for Knowledge and Social Research', in Cyrille Fijnaut and Gary T. Marx, eds, *Undercover Policing in Comparative Perspective*. London: Kluwer, 1995, pp. 323–7.

Monjardet, Dominique and René Lévy. 'Undercover Policing in France: Elements for Description and Analysis', in Cyrille Fijnaut and Gary T. Marx, eds, *Undercover Policing in Comparative Perspective*. London: Kluwer, 1995, pp. 29–53.

Nemitz, Teresa. 'Gender Issues in Informer Handling', in Roger Billingsley, Teresa Nemitz and Philip Bean, eds, *Informers: Policing, Policy, Practice*. Uffculme, UK: Willan Publishing, 2001, pp. 98–109.

Neyroud, Peter and Alan Beckley. 'Regulating Informers: The Regulation of Investigatory Powers Act, Covert Policing and Human Rights', in Roger

Billingsley, Teresa Nemitz and Philip Bean, eds, *Informers: Policing, Policy, Practice*. Uffculme, UK: Willan Publishing, 2001, pp. 164–75.

Shelley, Louise. 'Soviet Undercover Work', in Cyrille Fijnaut and Gary T. Marx, eds, *Undercover Policing in Comparative Perspective*. London: Kluwer, 1995, pp. 155–74.

South, Nigel. 'Informers, Agents and Accountability', in Roger Billingsley, Teresa Nemitz and Philip Bean, eds, *Informers: Policing, Policy, Practice*. Uffculme, UK: Willan Publishing, 2001, pp. 67–80.

Williamson, Tom, and Peter Bagshaw. 'The Ethics of Informer Handling', in Roger Billingsley, Teresa Nemitz and Philip Bean, eds, *Informers: Policing, Policy, Practice*. Uffculme, UK: Willan Publishing, 2001, pp. 50–66.

Radio and Television Programs

File on 4: 'US Muslims', BBC Radio 4, 4 July 2006.

'Rewards for Justice Fund Integrated with Web Site Marketing', in National Public Radio *All Things Considered*, 13 November 2001.

'Rewards for Justice Program Expands to Encourage Reporting of Information About Possible Terrorists Domestically', in National Public Radio Weekend *All Things Considered*, 15 December 2001.

'State Department Rewards', in National Public Radio Weekend *All Things Considered*, 9 November 1998.

Index